MACHINE LEARNING:

Applications in expert systems and information retrieval

ELLIS HORWOOD SERIES IN ARTIFICAL INTELLIGENCE

Series Editor: Professor JOHN CAMPBELL, University of Exeter

MACHINE LEARNING:

Applications in expert systems and information retrieval

R. FORSYTH, B.A. Hons., M.Sc.
Technical Director
Warm Boot Limited, London

and

R. RADA, B.A., M.S., M.D., Ph.D.
Reseach Officer, National Library of Medicine
Bethesda, Maryland, USA

ELLIS HORWOOD LIMITED
Publishers · Chichester

Halsted Press: a division of
JOHN WILEY & SONS
New York · Chichester · Brisbane · Toronto

First published in 1986 by
ELLIS HORWOOD LIMITED
Market Cross House, Cooper Street, Chichester, West Sussex, PO19 1EB, England

The publisher's colophon is reproduced from James Gillison's drawing of the ancient Market Cross, Chichester.

Distributors:

Australia and New Zealand:
Jacaranda-Wiley Ltd., Jacaranda Press,
JOHN WILEY & SONS INC.
GPO Box 859, Brisbane, Queensland 4001, Australia

Canada:
JOHN WILEY & SONS CANADA LIMITED
22 Worcester Road, Rexdale, Ontario, Canada

Europe and Africa:
JOHN WILEY & SONS LIMITED
Baffins Lane, Chichester, West Sussex, England

North and South America and the rest of the world:
Halsted Press: a division of
JOHN WILEY & SONS
605 Third Avenue, New York, NY 10158, USA

© **1986 R. Forsyth and R. Rada/Ellis Horwood Limited**

British Library Cataloguing in Publication Data
Forsyth, Richard
Machine learning: applications in expert systems and information retrieval. —
(Ellis Horwood series in artificial intelligence)
1. Information storage and retrieval systems
2. Artificial intelligence
I. Title   II. Rada, R.
025.5'24   Z699

Library of Congress Card No. 86–3054

ISBN 0–85312–947–9 (Ellis Horwood Limited — Library Edn.)
ISBN 0–7458–0045–9 (Ellis Horwood Limited — Student Edn.)
ISBN 0–470–20309–9 (Halsted Press — Library Edn.)
ISBN 0–470–20318–8 (Halsted Press — Student Edn.)

Phototypeset in Times by Ellis Horwood Limited
Printed in Great Britain by Unwin Bros. of Woking

Contents

Preface

This book is dedicated to the proposition that there can be no genuine machine intelligence without machine learning.

If somebody makes a mistake and keeps on repeating it, we say he is stupid. Yet for three decades workers in Artifical Intelligence (AI) have laboured diligently to construct problem-solving systems that cannot improve their performance without re-programming. It is a tribute to the skills of AI programmers that they have got as far as they have (e.g. to master-level chess playing) while relying almost exclusively on pre-programmed intelligence.

Recently, however, there has been a resurgence of interest in machine learning. The prime motivation for this has come from the expert-system field. An expert system needs a high-quality knowledge base; but this is difficult to create. The 'knowledge acquisition bottleneck' refers to the difficulty of teasing out a domain specialist's knowledge, codifying it, testing it, and refining it until the system is functioning satisfactorily. Machine learning offers a way through this bottleneck: in effect, the system synthesizes its own knowldege.

As a result a number of effective techniques have been developed to enable computers to learn for themselves, and their success has implications outside the expet system field. As this book aims to show, there are many areas in AI (and even more outside it) where computer systems that could improve their own performance would be extremely valuable.

ABOUT THIS BOOK

The book is divided into two parts, each serving a different but complementary purpose.

Part 1 is a wide-ranging introduction to the concepts and methods of machine learning, with special reference to the development of expert systems. It surveys the major systems, describing how they work and how they may be put to practical use. In addition it considers future prospects for the field. This part of the book should serve as a thorough gounding in the principles and applications of machine learning in a variety of domains.

Part 2 delves more deeply into a specific subject area. It contains detailed case studies of learning experiments which help to bring the goal of intelligent information retrieval closer to realization. The objective of the second part of the book is to demonstrate machine learning in action within an important contemporary field of information technology. For readers without a background in information retrieval the central terms and concepts are explained and defined in Chapters 7 and 8.

Each chapter is followed by a list of references, for readers who wish to pursue particular topics further. In addition, there is a Bibliography at the end of the book which collates a large number of important books and articles in Artificial Intelligence which have special relevance to machine learning. There is also a specially-prepared Glossary of over 100 words and phrases, since many of the terms used have somewhat idiosyncratic technical meanings.

ABOUT THE AUTHORS

Richard Forsyth obtained a B.A. in Psychology from Sheffield University in 1970 and an M.Sc. in Computer Science from the City University, London, in 1980. From 1979 to 1984 he was a lecturer in computing, latterly senior lecturer, at the Polytechnic of North London. Since 1984 he has been running his own business, Warm Boot Limited, which has permitted him to concentrate on writing machine-intelligence software packages — and books. Mr Forsyth is the author of a number of books on computing topics, including *Experts Systems: Principles and Case Studies* and *The Hitch-Hiker's Guide to Artificial Intelligence* (with Chris Naylor), both published by Chapman and Hall.

Roy Rada is currently a research scientist at the National Library of Medicine at Bethesda, Maryland. This is one of the foremost centres of information science in the world, with an unparalleled wealth of information held on computer in documentary form. Dr Rada is in charge of a project involving the application of artificial intelligence to information retrieval problems. He obtained his B.A. in Psychology from Yale University in 1973, an M.S. in Computer Science from the University of Houston in 1976 and a Ph.D. in Computer Science from the University of Illinois in 1981. He is also a qualified medical doctor (M.D. Baylor College, Texas, 1977) and one of his special interests is the application of AI techniques in medicine. Since October 1983 he has been editor of the ACM's Newsletter for the Special Interest Group in Biomedical Computing.

The two authors have extensive knowledge of the latest machine learning research on both sides of the Atlantic. By virtue of combining expertise in both psychology and computer science they are able to act as guides to this exciting frontier territory of cognitive science.

ABOUT THE READER

This book has a practical orientation, aimed towards the system designer. In other words, we have written in the expectation that our readers will want to apply machine learning in their own problem areas either by making use of existing programs or by writing their own. Our book is a guidebook for people who want to find out how machine learning systems work and put that knowledge to use.

Machine learning is not, as we hope to show, a mysterious black art: it is a technique (or set of techniques) which are becoming increasingly important as software is forced to become more adaptable. There are few areas where learning systems cannot be effectively applied. We hope that students of many disciplines — including psychology and computer science — will gain insight from these pages.

Our ideal reader, therefore, has the book in one hand and a keyboard in the other. We have said a little about ourselves (in a professional sense); but who do we think you are? Someone who wants to learn about learning.

ACKNOWLEDGEMENTS

Many people, other than the authors, contribute to the making of a book, from the first person who had the bright idea of alphabetic writing through the inventor of movable type to the lumberjacks who felled the trees that were pulped for its printing. It is not customary to acknowledge the trees themselves, though their commitment is total.

The present writers wish to thank by name the following people and institutions for assistance of various kinds, on the understanding that no list of this kind can be exhaustive. (If you think you should have been on it, please call the relevant author and he will try to give you a mention next time.)

Richard Forsyth	**Roy Rada**
(mostly Part 1)	(mostly Part 2)
BUPA Medical Research Ltd.	E. Brown
J. Campbell	D. Bennett
Continental Shelf Institute (Trondheim, Norway)	C. Coccia
	L. Darden
M. L. Forsyth	J. Eng
C. M. Griffiths	George Washington University
M. Horwood	S. Humphrey
R. Michalski	R. Lewis
D. Robinson	F. Lu
R. Smolski	H. Mili
S. Smith	National Library of Medicine
M. Tawse	
Warm Boot Ltd.	
M. Yazdani	
	M. Peterson
	C. Smith
	A Suh

The order is purely alphabetical. Our debt to numerous prior authors and researchers is acknowledged, indirectly, in the references and bibliography.

Part 1

Machine Learning for Expert Systems
Richard Forsyth

1

Introduction to machine learning

Machine learning is the key to machine intelligence just as human learning is the key to human intelligence.

In the natural world, species that have only rudimentary learning abilities are called 'primitive' — insects, molluscs and worms, for instance. No one would dream of calling them intelligent. More advanced groups, such as Cetaceans and Primates, are characterized by a greater capacity to learn.

In the clinical world, there are case histories of patients with brain damage who lose the ability to remember new facts and events. If the condition develops in adulthood, the patient can still recall early memories and retains skills learned in childhood, but cannot modify his (or her) behaviour. Such people have to be institutionalized. They exhibit in exaggerated form a problem that is seen in senility — not so much loss of memory as loss of adaptability.

Yet, in the field of Artificial Intelligence (AI), researchers have persisted in trying to build fully-fledged 'adult' systems which cannot learn for themselves at all. Early attempts to devise learning machines, during the cybernetic days of AI, proved disappointing, so the whole idea was dropped. Only recently has it been revived.

Our contention is that this revival of interest in machine learning is important, and will continue until systems capable of self-improvement become the norm rather than the exception. Indeed we believe that many AI problems (such as speech understanding) are so difficult that they can only be solved by systems that go through a 'childlike' phase.

After all, we do not expect babies to emerge from the womb and ask politely for a drink of milk.

1.1 THE MEANING OF LEARNING

When a computer system improves its performance at a given task over time, without re-programming, it can be said to have learned something. We will accept automatic performance improvement with experience as a rough-and-ready definition of learning, without delving too deply into the philosophical implications. Note that this implies a yardstick for measuring performance: if we cannot evaluate a system's performance, we cannot say whether it has learned anything.

In practice, learning algorithms attempt to achieve one or more of the following goals:

— provide more accurate solutions;
— cover a wider range of problems;
— obtain answers more economically;
— simplify codified knowledge.

The last goal presumes that simplification of stored knowledge is valuable for its own sake. For example, a system might re-arrange its knowledge base so that it was more intelligible to human readers. Even if its performance at the task was no better, this could well be useful.

However, it is the first two criteria (accuracy of solutions and range of applicability) which usually have the highest priority.

1.2 THE PHILOSOPHY OF INDUCTION

Before discussing how machines (which almost always means computers) may be made to learn, it is wise to see what philosophers and psychologists have said about the subject. We, too, may be able to learn from the past.

Philosophers have long been fascinated by the process of induction — i.e. formulating general laws by examination of particular cases. Clearly induction is the foundation not merely for most of our day-to-day learning, but for the whole edifice of science as well. For this reason many philosophers have looked at the part played by inductive reasoning in scientific discovery.

A typical act of induction goes something like this:

I have seen lots of white swans.
I have never seen a non-white swan.

Therefore, all swans are white.

Another old favourite is the sunrise 'problem'.

Yesterday the sun rose in the East and set in the West.
Every day of my life it has risen in the East and set in the West.
Never in living memory has anyone seen it do anything else.
Throughout recorded history it has always risen in the East and set in the West.

Therefore, it will do so tomorrow as well.

Those innocuous acts of commonsense inference are in fact logically invalid, and philosophers have spent many sleepless nights attempting to find rational grounds for validating them — not because they expect the sun to rise in the West tomorrow, but because they would like to put such crucial conclusions on firmer footing. After all, Australian swans are in fact black.

Francis Bacon, John Stuart Mill, Bertrand Russell and, to a lesser extent, Ludwig Wittgenstein are the philosophers who have devoted most attention to the problems of induction. They have considered particularly its role in the scientific method.

Unfortunately, for our purposes, they have been less interested in how to do it than in how to justify it. Their objective was to frame rules governing inductive argument just as logicians, from Aristotle to Boole, have framed rules for deductive argument. As J. S. Mill said (in his *System of Logic*): 'what induction is, and what conditions render it legitimate, cannot but be deemed the main question of the science of logic'.

In this enterprise they have only been partly successful. Nevertheless, the AI practitioner who is chiefly interested in how to mechanize the process of induction can glean a number of hints from their work.

Bacon, for example (*First Book of Aphorisms*), stressed the importance of negative evidence, and the tendency of the human mind to overlook it. (See Hampshire, 1956.)

> It is the peculiar and perpetual error of human intellect to be more excited by affirmatives than by negatives; whereas it ought properly to hold itself indifferently disposed towards both alike. Indeed in the establishment of any true axiom, the negative instance is the more forcible of the two.

He also pointed out that an inductive leap, to be of value, must go further than the facts warrant. When it does so, and is subsequently confirmed by observation, our confidence in it is strengthened.

> But in establishing axioms by this kind of induction, we must also examine and try whether the axiom so established be framed to the measure of those particulars only from which it is derived, or whether it be larger and wider. And if it be larger and wider, we must observe whether by indicating to us new particulars it conform that wideness and largeness as by a collateral security; that we may not either stick fast in things already known, or loosely grasp at shadows and abstract forms; not at things solid and realised in matter.

One final remark from Bacon, is perhaps his most apt: 'the understanding must not therefore be supplied with wings, but rather hung with weights, to keep it from leaping and flying'.

Two centuries after Bacon, Mill laid down four primary 'experimental methods' for inducing general laws from particular cases. These were:

— the Method of Agreement
— the Method of Differences
— the Method of Residues
— the Method of Concomitant Variation.

For example, the method of differences can be summed up as follows: take away factors affecting the situation one by one, two by two, and so on, to find the 'invariable and unconditional' antecedent factors; then you have found the cause or causes of the phenomenon under investigation. (See Passmore, 1968; Russell, 1961.) The method of concomitant variation involves looking for factors that vary together, or in inverse proportions; for example, the height and momentum of a weight when it is dropped to the ground.

Mill's four methods, however, were specified before the computer age, and are hence too vague to serve as plans for a program designer.

Russell also wrestled with the problem of justifying inductive reasoning, and eventually admitted defeat. As he says in *The Problems of Philosophy,* the inductive principle is 'incapable of being proved by an appeal to experience'. Its role in human thought, however, is so fundamental that 'we must either accept the inductive principle on the grounds of its intrinsic evidence, or forgo all justification of our expectations about the future' (Russell, 1912). In other words, if you don't believe induction, you can't believe anything.

The inductive principle, as he saw it, was essentially probabilistic. In brief, when two things, such as smoke and fire, have been found to go together many times and never found apart, then 'a sufficient number of cases of association will make the probability of a fresh association nearly a certainty, and will make it approach certainty without limit'. No smoke without a fire, as they say.

Wittgenstein's contribution was to emphasize, or re-emphasize, simplicity. He asserted in the *Tractatus Logico-Philosophicus,* 6.363, that 'the procedure of induction consists in accepting as true the simplest law that can be reconciled with our experiences' (Wittgenstein, 1961). Thus he recognized that many generalizations could be consistent with the evidence, and resurrected Occam's Razor as a means of choosing between them. For instance, having noticed that lightning flashes are invariably accompanied by loud bangs, it is simpler to assume that lightning causes thunder directly than that there is a heavy-metal rock group in a Jumbo jet who fly around looking for electrical storms so that they can re-charge their batteries and give their drummer a chance to practice his drum rolls with the amplifier at full blast.

The latter sort of explanation is difficult to disprove on the gounds of evidence alone, as the resilience of numerous superstitions testifies. Often such theories are only rejected because of internal contradictions. Indeed the history of science is littered with discredited hypotheses that were embellished with so many baroque flourishes that they collapsed under the weight of their own implausibility, even though they coincided with the known facts.

Thus, although philosophy has not laid the blueprint for an inductive engine, it does provide some guidelines for people wishing to build one.

— Do not neglect negative evidence (Bacon).

— Look for concomitant variation in the causal factors and the result (Mill).
— The more cases of association observed, the more likely the association is to be generally true (Russell).
— Prefer simple to complex generalizations (Wittgenstein).

This may seem no more than common sense, but then induction is a commonsense process which philosophers seek to clarify and AI workers to emulate.

1.3   THE PSYCHOLOGY OF LEARNING

Induction in science is a public procedure. In daily life, however, induction goes on in private whenever we learn from experience. As such, it has been extensively studied by psychologists for over a century.

Broadly speaking, psychological theories of learning fall into two groups. The S–R (Stimulus–Response) theorists regard the organism as a black box. They are interested in rules or formulae relating inputs (stimuli) with outputs (responses), but do not claim to model what is going on inside the animals's brain.

For example, the formula

$$P[n] = 1 - (1 - P[1]) \ast (1 - \theta) \uparrow (n - 1)$$

can be used to predict the probability of a response on the nth trial, $P[n]$, in a learning experiment where θ is the probability of making a connection on any reinforced trial. This generates the familiar 'learning curve' depicted in Fig. 1.1. Its slope depends on the numeric value of θ. But the mathematical psychologists are interested purely in fitting behavioural data. They would deny that θ has the status of a mental construct. As far as they are concerned it is a parameter in an equation, and no more than that.

Cognitive theorists, on the other hand, do attempt to describe the mental structures which are constructed within the nervous system. Interestingly enough, they borrow extensively from computing concepts and terminology to describe what they think is going on in there.

S–R theorists speak of 'learning' and experiment mainly with rats and pigeons. Cognitive psychologists usually talk of 'memory' and do most of their experiments on human beings. At present cognitive theorizing is in the ascendant (partly at least because cognitive theories lend themselves to computer simulation), but the debate continues between adherents of the two approaches. It will be a very long time before a unified psychological theory of learning emerges that fits the multiplicity of experimental data concerning human and animal learning.

In the meantime the AI worker looking to psychology for ideas on how to build learning systems will be disappointed. To put it bluntly, the psychol-

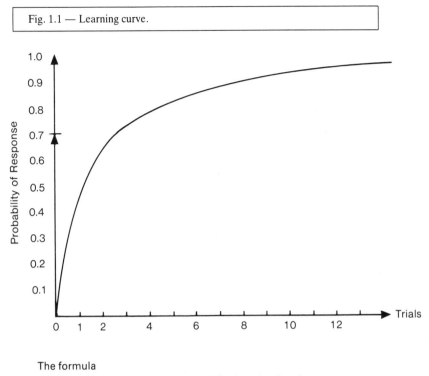

Fig. 1.1 — Learning curve.

The formula

$$P[n] = 1-(1-P[1]) * (1-\theta) \uparrow (n-1)$$

can be used to predict the probability of an animal making the correct response on trial *n* of a learning experiment. This may well match the form of observed results; but it does not attempt to explain how those results were generated. In particular the parameter θ does not have the status of a mental construct.

ogists do not know how it is done. For many years behaviourism was the dominant orthodoxy in experimental psychology, and behaviourists eschew mentalist concepts. The idea that a rat is forming and testing hypotheses when it runs a maze or that a pigeon is doing so as it pecks for food was anathema to behavioural scientists from about 1920 to 1970. It is hardly surprising, therefore, that psychologists cannot properly represent something they have only recently admitted to exist.

They can predict how rapidly (or slowly) people (or pigeons) will pick up various tricks in various situations. They can also tell you how fast they will be forgotten (on average). But the S–R theorists do not want to explain how it actually works, and the cognitive theorists are unable to do so.

This is not quite so disgraceful as it seems at first glance. Part of the explanation lies in the disparity between neurons and notions. The modern psychologist who trains a rat to run a maze knows that it has developed some sort of 'cognitive map' of the maze. The physiologist who cuts up the poor creature afterwards knows a good deal about how its nervous system works. But nobody yet knows how to put those two levels of description together. How is the software (the cognitive map) implemented in terms of the hardware (the neural interconnections)?

Ask again in a decade or two!

Only two conclusions have emerged that would command universal assent among psychological researchers into learning. One is that short-term memory (STM) is distinct from long-term memory (LTM) and very much smaller: STM is generally reckoned to be limited to about 7 'chunks' of information while LTM is for practical purposes unlimited. The second is that feedback, or knowledge of results, is absolutely crucial to the acquisition of novel skills, and must be provided quickly. (See Hilgard & Bower, 1966; Bolles, 1979).

1.4   A FRAMEWORK FOR LEARNING

Having gathered what we can from the researches of philosophers and psychologists, we will spend the rest of this book investigating computer systems which model the process of learning in some way. In order to be able to compare them, we need a general framework for discussion.

Looked at from a long way away, all systems designed to modify and improve their performance share certain important common features. Fig. 1.2 is a diagram of the four major components of a typical learning system. Essentially this sketches a pattern recognizer which learns to associate input descriptions with output categories, but as we shall see later many systems that are not overtly concerned with pattern recognition also fit into this general framework.

Note that the system contains a feedback loop. We will briefly describe its main components in turn, by going round this feedback loop.

The *Critic* compares the actual with the desired output. In order to do so, there must be an 'ideal system', as we call it, against which the system's behaviour is measured. In practice this may be a human expert, or teacher. For instance, if the task is medical diagnosis, the ideal may be the diagnosis given by a top consultant when faced with the patient whose history is being presented to the computer as input. The job of the critic is known as 'credit assignment' or alternatively 'blame assignment'. It must assess deviations from correct performance.

This can be simple or complex. In a simple case it might compare (for example) rainfall as forecast with actual rainfall. If 0.5mm of rain fell and the system predicted 1.9mm then it is only a matter of subtracting one number from another and passing the difference on as feedback to the learning module. In other curcumstances there may be more work for the critic to do to ascertain what went wrong. For example, after losing a game of chess, it may not be at all obvious where the computer blundered.

The *Learner* is the heart of the system. This is the portion that has responsibility for amending the knowledge base to correct erroneous

Fig. 1.2 — A typical learning system.

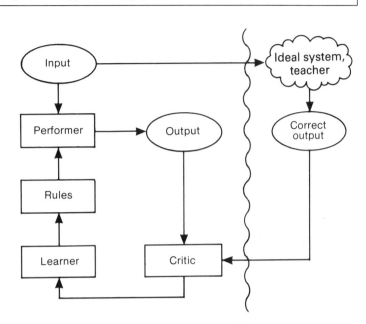

This outline shows the logical layout of a typical learning system. To the left of the wavy line is the learning system, to the right is the ideal system or teacher, whose behaviour it is trying to match.

The *Critic* compares the actual with the desired output and passes on feedback to the *Learner*. The learner attempts to modify the *Rules* (or knowledge base) to improve the system's performance. The *Performer* uses those rules to guide its performance at the task (but leaves the job of amending them to the learner module).

performance. A large number of learning strategies have been proposed, many of which we will examine in Chapters 2, 3 and 4.

The *Rules* are the data structures that encode the system's current levelof expertise. They guide the activity of the performance module. The crucial point is that they can be amended. Instead of a Read-Only knowledge base (as in today's Expert Systems) the rules constitute a Programmable-Erasable knowledge base. Obviously they must only be modified under strictly defined conditions or chaos will result. Other forms of knowledge representation than condition–action rules have been used successfully, but we use the term 'rules' as a kind of shorthand for the moment.

Finally, the *Performer* is the part of the system that carries out the task. This uses the rules in some way to guide its activity. Thus when the rules are updated, the behaviour of the system as a whole changes (for the better, if all goes according to plan).

Two other terms need to be defined before we begin our examination of practical learning methods — 'description language' and 'training set'.

The description language is the notation or formalism in which the knowledge of the system is expressed. There are two kinds of description language which are important. The first is the notation used to represent the input examples. One of the simplest of input formats is the feature vector. Each aspect of the input example is measured numerically, and the vector of measurements defines the input situation.

The second kind of description language is that chosen to represent the rules themselves. As we shall see in Chapter 3, the expressiveness of the description language in which the rules are formulated is ciritical to the success of any learning algorithm. It also has a bearing on how readily the knowledge can be understood, and hence on whether it can be transferred to people.

The notion of a 'training set' is important in understanding how a machine learning system is tested. Typically there is a database of examples for which the solutions are known. The system works through these instances and derives a rule or set of rules for associating input descriptions with output decisions (e.g. disease symptoms with diagnoses). But, as Bacon pointed out, rules must be tested on cases other than those from which they were derived. Therefore there should be another database, the test set, of the same kind but containing unseen data. If the rules also apply successfully to these fresh cases, our confidence in them is increased.

This preliminary definition of terms enables us to compare and contrast learning systems in a consistent fashion from now on. For example we can ask

what description language does it employ?
how does the critic evaluate performance?
how does the performer make use of the rules?

and so on.

1.5   WHY BOTHER?

Why is machine learning worth striving for? The answers are almost as various as the applications of computers. Here are just a couple of possibilities:

— a computer program that starts off knowing only the rules of the ancient oriental game of Go, and ends up defeating the world champion;
— a system that scans meteorological records of the past few decades and works out how to forecast the weather more reliably than at present.

In practice, the motivation for the resurgence of interest in machine learning has come from the new discipline of 'knowledge engineering'. Knowledge engineers are people who build expert systems, and their job is not easy. Traditionally (if one can speak of tradition in so new a field) they have had to work long and hard with a 'domain specialist', a human expert, to codify the expert's knowledge in symbolic form — e.g. as condition–action rules.

Experts are notoriously bad at formalizing their expertise — even if they are not worried about revealing trade secrets. The knowledge engineer must coax out of them know-how they are scarcely aware of possesing. Often this means building a flawed prototype system, submitting it to the expert's disparaging criticism, revising it, doing the same again, and repeating the cycle until the system reaches an acceptable level of performance.

This arduous process has come to be known as the 'knowledge acquisition bottleneck'. Machine learning offers one way through that bottleneck. Ideally a learning system could take a data base of example cases and come up with a set of rules for doing the expert's job. Even if completely automated knowledge acquisition of this kind proves too ambitious, the ability to refine a partial or inconsistent knowledge base derived from a human would be valuable.

And, of course, machine learning opens up the exciting possibility of synthesizing totally new knowledge — discovering concepts and patterns that humans have never even thought of.

1.6 REFERENCES

Bolles, Robert (1979) *Learning Theory*: Holt, Rinehart & Winston, New York.

Hampshire, Stuart (1956) ed. *The Age of Reason*: Mentor Books, New York.

Hilgard, E. R. & Bower, G. H. (1966)*Theories of Learning*: Appleton-Century-Crofts, New York.

Passmore, John (1968) *A Hundred Years of Philosophy*: Penguin Books, Middlesex.

Russell, Bertrand (1912) *The Problems of Philosophy*: Oxford University Press.

Russell, Bertrand (1961) *History of Western Philosophy*: Allen & Unwin, London.

Wittgenstein, Ludwig (1961) *Tractatus Logico-Philosophicus* tr. by Pears & McGuinness: Routledge & Kegan Paul, London.

2

Black box methods

One way of trying to understand a complex phenomenon is to ignore its internal structure and treat it as a 'black box'. This notion has proved useful in a number of disciplines ranging from enginnering to biology. The point about a black box is that no one really cares about what goes on inside it. Only the inputs and outputs of the system under scrutiny (which may be a natural phenomenon, a living organism or a man-made artefact) are studied. As long as the relationships between inputs and outputs can be specified precisely, it is not important how they are achieved (Forsyth & Naylor, 1985).

A black box is completely specified by its input-output behaviour. It does not matter whether that behaviour is realized electronically, hydraulically, mechanically, or by wet meat.

/ This methodology has obvious affinities with the S–R approach to the psychology of learning, as outlined in Chapter 1. Many behavioural scientists favour a black-box approach to learning because it is very hard to decide what is going on inside the brain of an animal (still less its mind) as it learns.

Some investigators in the field of machine learning have followed this lead. In this chapter we survey a number of black-box learning systems. They all share two distinguishing features:

(1) a mathematical bias;
(2) a 'write-only' description langauge.

The mathematical bias means that they tend to employ well-established procedures from the realms of statistics and control theory. Designers of such systems think nothing of multiplying or inverting matrices, calculating eigenvectors and so forth. These systems frequently require considerable processing power for heavy number-crunching.

Partly as a consequence of this, the knowledge that the system gains during its training phase is opaque. It may calculate a covariance matrix or optimize a set of coefficients; but even a mathematically sophisticated person cannot inspect knowledge in this format and readily determine what the system has learned. This is what we mean by saying that black-box learning systems have a 'write-only' knowledge base. It is computable, but not intelligible. Being able to look inside the black box is not one of the design goals.

In contrast, developers of structural learning systems tend to follow the footsteps of the cognitive psychologists. Their systems are intended to generate knowledge that is humanly comprehensible. But we postpone detailed consideration of such systems until Chapter 3.

2.1   INTRODUCTION TO PATTERN RECOGNITION

This book is concerned with all kinds of machine learning, but especially those which can be harnessed for the development of expert systems. Black-box learning systems, however, have almost all been applied in the area of pattern recognition.

The two fields, pattern recognition and expert systems, have different historical roots, different learned journals and, above all, different practitioners (very often in different academic departments). They belong to different subcultures, so it is worth spending a few paragraphs pointing out the similarities in their aims and methods. In particular, it is worth stressing that pattern recognition lies at the heart of all expertise, whether human or computerized.

Here are some typical pattern recognition tasks:

equipment fault diagnosis;
medical diagnosis;
fingerprint identification;
voice recognition.

In all pattern recognition tasks there are a number of measurements made of an event or object. These raw measurements are transformed in some way into a set of features, and the features are used by a decision procedure to assign the event to one category or another. Thus the typical pattern recognition system is a classifier. This is illustrated in Fig. 2.1.

Clearly, classification is a process of information reduction. The central operation (feature extraction) is logically unnecessary; but all practical sytems have this intermediate step. Coupling the decision algorithm directly to the raw data is computationally infeasible. In fact the choice of features is crucial to the success of any classifier.

Let us take birdsong recognition as an example. Suppose a system is required to distinguish nightingales from thrushes, by listening to their songs. It will have to go through the following three stages.

(1) Measurement. Birdsong is recorded via a microphone and pressure

Fig. 2.1 — Pattern recognition.

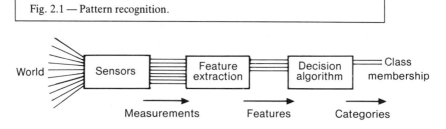

Pattern classification is a data-reduction process. Normally three stages are involved. First the attibutes of the outside world are sampled or measured in some way. Next these raw measurements are processed to give a smaller number of features. Finally the features are examined and the system picks one of a small number of classes and assigns the pattern to that class.
The problem is the many-to-one mapping of inputs to outputs.

waves are transformed into a time-varying amplitude signal. (See Fig. 2.2)

(2) Feature Extraction. This electrical signal is converted into a vector of parameters giving (for instance) number of zero crossings, maximum energy level, total duration of silence, number of detectable silences, average energy in the 10–20 KHz bandwidth, and much else besides.

(3) Classification. The feature vector is processed mathematically and a decision algorithm applied to decide category membership.

None of these stages is particulary simple. In particular, an informed choice of features at stage 2 can make all the difference. This is where human expertise is most needed at the design stage.

Before carrying out this three-step classification process, the system must be trained. In the training phase, the decision algorithm is optimized, in some sense, for the discriminations it has to perform.

Note that although learning is commonly used for tuning the decision algorithm, it is only rarely used for the feature extraction process. There are examples of systems that pick useful features from a large set of potentially useful ones; but there are very few that make up their own features from scratch.

After this detour into the field of pattern recognition, let us return to expert systems. Here is a list of some expert system applications:

equipment fault diagnosis;
medical diagnosis;
fingerprint identification;
voice recognition.

It is identical to the pattern recognition tasks that we listed earlier (delibera-

Fig. 2.2 — A typical acoustic waveform.

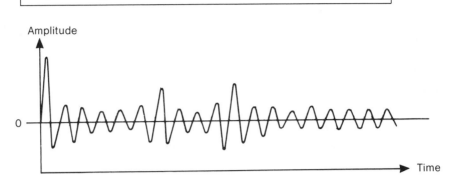

A microphone converts waves of air pressure into voltage, varying with time.
The raw temporal signal is difficult to process as it stands, so it is usually
transformed futher into a vector of numeric features.

    One commonly used feature is the number of zero-crossings. This is an
index of the overall frequency of the sound: the more times the wave form
crosses the zero line, the higher the frequency.

tely, of course). This overlap is not complete; but expert systems have to
recognize patterns, and once they have done so, the rest of their task is often
trivial. For example, in a medical consultation, the difficult part might be to
tell whether the patient is suffering from gastric ulcer or stomach cancer.
Once that diagnostic problem is solved, the choice of therapy is highly
constrained. It may simply be a matter of looking up the prescribed therapy
in a table.

    Expert systems, therefore, need to recognize patterns. From now on we
will treat systems that learn to recognize patterns as directly relevant to our
quest for self-improving expert systems.

    The systems described in this chapter use a description language in which
input patterns are presented as feature vectors, always numeric and sometimes binary. Thus an input example is a vector of numbers. If there are F
features, then this vector defines a point in F-dimensional space. Various
mathematical/geometric terms are used to describe regions in this abstract
space. Many of the methods attempt to partition the feature space so that
clusters of examples of one kind are together and clusters of another kind in
a different region. It is quite easy to imagine examples in 2D or 3D feature
space (e.g. with up to three features, such as age, weight and height); but the
terminology for multi-dimensional feature space can become confusing, so
we list the correspondences in Table 2.1.

2.2   BLACK BOXES AND GREY MATTER

The brain really is a black box (at present); but the digital computer is not.
At its darkest it is dirty grey: it is always possible, in principle, to look inside.
In practice, however, it may not be desirable or profitable to do so.

Table 2.1

2D	3D	Multi-D
space	3-space	hyperspace
area	volume	volume
curve	surface	hypersurface
line	plane	hyperplane
circle	sphere	hypersphere
square	cube	hypercube
polygon	polyhedron	polyhedron

However, from our vantage point, we can peep into the box and say that learning systems of this type fall into two main groups, on the basis of how they store their knowledge. There are those that adjust the parameters or coefficients of a discriminant function until it is optimal, or at least satisfactory, according to predefined criteria; and there are those which perform what amounts to an indexing operation. Borrowing the terminology of Samuel (1967), we say that systems of the second type construct 'signature tables'.

We can illustrate the difference with a simplified example. Suppose the objective is to classify military aircraft as fighters or bombers. There are two features: maximum speed (in km/h) and maximum load at take-off (kg). Table 2.2 gives two examples of each class.

Table 2.2

	Fighter			Bomber	
	Speed	Load		Speed	Load
F-15C	2443	20185	Blackjack-A	2200	267000
SU-27	2445	28800	TU-22M	2036	118000

There would be many more examples than this in a realistic training set.

A parameter adjustment system would typically look for weightings by which to multiply the features S (speed) and L (loading) in a function such as

$$F = W_0 + W_1 * S + W_2 * L$$

where $F > 0$ would be taken to indicate that the aeroplane was a fighter and $F \leq 0$ would indicate that it was a bomber. (This is a simple linear discriminant function.)

Since the bombers are heavier and (on the whole) slower, the final weightings might be: $W_0 = 640$, $W_1 = 1$, $W_2 = -0.0566$. This would give the discriminant function

$$F = 640.00 + 1.00*S - 0.0566*L$$

where a positive result indicates a fighter, as above.

A system based on signature tables, on the other hand, would attempt to quantize the feature range by establishing cut-off points or thresholds, giving S and L a small number of levels, and come up with a decision table such as Table 2.3.

Table 2.3

	$L < 22000$		$L > 100000$ kg
	Light	Heavy	Very Heavy
Very fast	Fighter	Fighter	Bomber ($S > 2400$ k/h)
Fast	Fighter	Bomber	Bomber
Slow	Bomber	Bomber	Bomber ($S < 1000$ k/h)

The two variables have been divided at two threshold points into three levels each, giving a table with nine entries altogether. In fact the entries in this table might well be probabilities (based on frequencies of fighters and bombers in the training data) for each class, rather than just class labels as shown here.

The relationship between these two different kinds of knowledge representation is depicted in Fig. 2.3. It is evident from the diagram that the parameter-estimation approach involves creating a function to define the boundary between the two classes, while the signature-table approach produces a jagged or zigzag decision line. (Both methods can be elaborated greatly compared to the examples presented here.)

The two methods have slightly different strengths and weaknesses. One advantage of signature tables over functional parameters is that they are somewhat more transparent: the box is a lighter shade of grey. Another advantage is that tables can be used to partition the feature space in more diverse ways than linear functions. In general, however, a decision function can be tabulated and a signature table can be functionalized if the need arises.

2.3   PARAMETER ADJUSTMENT

Parameter adjustment (PA) is one of the simplest forms of learning. We shall look briefly at four different systems which, between them, exemplify the most important parameter-adjustment techniques.

Fig. 2.3 — Parameter adjustment versus Signature Tables.

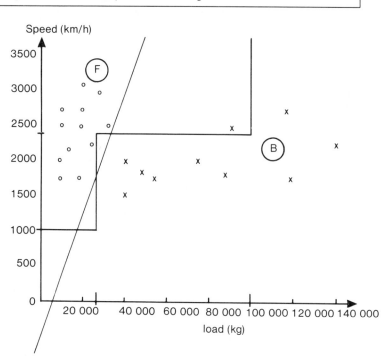

With only two features the objects in the training set can be displayed as points on a graph whose positions are fixed by plotting speed against load. Dots mark fighter planes (F) and crosses mark bombers (B).

To distinguish the two classes a parameter adjustment (PA) system fits the parameters of a function. In this example, the steeply sloping diagonal divides *F* from *B*, though it is not always a straight-line that is used.

A signature-table method (ST) creates, in effect a jagged boundary, as shown here by the stepped line. The axes are divided at threshold points.

2.3.1   The Perceptron

One of the earliest, and still one of the best known, PA systems was the Perceptron (Rosenblatt, 1958, 1962). Originally it was put forward as a simple neurological model, but it is perhaps better regarded as one of a family of trainable classifiers with certain interesting properties.

The device which Rosenblatt came to call the Mark I Perceptron has received most attention in the literature. This is the version we shall describe here. Its operation is sketched diagrammatically in figure 2.4.

In the first place an image is projected onto the picture plane and digitized as a grid of zeroes and ones, with 1 representing light and 0 dark. This is a crude approximation to the retina. The next level consists of a number of 'Associator Units'. Each of these receives inputs from several pixels in the digitized image. The associator units are the feature-detectors: they are threshold devices which produce binary outputs (rather like miniature Perceptrons themselves). For example, unit A7 may sample six

Fig. 2.4 — Mark I perceptron.

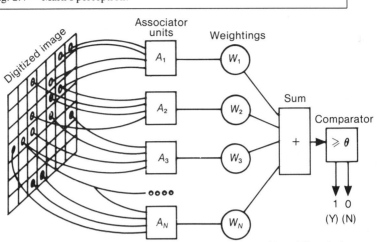

Outputs from the Associator Units are 1s or 0s computed by adding the inputs and comparing to a threshold. In other words, each Associator unit (or feature detector) is a Perceptron in miniature.

These are multiplied by the Weightings then totalled and compared to a threshold θ.

$$\sum_{i=1}^{N} A_i W_i \geqslant \theta$$

If the sum is greater the system says Yes (1); if not, it says No (φ).

randomly distributed pixels and 'fire' when four or more are lit. Firing just means transmitting a 1, rather than a 0, to the next level. Thus associator units are predicates which detect subpatterns in the input by local computations.

The outputs from the associator units are passed on to weighting units. Each binary value is simply multiplied by a numeric weighting. These weighted values are added up and compared to a threshold by the comparator. If the sum equals or exceeds the threshold, the system says Yes (pattern observed), otherwise it says No (pattern absent).

The only things that vary are the weightings. The Perceptron uses an error-correction learning algorithm in which the weightings after an erroneous response are adjusted, as follows

$$w[j]: = w[j] - a[j]*d$$

where $d = 1$ if the system said Yes and the teacher said No, and $d = -1$ if the system said No and the teacher said Yes.

In other words, no changes are made after a correct response, but after a mistake all the feature values ($a[j]$) are either added to or subtracted from the weightings ($w[j]$), depending on whether the system's output was too high or too low on the previous trial.

This is known as the proportional increment training strategy (Sklansky

& Wassel, 1981). It can be proved to converge on an optimal set of weightings only when the two pattern classes are linearly separable — i.e. when a linear function can separate the two groups in feature space. In many practical problems the classes are not linearly separable, although even in these cases the Perceptron may still give acceptable results.

There are many variations on the Perceptron theme. We will consider just one, in which it is given two minor extensions. First, we extend the number of pattern classes beyond two. Secondly we allow features to have unrestricted numeric values, not just zero and one.

The knowledge base for such an augmented Perceptron is simply a numeric matrix, as below.

Fig. 2.5 — Weighting matrix.

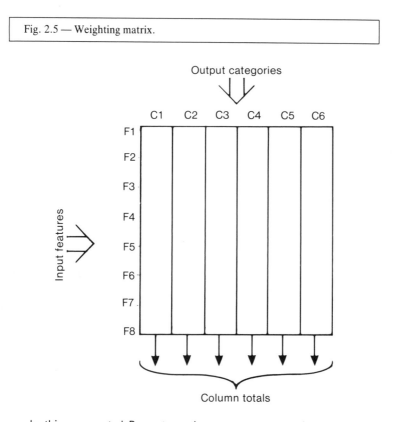

In this augmented Perceptron, there are as many columns as there are categories in the classification task. When the input features are presented, they are multiplied by each column in turn. The total for each column is added up and the largest total picked as the systems output.

The error-correction algorithm subtracts the F values from the corresponding C values for the column that gave the wrong answer, and adds the F values to the column that failed to give the right answer.

In this example we have eight input features $F1$ to $F8$ and six pattern classes $C1$ to $C6$. In each cell of the array is stored the weighting for the contribution of the feature in that row to the category in that column. In operation the features *F*1 to *F*8 are presented as input. For each column, the feature values are multiplied by the appropriate weights, and the column totals added up. The column with the highest total is chosen as the output class.

When the system makes a mistake, all the *F* values are subtracted from the weightings in the column that gave the incorrect response, and the *F* values are added to the column that should have given the response (but failed to do so). Other columns are left unaltered. Weights that are too large are thereby reduced and those that are too small are increased.

In this form the Perception can be taught to perform a variety of useful classification tasks, but it can still only be guaranteed to work when the classes are linerly separable. This is becuase any weighted sum is a linear function. Few interesting problems involve linearly separable classes. This and other deficiencies of the Perception were pointed out by Minsky & Papert (1969).

2.3.2 Pandemonium

Another pioneering pattern recognizer was the picturesquely named Pande-monium — a model put forward by Selfridge (1959) as a 'paradigm for learning'. Pandemonium learns in the sense that, having been given some examples of patterns and told what they are, it can then 'guess correctly which pattern has just been presented before we inform it'.

Selfridge describes the architecture of Pandemonium in therms of four levels of 'demons'. At the lowest level, data demons supply coded versions of the physical input — typically a digitized picture. At the next stage the computation demons respond to various elementary features in the input and pass their output up in turn to a number of cognitive demons — each one responsible for one identifiable pattern in the set of possible reponses. Their job is to 'shriek' at a single decision demon, with a loudness proportional to the degree to which their pattern matches the features on display. The decision demon picks the loudest as the correct response.

Pandemonium 'contains the seeds of self-improvement' in two ways. It can alter the strength of the connections between computation demons and cognitive demons; and it can alter computation demons. New ones are obtained by mutating old demons. This may mean changing some para-meters of a subdemon more of less at random, or creating one which is the logical combination of two existing ones. (See also Chapter 4.) Cognitive demons are specified by the task, and do not change.

Selfridge & Neisser (1960) reported that programs based on the Pande-monium concept were successful at transliterating manually keyed Morse code and in recognizing hand-printed letters of the alphabet. Uhr & Vossler (1961) took this approach one stage further by developing a program that generated its own operators (i.e. demons). An operator, in their termino-logy, is a 5×5 submatrix, set to respond to a particular pattern of zeros and ones, that scans a larger 20×20 image matrix and records the number of matches found, and their average horizontal, vertical and central position. Further opertors then combine characteristics.

Fig. 2.6 — Pandemonium.

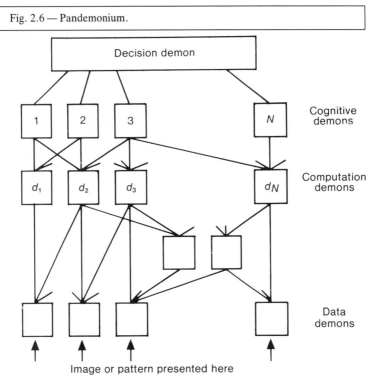

Image or pattern presented here

Computation Demons perform calculations on Data Demons to extract features. Cognitive Demons are specified by the task and do not change, but Computation Demons can be mutated according to their performance.

The resulting characteristics are then compared with lists in memory representing patterns, and the most similar chosen. The program gets better by varying amplifiers associated with each of the operators; by changing the lists in memory; and by creating or discarding operators. Novel operators are generated either as random 5×5 configurations or, more interestingly, as submatrices actually found in the large pattern. They are checked against stored operators before adoption, to avoid duplication.

This program has been tested against human performacne in an experiment (Uhr, 1963). Subjects were required to lean to classify five variants of five types of 'meaningless' forms. The program consistently outperformed the people; but the program's authors commented that this superiority 'should not be taken too seriously'.

Both Selfridge and Uhr gave their models neurological interpretations. (Uhr, 1966); but they are not very good neural models. They are mainly interesting as pioneering examples of machine learning, although (like the Perceptron) neither of them is capable of learning, for instance, whether an input field contains an odd or even number of figures of a kind that it can recognize in isolation.

Pandemonium, though it attracted less attention, was actually more powerful than the Mark I perceptron. Its main advance was that it could generate new demons, whereas the Perceptron's associator units are fixed.

2.2.3 Hyperspher classifiers

Another kind of PA system is the hypersphere classifier described by Batchelor (1974). This a generalization of an earlier technique known as nearest-neighbour classification (NNC).

In the NNC method a number of training examples are stored as representative points in the feature space. The feature vecotr of each example defines a point in a multi-dimensional space with as many dimensions as there are features. When a new case is presented to the classifier, it measures its distance from each of the known exam ples and assigns it to the same class as the nearest one. For this purpose, a distance measure must be defined. Usually the system minimizes the sum of squared deviations, and thus uses a straight-line, or Euclidean, distance metric; but other measures are occasionally employed. A diagram plotting example bombers and fighters on a 2D feature space shows how this method works (Fig. 2.7).

Fig. 2.7 — Nearest-neighbour classification.

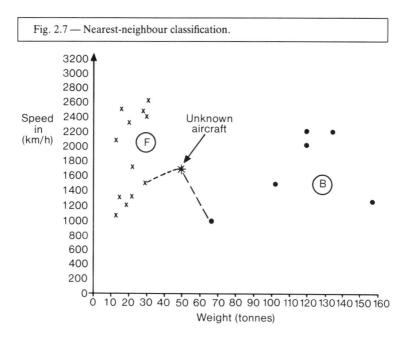

Nearest-neighbour classification (NNC) works by measuring the distance of a given point in the feature space to the nearest point of known class, and assigning the unknown point to that class.

Here the objects are aircraft measured by maximum speed and fully-laden weight. Dots represent bombers (group B) and crosses represent fighters (group F). The inidentified flying object indicated by the asterisk would be classified a fighter (group F) because its nearest neighbour is a fighter plane. The nearest bomber is about 50 km further away in a straight line.

NNC systems suffer two problems which the hypersphere method attempts to overcome. First, they require a great deal of storage, since all or most of the training instances need to be stored. Secondly they are sensitive to 'rogue' or 'quirky' exemplars. Various statistical techniques have been proposed to remove outliers, though none is wholly satisfactory.

The hypersphere method tries to get round these problems by storing only prototypical exemplars called 'locates', which represent clusters of observed cases. In fact the precise feature values of the locates may never have occurred in any single training example.

The training procedure works as follows.

(1) Initialize the classifier with a few (i.e. one or two) locates.
(2) Optimize the positions and sizes of the hyperspheres surrounding each locate, using the training data one by one with the error-correction procedure described below.
(3) Test the clasifier's performance. 3a. If the error rate is sufficiently low, halt. 3b. If it is unsatisfactory, add a new hypersphere.
(4) Repeat from step 2, unless there are enough hyperspheres.

The error-correction procedure adjusts the parameters of one or more hyperspheres. there are four distinct outcomes after each test case, where M stands for the machine's response and T for the teacher's response, either of which can be $+1$ or -1.

(A) $M = T$. No modification.
(B) $M = -1$; $T = +1$. (Latest point X lies outside al hyperspheres). The hypersphere closest to X is found, moved slightly closer to X and enlarged.
(C) $M = +1$; $T = -1$. (Lastest point X is in the wrong hypersphere.) The hypersphere enclosing X is moved away from it and reduced in size.
(D) $M = +1$; $T = -1$. (X is in more than one hypersphere.) All the hyperspheres enclosing X are moved away from it and reduced in size.

Note that C is a special case of D.

To understand this process you should imagine the locates as the centres of multi-dimensional bubbles in the feature space. They move around, growing and shrinking, until nearly all the positive training examples are within their radius but hardly any of the negative ones are so enclosed. With two or three dimensions this is easy to visualize. With more dimensions it is harder, but the mathematics are essentially the same.

Moving a hypersphre means adjustting the coordiantes of its locate, i.e. its feature values. Growing or shrinking one means altering an additional parameter, which gives its radius of influence.

The outer loop of the procedure starts with a single hypersphere (or only a few) and adds new ones until there is no gain from doing so. Batchelor suggests some heuristics for deciding where to place a new hypersphere. One idea is to take the least satisfactory hypersphere and split it in two. Another is to look for misclassified examples and take their centroid, or average on all dimensions.

In any case this incremental process can sometimes create degenerate hyperspheres, which have near-zero radius or which are completely enclosed by another one. So it is advisable to append a pruning phase afterwards which removes redundant hyperspheres until performance begins to deteriorate.

Batchelor gives various hints on the practical implementation of hypersphere classifiers.

(1) Put the initial (single) locate at the centroid of the positive training instances.
(2) Make the radius of the first hypersphere 'small'.
(3) Do not generate more than
$$N/10*(F+1)$$
locates, where N is the number of training samples and F is the number of features or dimensions.
(4) Use approximately $100/E$ training patterns, where E is the desired percentage error rate.

These rules of thumb do not, however, address the problem of deciding whether to classify positive or negative instances. This sort of classifier is asymmetrical; so it can make a difference which way round the two classes are assigned. For instance, Bomber $= +1$ and Fighter $= -1$ might give significantly better results than Fighter $= +1$ and Bomber $= -1$ (for the sake of argument). This question can only be answered by experiment, which implies that such systems have to be run twice to attain optimum performance.

Another disadvantage is that the extension to multiple classes is not a trivial matter. In fact such systems become impractical with a large number of pattern categories. The printable set of 96 ASCII characters would be far too large a domain.

However, with a small number of pattern classes (less than a dozen), hypersphere classifiers will generally outperform simple Perceptrons or Pandemonium-type systems. This is because they can adapt to much more diverse distributions within the feature space than systems based on linear functions. The hypersphere, naturally, is a non-linear decision surface.

2.3.4 The Boltzmann Machine

After Minsky & Papert's book on Perceptrons (1969), pattern recognizers based on overtly neurological principles virtually disappeared fro the AI literature. Research on pattern recognition continued in other fields, such as applied mathematics and engineering, but without the neurological overtones.

Nevertheless, the fact that the brain is a trainable pattern recognizer cannot be disputed, and recently AI researchers have started to re-examine the idea of simulating neural networks. Why should they think it might be worth resurrecting the old 'discredited' notions of Rosenblatt, Selfridge and others?

First, there has been some progress in neurophysiology during the intervening 20 years. Second, and more important, there has been extraordinary progress in micro-electronics during the same period. Fabricating machines that simulate the brain is beginning to seem feasible.

A team at Carnegie-Hellon University, led by Geoff Hinton (1985), has designed a system to do just that. They call it the Boltzmann Machine, in honour of Ludwig Boltzmann, one of the founders of statistical mechanics. (We shall see late why his name is appropriate.) Theirs is a deliberate attempt to mimic the behaviour of neural networks, though admittedly their model is highly idealized.

A Boltzmann Machine is composed of a network of multiple computing elements, all of which work in parallel. It can be simulated on a conventional computer, but the ultimate aim is to use it as a blueprint for a novel form of computer archietecture.

The Boltzmann Machine learns by trying, in effect, to construct internal representations of the input–output relationships it encounters in its environment. Its model of the world is represented by the strengths of association betwen elements, which are not meant for public scrutiny. It is a very dark box.

The elements in the network are threshold units, which produce a binary output (0 or 1) by adding up their inputs and 'firing' if the sum exceeds a certain quantity. Thus each processing element is a simplified, abstract neuron. The important point is that the elements react probabilistically. The threshold can be said to waver: the bigger the input, the more likely the unit is to fire, but the same input does not invariably trigger the same response. (See Fig. 2.8.)

All processing units in a Boltzmann Machine are of the same type; and they all have the same threshold, zero. But the connection strengths between them may vary. Connection strengths are symmetrical, so that if the link in one direction (X to Y) has a weighting of 7.5 then so does the link in the opposite direction (Y to X). (This is not like the real nervous system.)

The network of interconnections can be far more complex than that of a Perceptron. There are input units from the outside world which receive the feature vector (coded as a string of zeroes and ones), and output units which, in effect, give the system's decision. In between, all kinds of links are permitted. There may be backward links on many levels, with feedback loops and so on, as illustrated diagrammatically in Fig. 2.9.

The system can be made to learn input-output relationships (i.e. to recognize patterns) by adjusting the interconnection weights in the following manner.

Phase 1

1(a) Clamp the training pattern to the input units, and the desired response pattern to the output units.

1(b) Allow the network to settle down to equilibrium.

1(c) Increment the weights between any two elements (by a small amount, delta) whenever they are both active together.

Fig. 2.8 — Probability of processing unit firing.

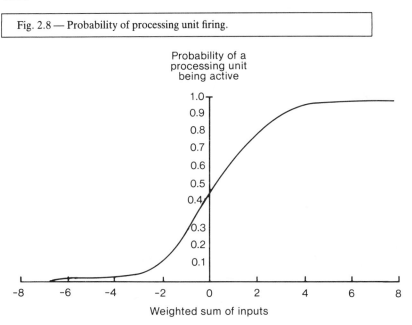

Probability of a
processing unit
being active

This graph shows the probability that a given element will fire as a function of the weighted sum of its inputs.

The whole network can be made more deterministic by making this curve steeper, and it can be made less deterministic by making the curve flatter. The simulated annealing process begins with all the units having a flat curve and gradually makes them all steeper.

Fig. 2.9 — Boltzmann Machine network layout.

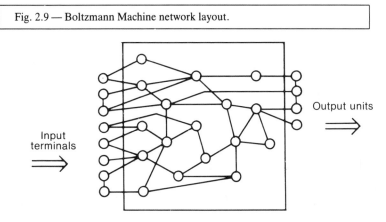

Output units

Input
terminals

The connection network in a Boltzmann Machine can be much more complicated than that of a Perceptron. There are typically many layers, and links may exist between different layers.

The 'black box' is enclosed in the rectangle.

Phase 2

2(a) Remove the output connections (i.e. take away the teacher), but leave the inputs connected.

2(b) Let the network stabilize again.

2(c) Decrement the weights between any two elements whicha re simultaneously active, by delta.

The two phases are repeated alternately for as many iterations are required
to give satisfactory input-output behaviour in phase 2 (the unsupervised
response).

   This method has been proved to minimize the discrepancy between the
structure of the network's internal model and the actual structure of the
input–output relationship. Thus the system learns to give the same responses in phase 2 that it has been taught in phase 1.

   Steps 1(b) and 2(b) are both instances of a procedure known as
'simulated annealing', by analogy with the hardening of metal as it cools.
When a substance is hot, there is plenty of essentially random motion among
the molecules that compose it. As it cools, they settle into fixed positions.

   Likewise in steps 1(b) and 2(b), the input–output relationship of all the
units in the network starts off with a greater degree of randomness and
becomes increasingly deterministic. This analogy with temperature reduction is intended to avoid a well-known 'pitfall' in machine learning — the
problem of local optima.

   To simplify maters, for the time being, imagine a ball bearing on a jagged
surface, as outlined in Fig. 2.10.

Fig. 2.10 — The shallow pitfall problem.

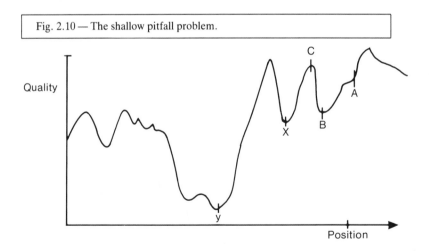

Here the vertical axis represents solution quality and the horizontal axis
represents position in the space of potential (stable) solutions. The problem of
finding an optimal solution is like the problem of getting a marble or metal ball
into the deepest trough of a jagged surface.
   The ball easily rolls down from A to But to get it to X & then Y requires that
the whole 'mountain range' is shaken by an 'earthquake'.

   If the metal ball starts at point A, it will rapidly roll down to point B and
stay there; but point B is not by any means the deepest trough. If we shake it
gently (adding some random disturbance) it will bounce around: sometimes

it will go upwards, but the tendency will be for it to jump over barriers like point C and come to rest at a lower minimum like point X. However the lowest point is at Y. To make it likely that the ball reaches that global minimum, we would have to shake it fairly violently for quite a long time.

Scott Kirkpatrick of IBM (Kirkpatrick *et al.*, 1983) have shown that the behaviour of a Boltzmann Machine in seeking an optimum set of weightings is similar to that of a ball rolling about on a bumpy surface. He introduced the concept of thermal disturbance for shaking such systems out of local minima into deeper ones, and showed that starting at a high temperature and gradually reducing it (simulated annealing) was effective. The fact that Boltzmann first studied the physics of such random thermal motion explains why his name was chosen for this computing procedure.

The Boltzmann Machine has brought neural modelling back to the forefront of AI. Such systems can be taught virtually any stimulus–response behaviour; but there is a price to pay for this flexibility. they are very slow. As Hinton himself says (1985):

> Our current simulations are slow for three reasons: it is inefficient to simulate parallel networks with serial machines, it takes many decisions by each unit before a big network approaches equilibrium, and it takes an inordinate number of I/O pairs before a network can figure out what to represent with its internal units. Better hardware might solve the first problem, but more theoretical progress is needed on the other two. Only then will we be able to apply this kind of learning network to more realistic problems.

The Boltzmann Machine is extremely versatile, but it is not yet a practical device. It learns far too slowly for prctical applications. For the present it is best viewed as an exciting idea thrown into the melting-pot of current proposals on how to design the next generation of parallel computers — with suggestive implications for students of the nervous system.

2.4 SIGNATURE TABLES

The signature table (ST) approach to machine learning seeks to construct little boxes in feature space such that each box contains only (or mostly) one kind of pattern. It is a slighly more comprehensible process than parameter adjustment (PA), and is clearly akin to the widespread computing technique of indexing — using attributes of an object to decide where to store that object.

2.4.1 Bledsoe and Browning's program

An early program of this type was the character recognizer of Bledsoe and Browning (1959).

In their system the image of a character was projected onto a 10×5 matrix and digitized. Each pixel in the matrix was given a binary value — either on or off. The 150 pixels were paired up, at random, into 75 couples.

A pairing can be in one of only four states — 00, 01, 10, 11 — and these are used to address one of four different locations in memory. As each couple is connected to four memory words and there are 756 couples, this uses 300 words of storage. The words in this case are 36 bits long, with one bit allocated to each of the 26 capital letters and 10 digit characters. Initially all 300 words are filled with zeroes.

What happens when a character is presented to the system during training is that each couple responds in one of its four ways. For each couple one (and only one) of its four associated words is selected, and in that word the bit belonging to the character on display is set to one, as shown in Fig. 2.11.

Fig. 2.11 — Bledsoe and Browning's program.

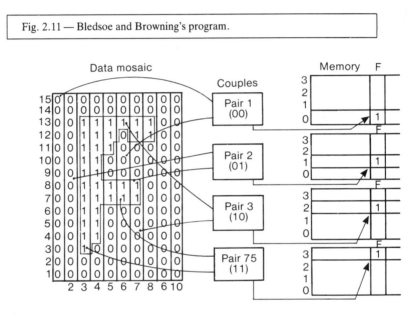

The diagram illustrates what happens when an F is presented (pattern 16) during the training phase. Each paining responds in one of four ways, and thus selects one out of the four memory words to which it is connected. At that work, in the column (or bit position) reserved for F, a one is set. If F is the 16th pattern, then the bit is set at the 16th position, or column, within that word.

Bits that never get set mark 'forbidden' subpatterns — where a pairing has never been in the given state with the given pattern.

If F is the 16th pattern, and an F is presented, the 16th bit in 75 of the 300 words will be set — one associated with each of the 75 couples. Which one, of the four, is determined by the state of that couple.

During the learning phase several examples of each possible pattern are presented, and the memory gradually fills with ones. However some bits are never set, because some couples cannot be in certain states given certain characters. For instance, it is hard to imagine an O or a Q causing the central pair at [row 8, column 5] and [row 8, column 6] both to be on together. In effect the system learns about forbidden sub-patterns in the various characters, as defined by the state of pairs of pixels.

After training, when test characters are displayed, each of the 75 words addressed contributes one or zero to 36 totals, one for each possible pattern. the bit position with the highest total is chosen as the correct decision. Ties are resolved randomly.

A bit set in any column says that such a configuration of the relevant couple has been seen before for the character assigned to that column. If the bit is zero, it means that the configuration has never occurred with that character.

This is not a particularly sophisticated algorithm by today's standards, but it is instructive as an early example of some principles that are still in use — in particular, the idea of using computed features of the input as addresses. Each pair of pixels functions as a simple feature detector, and the state of that pair is used to point to a position in memory associated with that state.

The system could be improved by storing integers, not just single bits, at each location, reflecting how often the feature-state had been encountered for each character, not merely whether or not it had been seen. But this would use up $36 \times 300 = 10\ 800$ words in memory. As we shall see, ST systems often prove rather greedy in their storage requirements.

2.4.2 Samuel's checker-playing program

Arthur Samuel (1959, 1967) conducted two of the classic AI studies of machine learning. He used the game of checkers (or draughts) as a test-bed for ideas on searching, planning and — more to the point — machine learning.

His first program (1959) was essentially a PA system. It introduced some important ideas about game-playing by computer, but it was not so interesting as a learning machine — although he did emphasize the role of 'selective forgetting' in rote-memory systems. In his 1967 paper, however, he introduced the key notion of 'signature tables' to describe a method he found more effective than adjusting the parameters of a polynomial evaluation function. This is the aspect of his work we concentrate on here.

At first glance, game-playing would seem an ideal arena for machine learning. It is, after all, quite easy to arrange for two programs, or two versions of one program, to play each other overnight and record the results. One might hope to leave the machine on all night and come back to find it playing at expert level.

The reason it is not this easy is that the credit-assignment problem is especially acute. At the end of a lost game, the program has to decide which moves were the bad ones. Various solutions have been proposed — one of which is to retrace all the moves from the winner's point of view and regard all those moves where the loser would have played diferently as mistakes. But in fact the winner is likely to have made mistakes too. If the winner makes six blunders and the loser makes seven, the loser is likely to pick up more bad habits than good ones. In general, there is no credit/blame assignment algorithm that is both simple and effective.

Samuel neatly sidestepped this dilemma by turning the game into a pattern recognition task. The problem then becomes one of looking at a board state (the pattern) and deciding which move is the best (classifying moves). To provide grist for the learning mill he had several hundred thousand moves from published master-level games encoded on magnetic tape. Only moves by players that led to wins or draws were stored. Thus all moves by losers were ignored. The game-state together with the move actually chosen constituted a training instance. The program examined up to 180 000 of these instances to form its signature tables.

There were actually three levels of the table in his experiments, as shown in Fig. 2.12.

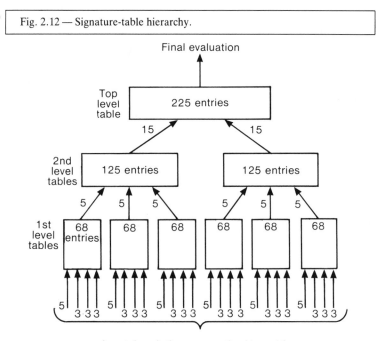

Fig. 2.12 — Signature-table hierarchy.

Input description as quantized board features.

At the bottom level are 24 features which are computed from the board state. these are numeric measures of such factors as centre-control, piece advantage, threat to opponent's kings and so forth. Such features are used routinely in game-playing programs to describe the board state.

The learning process begins by quantizing these features into one of three or five levels. In effect the raw value is converted to one of low, medium and high (three levels) or one of very low, low, medium, high and very high (five levels). This enables it to be represented by a small integer.

The 24 quantized features are then divided into six groups of four, as shown in Fig. 2.12, one per table; and the state of each of the four features is used as an index into the table it belongs to. thus the tables are $5 \times 3 \times 3 \times 3$ arrays containing 135 entries (but because checkers is a zero-sum game and the features are defined symmetrically, only 68 entries need to be stored).

Each cell in the arrary is associated with a particular combination of feature values, and thus with a particular board configuration. This constitutes a kind of signature of that board state.

Given a game-state, each of the 24 features is computed and used to select a single cell in each of the six low-level signature tables. What actually happens during the learning phase is that the game-states corresponding to all the possible next moves are generated, and each of them produces a set of six signatures for the six tables. In fact each cell contains two numbers (initialized to zero) called D and A. When a signature is formed from a move that the expert did not pick, D is incremented by one. When a signature is generated by a move the expert did make, A is incremented by N, where N is the number of alternative moves that the expert could have made (but rejected) at that point. This gives greater positive weight to the moves the expert did choose than negative weight to those not played by the expert — some of which may be quite good moves.

As and Ds are accumulated separately for all signatures in all tables. After a large number of examples, the program can compute an evaluation for any proposed board state (and hence for a proposed move) from the formula

$$C = (A - D)/(A + D)$$

where C is interpreted as a coefficient expressing correlation with the expert's choice. C can vary from $+1$ to -1, with higher values indicating better moves.

In this manner each signature (corresponding to a board configuration) points to a location in its table where the information can be found for estimating its value, by reference to numerous examples of expert play.

But how are the six tables to be combined into an overall assessment? At one stage Samuel simply added their outputs up and took the total (in the same way as Bledsoe and Browning had done), but later he hit on the idea of applying the same procedure to them. This is the purpose of the second-level tables in Fig. 2.12. Just as the first-level tables store information about combinations of feature values, so the second-level tables hold information about combinations of signature-table vaues. Once the first-level tables have been filled, the process can be repeated, quantizing the output of the first–level tables (to five discrete levels in this case) and using them to index into two $5 \times 5 \times 5$ tables where the values of various first-level combinations can be accumulated. In effect the second-level table learns the weightings to apply to its first-level tables.

The third-level table is filled in the same way. The outputs from the two second-level tables are quantized to 15 levels each, and used to address cells in a 15×15 array. Again, it is effectively weighting the contributions of the mid-level tables.

Samuel found the ST procedure far more effective than a comparable PA method using linear functions. After 184 000 sotred moves had been analyzed the correlation coefficient of the computer's evaluation with the expert's evaluation was nearly twice as high (0.48 to 0.26) with the signature tables than with parameter adjustment. In another test, on 895 unseen examples, the ST program rated the master's actual move as its first or second choice on 64% of the occasions. (By searching forward using aplha-beta minimaxing, the program could do even better in actual play.)

The ST procedure gives better performance than a linear PA method because it is capable of handling non-linear interactions among the board features. These are actually quite common in practice.

Its chief defect is that the groupings are fixed. The selection of which four features should be grouped together to address a single table was done by Samuel. The program has no way of altering this choice, and an exhaustive search of all possible 4-form-24 groupings would be out of the question. If low-level tables were allowed to have three of five or six inputs as well, the number of combinations would become astronomical.

2.4.3 Michie's Boxes

Another system in the ST tradition but with a markedly different application was Boxes, designed by Donald Michie and colleagues at the University of Edinburgh (Michie & Chambers, 1968). This was a program that learned to balance a pole on a moving cart.

A small cart driven by an electric motor runs along rails carrying a pole hinged at the bottom. The cart must move back and forth to keep the pole from falling, rather like a Scottish Highlander preparing to toss a caber. In addition, the cart must not run off the ends of the track. This sort of set-up, illustrated in Fig. 2.13, is often posed as a problem for students of control

Fig. 2.13 — The Boxes balancing act.

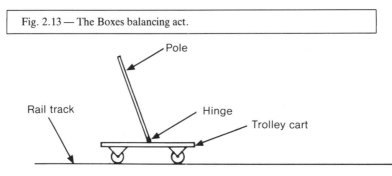

The Boxes computer system learned to control the movement of a wheeled cart on rails, so that it could keep the pole upright and avoid falling over the ends of the track for up to 30 minutes at a stretch.

The computer's output could be either L or R, to send the cart left or right. Its inputs were the position and velocity of the cart and the angle and rate of change of the pole.

engineering to solve using complex analogue circuitry.

The program has two outputs, L and R, which cause the cart to move left or right, and four inputs. The input signals are shown in Table 2.4.

These features are quantized, two with three levels and two with five. The intention is the same as with Samuel's program described in the previous section, to reduce an unrestricted numeric range to a range of small integers. This divides up the 4-dimensional space of possible states into $5 \times 5 \times 3 \times 3 = 225$ compartments. A typical situation might be: cart near righthand end; cart moving leftwards; pole slightly inclined to the left; pole swinging towards the left. Each situation thus addresses its own box within the state-space.

One way of looking at this knowledge representation is to say the system starts with 225 rules in the

$$\text{situation} \rightarrow \text{action}$$

format with the left-hand sides predefined but the right-hand sides (actions) to be determined by experience.

At the start of the learning process move-left and move-right decisions are distributed at random among the 225 compartments. As the program goes along it updates the decision frequencies in each box after each run, according to the length of time the pole stayed upright and the number of times the box was addressed during the run. In consequence, its relative preference between the two actions in each box varies. Eventually it learns to perform as an expert pole-balancer. After about 60 hours of practice, for instance, the system can balance the pole for 25 minutes at a stretch.

It is noteworthy that some regions in the state-space require counter-intuitive responses. Sometimes, when the cart wanders almost off the rails, it is necessary to push it a little further towards and danger zone in order to swing the pole in the opposite direction and then follow the pole to safety. Boxes was capable of learning this counter-intuitive skill.

Although this is a task that appears to demand little intelligence, it is very difficult to program a computer to perform equally well from first principles — i.e. by using the laws of dynamics. The conventional solution using differential equations requires inordinate processing power to run in real time.

2.4.4 Aleksander's WISARD

Our final example of a signature-table mechanism is not a computer program at all, but a piece of special-purpose hardware. WISARD (Wilkie, Stonham and Aleksander's Recognition Device) was developed at Brunel University, and can be taught to distinguish, for example, smiling from frowning faces (Aleksander & Burnett, 1984). It is the basis for a commercially successful vision system that can detect sub-standard produce on a moving conveyor belt. The system operates in real time (25 frames a second) connected to a closed-circuit TV camera.

Briefly, WISARD works by assigning groups of eight pixels at a time (octuples) to selected banks of RAM (Random Access Memory). An octuple is essentially an enhancement of Bledsoe and Browning's couple: it acts as a feature detector which can be in one of 256 states (0 to 255)

Table 2.4

Parameter	Range	
Position of cart	− 35 ... + 35	inches
Velocity of cart	− 30 ... + 30	in/sec
Angle of Pole	− 12 ... + 12	degrees
Rate of change of angle	− 24 ... + 24	degrees/sec

Fig. 2. 14 — WISARD schematic.

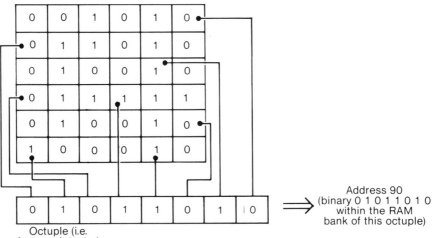

Octuple (i.e.
feature detector)

Address 90
(binary 0 1 0 1 1 0 1 0
within the RAM
bank of this octuple)

Each octuple is connected to 8 pixels and uses their status as a kind of address
to select one out of the 256 RAM locations it controls. There may be thousands
of octuples, or feature deflectors.
    Quiz: Is this an A or an H on display? Perhaps the compute can tell?

depending on the status of the pixels it monitors. During training, a one is
stored at the location within its RAM-bank specified by the state of the
octuple when a given image is present. Later, in the recognition phase, the
presence of a one at the addressed location within that octuple's RAM-bank
is evidence that the taught image is again presnt, since the same configuration was seen previously.

By using a very large number of octuples, the system becomes relatively
impervious to spurious data in the image. Aleksander's system uses a 512-by-
512 grid for the digitized image and more than 32 000 octuples as feature
extractors. Each octuple has its own bank of 256 memory addresses, so this
requires over 8 million bits, or a megabyte, of RAM. Only in recent years
have such memories become affordable.

The great advantage of WISARD is that all the RAM-banks are
addressed in parallel. Thus it can work at high speed with moving TV

pictures. By contrast, many 'state-of-the-art' vision systems running on conventional computers can take several minutes to process one image!

Note that the assignment of pixels to octuples is random, though it must be repeatable. The features are not pre-programmed.

Each octuple, or discriminator, is arbitrarily connected to 8 cells, and samples the status of these 8 pixels. The status is converted into a binary number such as 10110001 (177 decimal) and used as the address of one of the 256 memory locations within the bank to which that octuple is linked. During training a one is written at that location when the image is present. During recognition a one is read from that location when the octuple is in the same state.

Each octuple is evidence that the taught pattern is present when a one is read out and evidence of its absence when a zero is read out. The system decides by adding up the numbe of ones read out for each category and picking the one with the highest total. Aleksander has experimented with providing positive feedback for the system, but essentially the decision algorithm is a voting procedure.

WISARD is interesting because it demonstrates that practical adaptive recognition systems can be built on relatively simple principles and because it shows that there is more to machine learning than programming computers. It works as a parallel computer, using microelectronic components designed for the computer industry in a novel way. As a program on a serial computer it would be horribly slow; as a parallel machine it is impressively quick.

2.5 SUMMARY AND CONCLUSIONS

We have reviewed a variety of black-box learning systems. What lessons have we learned?

2.5.1 The wheel of fashion
One of the most interesting points to emerge is the cycle of fashion.

Table 2.5

	Parameter adjustment	Signature tables
Old:	Perceptron	Bledsoe and Browning's program
New:	Boltzmann Machine	WISARD

Table 2.5 above shows the oldest and the latest example in each of our two categories. In hardware terms, they are worlds apart; but as far as the software is concerned, they are strikingly similar. Once someone has a good idea, it keeps re-surfacing in a multitude of guises.

Let us first compare the Perceptron with the Boltzmann Machine. It is clear that the Boltzmann Machine is a far more powerful design, since it has several layers of processing units with feedback loops and so on. Fundamentally, however, both systems share a common heritage, based on similar ideas about how to simulate the nervous system using threshold units.

It is interesting to note, moreover, that the Boltzmann Machine is not much more useful than the Mark I Perceptron. Even if it were realized in custom-built hardware it would not, in its present form, be an efficient learning machine.

One problem with the Boltzmann Machine is that it is not whole-hearted enough as a neural model. For example, the assumption that all interconnections are of equal strength in both directions is not grounded on any neurophysiological findings, but is convenient when it comes to proving theorems about the system's behaviour. It is reminiscent of the story about a drunk who, when asked why he is looking for his wallet under a lamp-post after dropping it on the other side of the street, replies: "becuase the light is better here".

The Boltzmann Machine will doubtless fall from grace, like the Perceptron, as its practical limitations become widely appreciated. But the idea of simulating the brain will not go away. People will continue to build neurologically inspired models, and one day may well construct devices of comparable power to the human brain — probably by imitating it more slavishly than anything we have seen so far. But even then it is unlikely that they will truly understand how it works in a theoretical sense.

The lesson here is that the brain is a seductive, but unrewarding, model — given our present level of understanding.

The contrast between WISARD and its predecessor, on the other hand, shows that much progress has been made. Why should WISARD be a practical success while connectionist devices like the Boltzmann Machine remain a pipedream? This is not an easy question to answer. It may be simply that it was designed with a practical application in mind. Or perhaps the secret is that WISARD matches up-to-date equipment (where we have made great strides) with a well-tried conceptual scheme (where we have not).

In any case it seems that some ideas that are rather antiquted — in computing terms — gain a new lease of life when implemented on modern hardware. Thus the designer of learning systems can expect to find useful ideas in systems that are several decades old.

2.5.2   The critics
The critic is the part of the learning system that has to evaluate its performance (as explained in Chapter 1). All the systems so far described try to simplify the critic's job as far as possible. The easiest thing is simply to compare the machine's answer with the teacher's, and several systems do just that.

Among the systems where the critic has a bit more work to do are Samuel's and Michie's. Both go to considerable lengths to turn multi-step tasks into single-shot tasks — i.e. to remove the time dimension. This simplifies the credit-assignment problem, and in the present state of the art is probably a good plan to follow.

Michie's Boxes program maintains usage and length counts for the alternative actions (L or R) in each compartment of the state space. It probably has the most complex of the credit-assignment procedures used, but even this is relatively straightforward.

The lesson for system designers is: keep you evaluation measure as simple as you can.

2.5.3   Feature extraction

All the systems we have considered reduce information from a mass of raw data to a smaller number of computed features. It is far from clear, in general, how to reduce the amount of incoming data to a manageable level without throwing away vital information. Yet several of the systems surveyed (e.g. Pandemonium and WISARD) generate their feature detectors randomly, and still perform acceptably well.

This suggests that even if you do not know what features are significant, you can achieve good performance by letting the machine make them up. Indeed this technique has a distinct advantage: the machine is not biased to respond to only a few expected types of pattern.

2.5.4   The description language

All the systems in this chapter use numeric features to characterize input patterns. Thus an input is simply a vector of numbers. Some go as far as reducing input to an array of bindary numbers (0 or 1).

This makes it possible to think in terms of a feature space in which examples are located; or (after the features have been reduced to a small number of discrete values) a state space. However it may take a good deal of pre-processing to turn raw data — a speech spectrogram, say — into a list of features. Although the feature vector is helpful for certain learning algorithms, it is not very convenient for people. In addition, as we shall see in the next chapter, feature vectors are extremely cumbersome when it comes to representing relationships between components of a pattern.

As for the rule description language, it is either a set of weighting factors (PA) or a table of some kind (ST). However effective these representations have proved, they are bound to be inscrutable. This is a severe liability as far as expert systems are concerned, since an expert system may have to explain its own reasoning. If all it can do is say 'I looked it up in the table' or print out a row of coefficients (to six places of decimals!) then the user is likely to remain baffled.

This criterion alone means that black-box methods are the last resort when it comes to applying machine learning to expert systems, though it is usually possible to present table-lookup in a more comprehensible way than function evaluation.

2.5.5 Noise immunity

One very useful attribute that all the systems here share is a degree of tolerance for 'noisy' data. (Indeed, the Boltzmann Machine actually works better when the data is slightly 'noisy'.)

Noise is a concept borrowed from communications theory. Communications engineers frequently need to send messages along channels (such as short-wave radio) with background noise or interference. the signal is inevitably distorted during transmission. The receiver's problem is to pick out the signal from the noise.

By analogy, a pattern recognizer has to pick a category (the message) given input which may be spurious or garbled in some way. 'Noise' in this context covers a multitude of sins, for example:

— the teacher sometimes gets it wrong;
— instrument readings are not wholly reliable;
— random processes affect the input signals;
— the causal link between symptoms and diagnosis is tenuous at best.

Despite being such a rag-bag concept, it has proved useful in pattern recognition because the relationship between a pattern and its classification is seldom clear-cut. See Fig. 2.15.

Fig. 2.15 — AH!

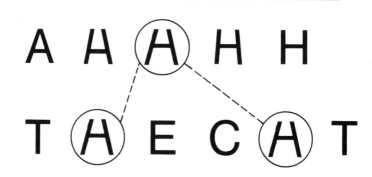

Pattern Recognition systems have to deal with uncertainty in various forms. It is not really possible to say that there are 3 As and 2Hs in the top line, or that there are 2As and 3Hs. As the lower line (THE CAT) shows, the central letter can be pressed into service as A or H.

This is one reason why the information-theoretic concept of 'noise' has been borrowed from the communications engineers.

None of the black-box systems expect 'perfect' training data. This makes them robust enough to cope with the fuzziness of the real world; though obviously there has to be a message hidden amidst the noise, or the best system in the world will find only phantoms and illusions — as we do when gazing into a fire and seeing dragons, or hearing voices in a sea shell.

2.6 REFERENCES

Aleksander, Igor & Burnett, Piers (1984) *Reinventing Man*: Penguin Books, Middlesex.

Batchelor, Bruce G. (1974) *Practical Approaches to Pattern Classification*: Plenum Books, London.

Bledsoe, W. W. & Browning, I. (1959) *Pattern Recognition & Reading by Machine*: Proc. Eastern Joint Computer Conf. [Reprinted in Uhr (1966).]

Forsyth, Richard & Naylor, Chris (1985) *The Hitch-Hiker's Guide to Artificial Intelligence*: Methuen/Chapman & Hall, London.

Hinton, Geoff, E. (1985) Learning in Parallel Networks: *Byte Magazine*, **10**, 4.

Kirkpatrick, S., Gellatt, C. D. & Vecchi, M. D. (1983) Optimization by Simulated Annealing; *Science*, **220**.

Michie, Donald & Chambers, Roger (1968) Boxes: an Experiment in Adaptive Control, in Dale & Michie (eds.) *Machine Intelligence* 2: Edinburgh University Press.

Minsky, Marvin & Papert, Seymour (1969) *Perceptrons*: MIT Press, Massachusetts.

Rosenblatt, Frank (1958) The Perceptron: a Probabilistic Model for Information Storage and Organization in the Brain: *Psychological Review*, 65.

Rosenblatt, Frank (1962) *Principles of Neurodynamics*: Spartan Books, New York.

Samuel Arthur (1959) Some Studies in Machine Learning Using the Game of Checkers: *IBM Journal of Research & Development*, **3**.

Samuel, Arthur (1967) Some Studies in Machine Learning Using the Game of Checkers, Part II: *IBM Journal of Research & Development*, **11**.

Selfridge, Oliver & Neisser, Ulric (1959) Pandemonium: a Paradigm for Learning in *NPL Symposium on Mechanization of Thought Processes*: HMSO, London. [Reprinted in Uhr, 1966.]

Selfridge, Oliver & Neisser, Ulric (1960) Pattern Recognition by Machine: *Scientific American*, **203**.

Sklansky, Jack & Wassel, Gustav (1981) *Pattern Classifiers and Trainable Machines*: Springer-Verlag New York and Berlin.

Uhr, Leonard (1963) Pattern Recognition Computers as Models for Form Perceptors: *Psychological Bulletin*, **60**.

Uhr, Leonard (1966) ed. *Pattern Recognition*: Wiley, New York.

Uhr, Leonard & Vossler, C. (1961) A Pattern Recognition Program that Generates, Evaluates and Adjusts its own Operators: Proceedings, Western Joint Computer Conference.

3

Learning structural descriptions

The procedures of the last chapter have proved useful in a number of pattern-recognition tasks, but the knowledge they acquire tends to be rather opaque. We now turn from black-box learning techniques, where only the effectiveness of the system matters, to methods where the resultant knowledge is intended to be accessible to people as well as machines. This makes them more suitable for generating rules that can later be used as part of an expert system's knowledge base, because the knowledge in an expert system should be intelligible to humans.

In this chapter, therefore, we consider some description languages which are more sophisticated than those of the previous chapter. We will discuss representation schemes capable of expressing structural descriptions, where the relations between parts of an object are important as well as the elementary attributes (or features) of the object.

For example, in teaching a system to acquire the concept of 'arch' (Winston, 1975), it is necessary to capture the relationships of 'on-top-of' and 'touching', as illustrated in Fig. 3.1.

Fig. 3.1 — An arch and a near-miss.

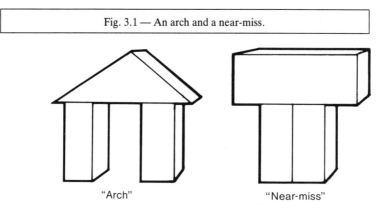

"Arch" "Near-miss"

The most important property distinguishing the arch from a non-arch is the fact that the two pillars supporting the cross-piece are touching in the latter case. To express such properties succinctly requires a language in which two-term relationships (not merely single-term features) can be stated.

The things that distinguish an arch from a non-arch are the relationships among its components — e.g. A-above-B, B-touching-C, C-below-A etc. To express such relations in terms of feature vectors would be hopelessly cumbersome.

3.1   THE DESCRIPTION LANGUAGE

As we have pointed out, the choice of representation for encoding a system's knowledge is at least as important as the details of the learning algorithm it uses. One of the most successful of recent discovery programs, Eurisko (Lenat, 1982), owes its success largely to its highly flexible description language. All Eurisko's concepts and heuristics are expressed in a common formalism, as 'Units'. Units are record-like structures that are modified by the discovery rules (other units). Simple syntactic changes in a unit usually lead to meaningful, and possibly valuable, new units. By contrast, small alterations in a conventional program or its data structures are likely to produce nonsense.

So before building a learning system it is essential to ensure that the description language is capable of expressing the kinds of distinction which will be needed. This is not a trivial problem.

It is very convenient if the representation for the input data is the same as that for the descriptions (or rules) but this is not always the case. Some representations that have been used in practice are given in Table 3.1.

Table 3.1

System	Input format	Rule format
Perceptron	Feature Vector	Weight Vector
Winston's Prog.	Semantic Net	Semantic Net
ID3	Feature Vector	Decision Tree
AQ11/Induce	Predicate Calculus	Predicate Calculus
LS-1	Feature Vector	Rule-strings
BEAGLE	Data Record	Boolean Expression
EURISKO	'Units'	'Units' (Frames)

A feature vector, as described in previous chapters, is just an array of numbers. Each number characterizes the state of one attribute of the input. In the simplest case the numbers are binary (0 or 1 only), meaning that the input is a bit-string.

Winston's system learns simple concepts describing structures built from children's blocks, like the arch in Fig. 3.1. Both the training examples and the concepts are expressed as semantic networks. We discuss Winston's method briefly in section 3.5.

The ID3 induction program (Quinlan, 1979) uses feature vectors for the input but a tree structure for the decision rules that it builds up. (An example is given later in this chapter.)

The series of programs devised by Michalski and his associates including AQ11 and Induce (Larson & Michalski, 1978; Dietterich & Michalski, 1981) employ logical expressions in an extended predicate calculus notation to represent both input examples and class descriptions. The AQ11 program successfully induced descriptions from examples that enabled it to classify soyabean diseases better than an expert in agricultural biology. AQ11 and its successor, Induce 1.2, are described in section 3.4.

LS-1 is a program that we shall describe in the next chapter. It is a genetic learning algorithm (Smith, 1983). It was tested on a poker-betting task using simple feature vectors to represent the state of the game and fixed-length strings to represent production rules in a special language. These strings were manipulated by pseudo-genetic operators and represented the system's expertise by controlling its betting decisions.

BEAGLE is another evolutionary learning program described in the following chapter. It used 'flat-file' database records for its input examples and Boolean expressions, held internally as tree structures, for its rules.

Finally Eurisko as mentioned above, which is one of the most impressive current discovery programs, uses framelike data structures called units to represent practically everything in the system — including objects, concepts and the discovery rules themselves. Each field in a unit is called a 'slot' and describes one facet of the concept. For instance, the IS-A slot specifies subclass/superclass relationships. There is also a WORTH slot that specifies the value of a unit, on a scale from 0 to 1000. It is important to note that rules and meta-rules can be described as units as well as concepts: this is one of Eurisko's strengths. (To describe Eurisko's mode of operation would take too long: it is a most complex system. In a nutshell, however, what it does is wander around its conceptual space making small alterations to its concepts and rules and testing the consequences.)

From the variety of notations successfully used we can conclude that there is no ideal representation language for all machine learning problems. However, it is important that the representation used is expressive enough for the task in hand.

3.2   LEARNING AS SEARCHING

Assuming that we have an adequate description language, the next problem is to automate the generation of useful descriptions in that language.

One way of looking at this problem is as a search through the space of all possible descriptions for those which are valuable for the task in hand (Mitchell, 1982). The number of syntactically valid descriptions is astronomical; and the more expressive the description language, the more explosive is this combinatorial problem.

Clearly some way has to be found of guiding the search and thereby ignoring the vast majority of potential descriptions, or concepts, which are useless for the current purpose.

We can try to illustrate the link between the two fundamental AI notions of Search and Learning with a simplified weather-forecasting example. Let us suppose that we have a database of weather records and the job of the learning algorithm is to learn how to classify records on the basis of whether the next day will be fine or not. The machine must find a rule for making this discrimination.

Assume further for simplicity's sake that each record contains only four fields. These four variables are: rainfall in millimetres, sunshine in hours, maximum wind gust in knots, and pressure at noon in millibars. Thus two typical records from the training set (the instances used in forming the rule) might be as below.

(17-Apr-85)		(12-Apr-85)	
Rainfall	0	Rainfall	0.5
Sunshine	10.6	Sunshine	7.6
Windmax	15	Windmax	44
Pressure	1030	Pressure	1008
[Nextday	Fine]	[Nextday	Not-Fine]

The extra item, Nextday, indicates whether the next day turned out fine or not. For the present purpose, a fine day is defined as having

$$(\text{Rainfall} < 0.5) \quad \text{AND} \quad (\text{Sunshine} > 3.6)$$

i.e. less than half a millimetre of rain and more than 3.6 hours of sunshine. This is the value, derived from the following day's readings, that the system must learn to predict.

Rules can be composed by linking variable names and constants with the following operators.

Logical	AND, OR, NOT
Comparison	$> = <$

Thus the rule description language allows Boolean expressions such as

$$\text{Sunshine} < 4 \text{ AND Pressure} < 1000$$

with brackets if necessary to avoid ambiguity. This is a relatively simple description language, but it suffices for our purposes.

Given this sort of training data and description language, the learning system can start with an initial description (which may be randomly created) and apply transformation operators to generate its successors. These successors are new descriptions for testing. The most important transformation operators are generalization and specialization. The process is illustrated in Fig. 3.2. For training data we use the 30 days of April 1985 (London readings). Of course in a real meteorological application, we might have tens of thousands of example cases measured on scores of variables.

Each node in the search tree is a decision rule that can be evaluated according to how well it distinguished days followed by rain from days not followed by rain. We use here an extremely simple evaluation score, the percentage of correct cases; but rules that apply to less than five cases (out of the 30 in the training set) are discarded. They are too rarely applicable. Our search strategy is to generate successors only from ules that have a high evaluation score — i.e. to employ a best-first search method.

Fig. 3.2 — Learning as a search

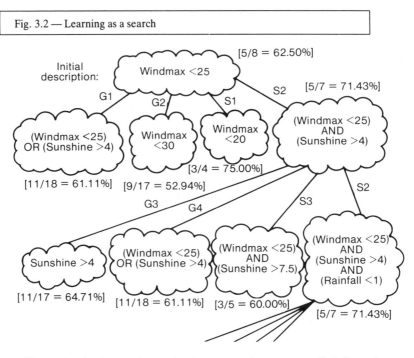

The top-level rule may be randomly generated or user-supplied. From then on, new rules are produced by applying generalization and specialization operators; such as

G1. Add OR condition   S1. Decrease LT-constant
G2. Increase LT-constant   S2. Add AND- condition
G3. Drop AND- condition   S3. Increase GT-constant
G4. Change AND to OR   (S4. Change OR to AND)
(G5. Decrease GT-constant)   (S5. Drop OR- condition)

Where do extra conditions like (Sunshine >4) come from? One possibility is that there is a 'plausible comparison generator', guided by elementary statistical principles.

The diagram shows that this process can be viewed as a search through a network where the nodes are descriptions (rules) and the arcs are transformations that modify descriptions and thus generate new ones. At each step we show only four successoprs being generated — two by generalization and two by specialization — from the best rule, as defined by our simple evaluation function. In reality, far more successors would be created at each step.

In this context generalization of a rule means that it applies to more cases and specialization means that it applies to fewer. Thus the operator G1, which adds an OR-condition, makes the resulting expression cover a wider class of examples. On the other hand, the operator S3, which takes an expression of the form

$$\text{Variable} > \text{Constant}$$

and transforms it to

$$\text{Variable} > (\text{Constant} + k)$$

where k is some small increment, makes the rule more specific. It covers fewer cases. There are several methods of automatic generalization and specialization, as we shall see in section 3.4.

Note that the search defines a tree-structure, but the underlying search space is a network, because repeated applications of the transformation can re-generate ancestral rules. This corresponds to re-visiting a node in the network, and there is an example in the diagram, where

$$(\text{Windmax} < 25) \quad \text{OR} \quad (\text{Sunshine} > 4)$$

is generated at two different levels in the tree.

A number of searching methods have worked well with noise-free training instances. Dealing with 'noisy' data like the weather, however, is a more challenging problem. We shall confine our attention principally to systems that can be used with noisy data.

3.3 QUINLAN'S ID3

Quinlan's ID3 (Interactive Dichotomizer 3) is a natural step forward from the signature-table methods of Chapter 2 (Quinlan, 1982). Instead of creating a decision table, it creates a decision tree.

It is not particularly robust in the face of noisy data, though it could be improved in this respect if it did not always seek a 'perfect' rule. The program works as follows.

(1) Select at random a subset of size W from the training set (the 'window').
(2) Apply the CLS algorithm (detailed below) to form a rule for the current window.
(3) Scan the whole database, not just the window, to find exceptions to the latest rule.
(4) If there are exceptions, insert some of them into the window (possibly replacing existing examples) and repeat from step 2; otherwise stop and display the rule.

This procedure actually throws away the latest rule and starts again from scratch on each cycle.

The method of window selection is sometimes termed 'exception-driven filtering'. The need for a window arises because the main database may contain hundreds of thousands of cases, and hence be too large to be processed (from backing store) in an acceptable time.

The CLS algorithm (Hunt *et al.*, 1966) acts as a subroutine of the main program. CLS stands for Concept Learning System and derives originally from work done by experimental psychologists in the 1950s and 1960s. It first appeared as a proposed model of what people do when given simple concept formation tasks, and only later became a computer algorithm, due to Hunt and others. Thus it is an example of AI borrowing from psychology, rather than the other way round.

CLS works by first finding the variable (or test) which is most discriminatory, and partitioning the data with respect to that variable. Quinlan used an information-theoretic measure of entropy (i.e. surprise) for assessing the discriminatory power of each variable, but others have suggested different measures, e.g. the Chi-Squared statistic (Hart, 1985). Having divided the data into two subsets on the basis of the most discriminatory variable, each subset is partitioned in a similar way (unless it contains examples of only one class). The process repeats until all subsets contain data of only one kind. The end-product is a discrimination tree, which can be used later to classify samples never previously encountered.

ID3 trees performed well on King–Rook versus King–Knight chess endgame problems, where the data is clear-cut and free from uncertainty. Really noisy data, however, such as weather records, leads it to grow very bushy decision trees which fit the training set but do not carry over well to new examples. In the worst case it can end up with one decision node for every example in the training set!

ID3's main shortcomings are listed below:

(1) the rules are not probabilistic;
(2) several identical examples have no more effect than one;
(3) it cannot deal with contradictory examples (which are commonplace outside the rarified setting of chess endgames);
(4) the results are therefore over-sensitive to small alterations to the training database.

These objections would lose much of their force if ID3 stopped before it reached a subset with no counterexamples at all.

To give an illustration of ID3 in action, let us imagine that we are giving it data about the flags of various states in the USA. The objective is for it to learn how to distinguish states that joined the Confederacy in the US Civil War (1860–65) from those that stayed loyal to the Union. It is an artificial example, but it serves to illustrate the way the system works. In fact, there are reasons for thinking that confederate states might choose different emblems from those that remained in the Union.

First of all, here is the training data. We have picked 23 states that existed at the time of the Civil War, and augmented our set with the Union and Confederate flags themselves, as well as that of the District of Columbia (which is as federal as you can get, though not really a state at all). This gives 26 examples in all.

The data is presented in conventional feature–vector form, which is the way ID3 expects it. There are nine variables, plus the Type column (U or C) which is the one we want to predict.

The variables used are as follows. Stars is a count of the number of stars on the flag. Bars are vertical lines. Stripes are horizontal lines. Hues is the number of colours in the flag. Xcross indicates the presence of an X-shaped cross on the flag. Icon is Y if there is a pictorial design and N if the flag is purely abstract. Humans is a counter of the number of human figures depicted on the flag. (If Icon=N then obviously Humans=0.) Word is

Table 3.2

Flag	Stars	Bars	Stripes	Hues	Xcross	Icon	Humans	Word	Num	Type
Union	50	0	13	3	0	N	0	0	0	U
Confederate	13	0	0	3	1	N	0	0	0	C
Alabama	0	0	0	2	1	N	0	0	0	C
Arkansas	29	0	0	3	0	N	0	1	0	C
Connecticut	0	0	0	5	0	Y	0	4	0	U
Delaware	0	0	0	6	0	Y	2	4	2	U
Florida	0	0	0	6	1	Y	1	15	0	C
Georgia	13	1	0	3	1	Y	0	3	1	C
Illinois	0	0	0	6	0	Y	0	6	2	U
Iowa	0	2	0	5	0	Y	0	10	0	U
Louisiana	0	0	0	4	0	Y	0	4	0	C
Maryland	0	12	0	4	0	N	0	0	0	U
Massachusetts	1	0	0	4	0	Y	1	6	0	U
Mississippi	13	0	3	3	1	N	0	0	0	C
New Hampshire	9	0	0	5	0	Y	0	7	1	U
New Jersey	0	0	0	5	0	Y	2	3	1	U
New York	0	0	0	6	0	Y	2	1	0	U
N. Carolina	1	1	2	4	0	N	0	3	4	C
Ohio	17	0	5	3	0	N	0	0	0	U
Rhode Island	13	0	0	3	0	Y	0	1	0	U
S. Carolina	0	0	0	2	0	Y	0	0	0	C
Tennesee	3	2	0	3	0	N	0	0	0	C
Texas	1	1	2	3	0	N	0	0	0	C
Virginia	0	0	0	5	0	Y	2	4	0	C
Wisconsin	0	0	0	5	0	Y	2	2	1	U
Washington DC	3	0	5	2	0	N	0	0	0	U

another counter, of the number of words appearing in the flag (as a motto or slogan). Finally Num gives the number of numbers represented: some states put dates, like 1848, on their flag. (Example flags are shown on the back cover of this book.)

Note that this input description language does not allow us to express structural relationships, such as 'a white star over a blue bar'. There is one of the problems with feature–vector notation.

CLS begins by looking for the most discriminatory variable, in order to create the root of the decision tree. To do this it constructs a number of frequency tables, such as those shown in Table 3.3.

To make these contingency tables the program must pick one or more thresholds when dealing with numeric variables. The thresholds 0 and 1 were tried with Stars, giving (Stars > 1) as one test and (Stars > 0) as another. The second one turned out slightly better, but neither was much use. In fact the best test turns out to be

$$(Xcross > 0)$$

which is only true for confederate flags, though it is false for both kinds of flag. (The original ID3 could not cope with unrestricted numeric attributes, but it can easily be extended to do so, as we have done here.)

Table 3.3

Test	U	C
Stars >1	5	5
Stars ≤1	9	7
Stars >0	6	7
Stars ≤0	8	5
Stripes >0	3	3
Stripes ≤0	11	9
Xcross >0	0	5
Xcross ≤0	14	7

The test (Xcross > 0) is then established as the root of the tree, as shown in Fig. 3.3.

For the next stage, the left branch can be left alone: it only contains one type of data (confederate). But the right branch needs to be further subdivided, using essentially the same method on the subset of 21 cases for which the top-level test is false.

The next best discriminator, for that subset, turns out to be

$$(Num > 0)$$

which tests whether the flag has any numbers written on it. This divides the 21 remaining cases into five union and one confederate (North Carolina) which do have numbers, and nine union and six confederates that have none.

One of the weaknesses of ID3 appears at this point. It always subdivides the subsets until no single exception remains. So the group with five union and one confederate flags is split up on the basis of the test (Icon = Y) — i.e. whether they have an icon (pictorial image) or not. North Carolina does not while the others do, so the subdivision can halt. This striving for 100% correct rules can cause ID3 to generate very bushy trees whose nodes contain very few examples. These are unlikely to be statistically reliable when the tree is later used for classification. Furthermore, large branchy tree structures are difficult for people to comprehend.

Once the tree has been grown, it can be used to make decison about new examples, by applying the tests and following down the appropriate branches to a terminal node. Thus if we asked, in effect, 'is Britain a confederate state?' it would reply Yes, because the British flag does have an X-shaped cross. (Ask a silly question . . .)

More relevantly, to decide whether the state of Washington (not D.C.)

Fig. 3.3 — Example ID3 discrimination tree.

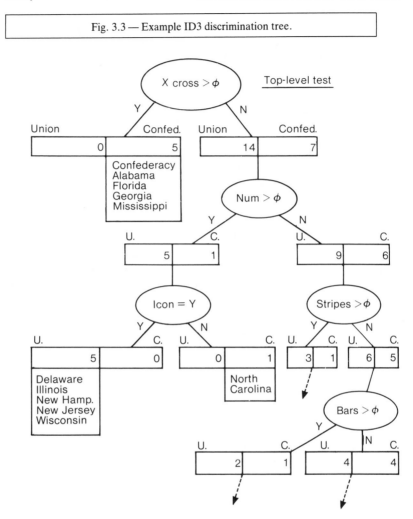

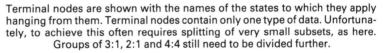

Terminal nodes are shown with the names of the states to which they apply hanging from them. Terminal nodes contain only one type of data. Unfortunately, to achieve this often requires splitting of very small subsets, as here. Groups of 3:1, 2:1 and 4:4 still need to be divided further.

was confederate, the system would ask: has it any X-shaped crosses? The answer is No, so it would go on to ask: are there any numbers on the flag? The answer is Yes (its date of admission to the Union, 1889), so it would then ask: does it have an icon? It does (the face of George Washington), so the decision would be that Washington was a Union state — because all 5 training examples with

$$(Xcross=0) \text{ and } (Numbers>0) \text{ and } (Icon=Y)$$

were union states. (It surely would have been, if it had been founded early enough, being about as far as you can get from the old Deep South.)

It will be seen that ID3 has much in common with the signature–table methods we encountered earlier. The decision tree can be thought of as a compressed signature table: the tree could be held as a multi-dimensional matrix, except that it would take far too much room. The decision tree is also more natural for human readers. We are accustomed to using such trees in biology and other fields.

The problem of excessive subdivision could be cured simply by stopping early. For instance, any subgroup that contained fewer than, say, 5% of the training examples could be deemed too small for further division. When the tree was used to categorize new cases and such a node was reached, the system could give a probabilistic answer. Thus, in the diagram, on reaching the node with 3 union and 1 confederate instances, the system could respond with '75% Union' instead of saying 'don't know'. Realistically, such a group is too small to split up any further. There are many domains where certainty is not attainable, and a probabilistic answer based on a reasonable sample is preferable to an exact answer based on a tiny sample.

A more serious problem concerns the nature of the description language itself. The decision tree is actually a rather restrictive language. All tests have to be in the form of a comparison between one variable and one constant, such as (Hues > 3). Tests like

$$(Stars \geq Stripes)$$

and

$$(Hues > 4) \quad OR \quad (Humans > 0)$$

might prove to be useful, but the system could never find them. They are literally inexpressible.

This is the price paid for ID3's efficiency. It is relatively quick, but this speed is purchased at a cost. Clearly a more expressive description language would make the tree-growing far more complex; but the poverty of its description language places the burden of devising an effective set of descriptors squarely on the user. Any preliminary calculations or logical operations have to be incorporated in the attributes of the input data before running the program.

(ID3 forms the basis of a package marketed as 'Expert-Ease'.)

3.4 AQ11 AND INDUCE

The series of programs developed by Michalski and his colleagues at the University of Illinois use more powerful description languages than ID3.

3.4.1 AQ11 and the soybeans

The program AQ11 (Michalski & Larson, 1978; Michalski & Chilausky, 1980) is the one which found better rules for soybean disease diagnosis than a human expert. For that particular experiment, they collected 630 questionnaires describing diseased plants. Each plant was measured on 35 features (called 'descriptors') as in the abbreviated record below.

Environmental descriptors
   Time of occurrence   = July
   Plant stand   = normal
   Precipitation   = above normal
   Temperature   = normal
   Occurrence of hail   = no
   Number of years crop repeated   = 4
   Damaged area   = whole fields
[22 descriptors omitted for brevity]

Conditions of seed   = normal
   Mold growth   = absent
   Seed discoloration   = absent
   Seed size   = normal
   Seed shriveling   = absent

Conditions of roots   = abnormal

Diagnosis   : Brown Spot

The 36th descriptor is the diagnosis of an expert in plant biology . There were 15 disease categories altogether.

AQ11 generated rules in a language call VL1, where a description is a set of terms called 'selectors'. The rule below (D3), which the system produced for classifying Rhizoctonia Root Rot, illustrates the language.

D3; [leaves = normal] [stem = abnormal]
      [stem cankers = below soil line]
      [canker lesion color = brown]
      OR
      [leaf malformation = absent] [stem = abnormal]
      [stem cankers = below soil line]
      [canker lesion color = brown]

This rule consists of two descriptions linked by an OR: it is a disjunction. Each description happens to consist of four selectors, such as [stem = abnormal], which are linked by logical ANDs. That is to say, AND is implied between selectors, so that a description in VL1 is a conjunction of terms. Each selector compares one variable with a constant (or range of constants).

As a matter of fact, this particular disjunction is trivial. The only difference between the two descriptions, [leaves = normal] versus [leaf malformation = absent], would be unnecessary if the system realized that one was a special case of the other.

This diagnostic rule (D3) and 14 others were generated from 290 training instances. The training set was selected from the 630 cases by a program called ESEL, which picks examples that are 'far apart', or different from each other, to give a broad coverage. Michalski did not report what AQ11 would do with a randomly chosen training set, so the effect of this selection strategy is unclear.

The 15 computer-generated rules were used to classify the remaining 340 cases, with great success. Whereas the human expert's rules gave the correct first choice disease on 71.8% of the test cases, AQ11's rules were gave correct first choice on 97.6% of the unseen cases.

AQ11 works in an incremental fashion, each step appending another conjunctive term (i.e. a new selector) starting off from a null description. The idea is to introduce new items of evidence one at a time, or a few at a time, and extend the growing rule to deal with them. The AQ11 method can be outlined in four major steps.

(1) Pick a new training event.
(2) Generate a 'star' of new terms by extending the current description to cover as many positive events and as few negative events as possible (ideally no negative ones at all).
(3) Retain the most preferred description (e.g. the simplest) according to pre-specified criteria.
(4) If all relevant events have been covered, keep the description; otherwise go back to step 1.

If a single conjunctive description cannot be found to cover all positive examples, AQ11 will generate several, linked by ORs, as we saw with rule D3.

The 'star' method extends the current hypothesis (i.e. description of a given category) to cover the latest event or events. First it isolates all facts inconsistent with the hypothesis, both positive and negative exceptions. Then it derives two new descriptions — one that covers the positive cases that were not covered by the old hypothesis (D+) and another that covers the negative cases that were covered by the old hypothesis (D−). Next it updates the hypothesis by appending the D+ terms and removing the terms that caused it to include the D− events. Finally the descriptions so generated are tidied up.

In the soybean work, the system made a complete pass through the data for each disease type, treating cases of that disease as positive examples and all other cases as negative examples. It is also possible for AQ11 to treat previously generated rules as negative examples: this enables it to come up with non-overlapping rules where the categories are mutually exclusive.

3.4.2   Induction by Beam Search

AQ11 rules start off very general and become more and more specific. It adds new terms to exclude negative examples, while still covering as many positive cases as possible. The successor of AQ11, Induce 1.2 (Dietterich & Michalski, 1981), works the other way round. It starts with very specific descriptions and keeps on generalizing. It also uses a richer description language called VL2, a form of 'annotated predicate calculus'. This allows

quantifiers, functions and relational predicates with more than one argument. A VL2 description of the arch in Fig. 3.1, for example, could be

(EXISTS A, B, C)
[Touching (A, B)] [Touching (A, C)]
[Ontop (A, B)] [Ontop (A, C)]
[Shape (A) = Pyramid]
[Shape (B) = Block] [Shape (C) = Block].

Induce explores the description space by the method of Beam Search.
This is a modified Best-first strategy that preserves a small number of
descriptions at each stage.

The progress of a Beam Search is illustrated in Fig. 3.4. Here we show
the search fanning out upwards. At each level only the seven best nodes are
retained. All the other nodes are pruned away, and do not generate any
successors. Each node in the diagram represents a description. Upper levels
are more general (i.e. cover more cases) than lower ones. In this case the
tree grows upwards only. As in Fig. 3.2, the same node/description can
sometimes be reached by two or more routes.

Fig. 3.4 — Beam Search.

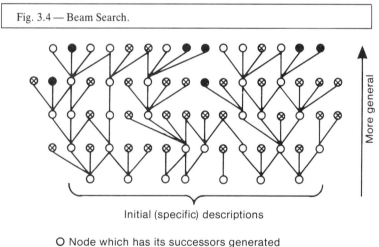

Initial (specific) descriptions

○ Node which has its successors generated
⊗ Node which is pruned
● Node which is saved (as a satisfactory rule or description

In this Beam Search, only the best 7 nodes are preserved at each stage and
allowed to generate successors. The generation process proceeds upwards
(towards more general descriptions). Nodes shown with more than one
'parent' are descriptions created in more than one way: this can easily happen

Induce employs the Beam Search, as outlined below.

(1) Set H to contain a randomly chosen subset of size W of the training
    instances. (These are also rules which happen to be very specific.)
(2) Generalize each description in H as little as possible.
(3) Prune implausible descriptions, retaining the best W only. The best are

those that are simple and cover many examples; the worst are those that
are complex and cover few examples.

(4) If any description in *H* covers ebnough examples, print it out. If *H* is
empty or enough rules have been printed, stop; otherwise continue from
step 2.

We have been deliberately vague here about the criteria for evaluating
descriptions, and hence deciding which ones to prune. This is the job of the
Critic (see Chapter 1). Obviously rules should be brief and they should cover
many positive and few negative examples, but various trade-offs are possible. Induce provides several preference measures which can be combined to
give an evaluation function tailored for a particular application.

Induce works from specific descriptions to more general ones. It is easy
to start it off with an initial set because it uses the 'single representation
trick'. In other words, the VL2 language expresses both the rules and the
training instances. A training instance can be regarded as a highly specific
rule — a class with only one member (or possibly a few members if there are
repeated examples).

To turn an event description into a rule, or a rule into a more general
one, Michalski's program uses a variety of generalization operators. We can
illustrate some of them by encoding another flag (this time the national flag
of Canada) in a version of VL2.

(EXISTS X, Y, Z) [Background = White]
[Hue (X) = Red] [Hue (Y) = Red] [Hue (Z) = Red]
[Type (X) = Bar] [Type (Y) = Maple Leaf] [Type (Z) = Bar]
[Left-of (X, Y)] [Left-of (Y, Z)] [Left-of (X, Y)]
[Width = 50] [Height = 25]
[Hues = 2]

As well as encoding simple features, such as [Width = 50], VL2 can express
structural relationships, such as [Left-of (Y, Z)], which is a step forward
from the flag descriptions we used in the previous section. To put it another
way, it can handle binary predicates as well as unary ones. It can in fact
handle predicates with more than two arguments, if required.

Let us now consider some ways of generalizing this description.

(1) Dropping Conditions:
e.g. delete the last four lines of the above description to create a new
description that applies to any flag with a white background and three red
objects or regions.

(2) Internal Disjunction:
     e.g. [Hue (X) = Red] 《 [Hue (X) = Red, Blue]. This now also covers a
     variant of the Canadian flag with a blue bar on the left-hand side.

(3) Relax a Condition:
e.g. [Height = 25] 《 Height > 24]
or   《 Height < 26].
     These effectively introduce disjunctions.

(4) Make a Constant into a (Don't-Care) Variable: e.g. [Type (X) = Bar] 《

[Type(?) = Bar], where the question mark stands for any object, meaning that any object can be a bar. Again, this is a way of introducing a disjunction.

Other methods of generalization were described in section 3.2.

The problem is not that machines cannot generalize. On the contrary, there are too many ways of generalizing. This is why Induce only makes minimal generalizations on each cycle (step 2). The successors of a node are produced by applying one generalization operator in only one way.

For example, the dropping-conditions method (no. 1) would cause the generation of 13 successors to the Canadian flag description, since it contains 13 terms. Each successor would differ from the original in having one condition dropped. The program would not drop two or more conditions at once. Nor would it drop a condition and apply another generalizing rule (such as relaxing a condition) in the same step. For that to happen would require at least two cycles. This is mainly a question of efficiency: if all generalization operators were applied in all possible ways, there would be an astronomical number of new nodes.

The trouble is that even single-change generalizations can lead to an enormous proliferation of descriptions at each stage, especially with an expressive language like VL2. It is highly likely that some which are unpromising in themselves, but which would lead to good descriptions a few more steps down the line, will be pruned away. This ensures that the Induce algorithm is non-optimal (though in practice it may perform very well).

One final point about Induce, not so far mentioned, is that it can run the search in two distinct phases. In the first phase it searches the 'structure-only space'. That is to say, it ignores the unary attributes and does a Beam Search using only multi-argument predicates, such as Ontop or Left-of. Then, having found a set of descriptions using relational predicates only, it enters a second phase, which is a search of the 'attribute-only space'. At this point the unary features are considered. It is not yet clear, however, whether this two-stage approach is generally useful.

3.5   OTHER SYSTEMS

Several other programs have been developed for learning concept descriptions. We do not have space to describe them here in detail. Nevertheless, some of them deserve at least a mention.

3.5.1   Meta-Dendral

The Meta-Dendral system (Buchanan, 1976; Buchanan & Mitchell, 1978) has discovered several rules of chemistry that were previously unknown. Specifically it founds new cleavage rules that describe how organic molecules, of the ketoandrostane group and others, fragment in a mass-spectrometer. These rules were later incorporated into the knowledge base of Dendral (Buchanan & Feigenbaum, 1978), one of the classic expert systems. Dendral interprets mass-spectra. Fig. 3.5 shows a typical mass-spectrum.

These patterns are produced by an instrument that bombards chemical

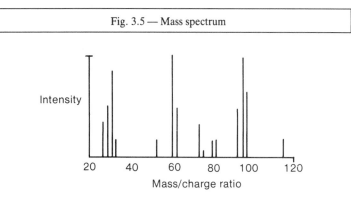

Fig. 3.5 — Mass spectrum

Organic chemists use such mass spectrograms, together with a knowledge of
the chemical composition of the compound, to deduce its chemical structure.
Different structures have different characteristic peaks at different mass-to-
charge levels.

samples with accelerated electrons, causing them to break up. The fragments are then passed through an electromagnetic field that separates out
the fragments with low charge and high mass, which are not deflected much
by the field, from those of low mass and high charge, which are deflected
considerably. This gives rise to the plot of intensity against mas-to-charge
ratio.

A trained chemist can look at such a plot and identify the molecular
structure of the compound that produced it by noting where the peaks are.
So can Dendral. In doing so it tests its own hypotheses against a simulation
of a maxx-spectrometer. Meta-Dendral was designed to enhance this
internal model of the device by discovering additional fragmentation rules.

Meta-Dendral contains two main programs, Rulegen and Rulemod.
Rulegen performs a relatively crude search of the space of potential cleavage
rules, using only positive training instances. It moves in the direction from
general to specific. It starts with the most general rule possible (that some
atomic bond will break) and gradually specializes it. At each stage it creates
offspringc of existing rules by making them more specific in various ways —
i.e. stating more precisely which bonds will break under what circumstances.
A descendant rule is retained if

— it predicts fewer fragmentations per molecule than its parent (i.e. is more
  specific);
— it still predicts fragmentations for at least half of the training molecules;
— it predicts fragmentations for as many molecules as its parent (unless the
  parent was 'too general').

Rulemod takes the rules produced by Rulegen and performs minor
alterations designed to improve their performance — both by generalizing and specializing. In particular, it takes account of negative evidence.

Meta-Dendral can handle noise, which can arise from impurities in
the samples, from imperfections in the instrument and from errors

introduced by the program that transforms the training instances into a suitable form for processing. In addition, it has achieved respectable performance: some of its discoveries were written up and published in a chemical journal (see Michie & Johnston, 1985).

The real weakness of Meta-Dendral is the fact that its description language is specifically designed to be good for expressing rules about molecular structures and how they split up — and for virtually nothing else.

3.5.2   Bringing home the Bacon

Another discovery system worthy of note is the Bacon series of programs (Langley, 1977, 1981).

One of these programs, Bacon.4, 'rediscovered' — among other things — Ohm's Law, Archimedes' Principle of Displacement, Newton's Law of Gravitational Attraction and almost all of 19th century chemistry. (It has not so far discovered any 21st century chemistry.)

Bacon.4 is presented with training instances such as Table 3.4.

Table 3.4

Planet	Day	Year	Dist.	Diam.	Mass	Moons
Mercury	58.00	0.24	0.39	0.38	0.05	0
Venus	244.00	0.62	0.72	0.95	0.82	0
Earth	1.0	1.0	1.0	1.0	1.0	1
Mars	1.03	1.88	1.52	0.53	0.11	2
Ceres	999.99	4.60	2.77	0.08	0.00	0
Jupiter	0.41	11.86	5.20	11.19	318.35	16
Saturn	0.43	29.46	9.54	9.41	95.30	15
Uranus	0.67	84.01	19.19	4.06	14.60	5
Neptune	0.75	164.80	30.07	3.88	17.30	2
Pluto	6.38	248.40	39.52	0.24	0.08	1
Trogstar Beta	2.22	680.00	77.22	16.48	444.44	4

Here the length of day, length of year, mean distance from the Sun, diameter, mass and number of satellites for all the members of the Solar System have been tabulated. (We have taken the liberty of including data for Trogstar Beta, the totally inconspicuous brown dwarf companion of our sun, which has not yet been discovered — even by Bacon.4!)

To emulate Kepler, and discover that the square of the orbital period (Year) of a planet is proportional to the cube of its distance from the sun, the program has to note concomitant variations. (See Chapter 1 on J. S. Mill.) For example the length of day appears to vary inversely with the diameter, while the year and the distance vary together. This sort of observation leads Bacon to create new columns in the table, formed by fairly straightforward arithmetical combinations of existing ones — using division, multiplication, etc.

Bacon proceeds step by step in its search for constancies. This is shown in Table 3.5, where all the variables apart from Y (year) and D (distance) have been ignored.

Table 3.5

	Y	D	Y/D	$(Y/D)/D$	$((Y/D)/D)*Y$	$(((Y/D)/D)*Y)/D$
Mercury	0.24	0.39	0.62	1.61	0.39	1.00
Venus	0.61	0.72	0.85	1.18	0.72	1.00
Earth	1.00	1.00	1.00	1.00	1.00	1.00
Mars	1.88	1.52	1.23	0.81	1.52	1.00
Ceres	4.60	2.77	1.66	0.60	2.76	1.00
Jupiter	11.86	5.20	2.28	0.44	5.20	1.00
Saturn	29.46	9.54	3.09	0.32	9.54	1.00
Uranus	84.01	19.19	4.38	0.23	19.17	1.00
Neptune	164.80	30.07	5.48	0.18	30.04	1.00
Pluto	248.40	39.52	6.29	0.16	39.51	1.00
T. Beta	680.00	77.22	8.81	0.11	77.55	1.00

The figures are correct to two decimal digits.

Bacon's first step, having noted that Y and D vary together, would be to divide one by the other, forming the Y/D column. This still varies with D so the next column, $(Y/D)/D$, is created. Now it has overdone it, but it notices that the new column varies inversely with Y, so it multiplies by Y, giving the fifth column $((Y/D)/D)*Y$. This now agrees almost perfectly with D. Eventually it finds a column like the last one, with a constant value. That is what it was looking for. It can be expressed more clearly as $(Y*Y)/(D*D*D)$. In a sense, the program has recapitulated Kepler's discovery that Y squared equals D cubed.

For exposition, our table has cut out the many blind alleys and red herrings which Bacon would probably explore. (Kepler, too, spent plenty of time on such things.) For example the program, give this data, might well go looking at the relationship of distance with rank position — perhaps even to the extent of re-formulating Bode's notorious 'law', or something like it. Or it might try to relate the number of satellites to the mass of a planet and its distance from the sun. (Readers may care to investigate this for themselves.)

Bacon, like most scientists, has rather strong preconceptions about what form scientific laws should take — i.e. that the relations between significant quantities should be mathematically simple. Human scientists often express this as an aesthetic principle: that Nature (or God) is clever but not devious; or that the beauty of Truth is its simplicity. Philosophers, however, sometimes take a different view, namely that the human mind is only capable of discovering certain rather simple regularities in nature.

The main drawback of Bacon.4 is that it cannot cope with noise. It needs a training set without significant exceptions, and thus cannot find approximate statistical laws.

3.5.3 Winston's work

Another concept learning system (Winston, 1984) which unfortunately is not much good at coping with noisy data is Winston's program. Still, his work is interesting from our point of view because it has been influential in stressing the importance of 'near misses' (cases that almost but not quite count as positive examples) and the importance of a good training sequence. In human terms, this amounts to saying that the role of the tutor is critical for effective learning.

One of the tasks Winston's program performed was learning to distinguish blocks-world objects, such as we saw in Fig. 3.1. The basic algorithm works as follows.

(1) Let the description of the first example (which must be a positive case) be the initial rule.
(2) For all subsequent instances:
    If the instance is a near miss, specialize the rule to exclude the latest example;
    If it is a positive instance not covered by the rule, generalize the rule to include the last example.

Nothing happens if the current rule covers the latest case. The algorithm only learns from its mistakes.

Notice that this is a strictly stepwise procedure. It maintains a single hypothesis and works with one training example at a time. Although it has trouble coping with inconsistencies in the training data, it is very efficient in that it does not need many passes over a large database (as many other systems do).

It is also interesting because it uses semantic networks to describe objects and the rules for classifying objects. This is an idiosyncratic choice of representation — illustrating the fact that there is not yet a consensus about the right kind of description language in this field.

3.5.4 Rulestorming

Another interesting rule-generator is the system described by Quinqueton and Sallentin (1983). Their method consists of iterating an algorithm composed of three modules, optionally followed by a fourth phase, called 'rule-storming'. The three main modules are: expansion, selection and compression.

Their input language is as basic as it can be. Data are bit-strings, recording truth values for a number of logical features. One of these is treated as the dependent variable — the one to be predicted.

The output rule is a logical combination of the variables using only symmetric operators, namely conjunction (AND) and logical equivalence (EQV). The method works as follows.

(1) Expansion: combine each pair of descriptors (logical features) with a logical operator in five permissible ways to create new, derived, descriptors. Thus from two basic features (A, B) the descriptors

$$A \& B, A \& \bar{B}, \bar{A} \& B, \bar{A} \& \bar{B}, A = B$$

would be created.

(2) Selection: eliminate the descriptors that correlate poorly (according to Chi-Squared or some similar measure) with the dependent variable.

(3) Compression: attempt to combine associated descriptors into clusters so that only one representative of each cluster needs to be preserved for the next stage (or just a few).

These steps are iterated. At the end of the process a rule-storming phase may take place. This attempts to construct a hierarchy of the surviving descriptors, and to devise a voting procedure for combining them in subsequent forecasting.

This method is relatively resistant to noise, and it does not make the assumption that the descriptors are metrical: they can be based on underlying nominal, ordinal or metrical values. Apparently it has been used to forecast earthquakes.

However, with a large number of descriptors the combinatorial problem in the expansion phase is quite severe. Moreover, the system uses an impoverished input description language. Considerable work is required to make raw data suitable for the rule-induction program. The rule language is not particularly comprehensible either.

3.6 CONCLUSIONS

Several themes emerge from our study of rule learning programs. Among the most important is the idea of

Conjecture + Refutation

which is said to be at the heart of all scientific discovery (Popper, 1959). In one way or another, all the systems described here generate potential solutions and then test them, typically discarding the majority.

There are various methods of generation, various measures of quality for the generated rules, various ways of handling training data, and so on. For example, there are model-driven (top-down) generators, guided by prior assumptions about the form of hypotheses; and there are data-driven (bottom-up) generators, guided by patterns in the training data. However, the idea of learning as search provides a framework within which these divergent approaches can be unified.

The diagram in Fig. 3.6 shows a generalized outline of rule-generation as a search process. Numerous variations on the common theme can be obtained by making particular choices about how exactly to fill the boxes. For instance, the production of new descriptions from current descriptions

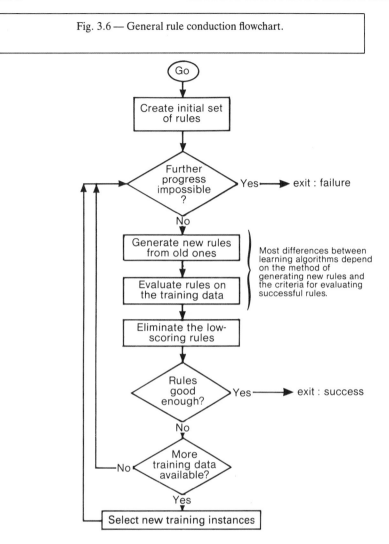

Fig. 3.6 — General rule conduction flowchart.

may be predominantly from specific to general, or vice versa, or either way. Indpendently, the evaluation may take account mainly of positive evidence, mainly negative evidence, or both equally.

Likewise the number of plausible rule structures retained on each cycle may vary. In Quinlan's and Winston's programs, only a single rule is kept. Other systems keep as many as will fit in RAM. In addition, different systems make different choices about how many training items to focus on at any one time. This can range from examining a single instance at a time, through the concept of a window of selected instances, to taking the entire training set.

Finally, of course, description languages differ greatly. The description language limits what can be learned. Even more important, it determines how well people can understand the results of the learning process.

If one single message comes over from the present chapter, it should be this: that these choices are inevitably compromises. You cannot have the best of everything.

You might choose a humanly comprehensible description language and find that it is hard to express the required kinds of concepts in it. You might want a very expressive description language, but find that it is hard for humans to comprehend and/or it slows down the learning procedure. Not all the desirable attributes of a learning system are mutually compatible. The art of AI in this field (as in others) lies in a successful balancing of conflicting requirements.

3.7 REFERENCES

Buchanan, Bruce (1976) Scientific Theory Formation by Computer: in Simon, J. C. (ed.) *Computer Oriented Learning Processes:* Noordhoff, Leyden.

Buchanan, B. G. & Feigenbaum, Edward (1978) Dendral and Meta-Dendral: their Applications Dimension: *Artificial Intelligence,* **11**.

Buchanan, B. G. & Mitchell, Tom (1978) Model-Directed Learning of Production Rules: in Waterman & Hayes-Roth (eds.) *Pattern-Directed Inference Systems*: Academic Press, New York.

Dietterich, Thomas & Michalski, Ryszard (1981) Inductive Learning of Structural Descriptions: *Artificial Intelligence,* **16**.

Hart, Anna E. (1985) Experience in the Use of an Inductive System in Knowledge Engineering: in Bramer, Max (ed.) *Research & Development in Expert Systems*: Cambridge University Press.

Hunt, Earl, Marin & Stone (1966) *Experiments in Induction*: Academic Press, New York.

Langley, Patrick (1977) Rediscovering Physics with Bacon-3: *Proc. 5th IJCAI*.

Langley, Patrick (1981) Data-driven Discovery of Physical Laws: *Cognitive Science,* **5**.

Larson, J. & Michalski, Ryszard (1978) Inductive Inference of VL Decision Rules: in Waterman & Hayes-Roth (eds.) *Pattern-Directed Inference Systems*: Academic Press, New York.

Lenat, Douglas (1982) The Nature of Heuristics: *Artificial Intelligence,* **19**.

Michalski, Ryszard & Chilausky, R. L. (1980) Learning by Being Told and Learning from Examples . . .: *Journal of Policy Analysis & Information Systems,* **4**.

Michalski, Ryszard & Larson, J. B. (1978) Selection of Most Representative Training Examples & Incremental Generation of VL1 Hypotheses . . .: Report 867, University of Illinois, Urbana.

Michalski, Carbonell & Mitchell, (eds.) (1983) *Machine Learning*: Tioga Press, Palo Alto.

Michie, Donald & Johnston, Rory (1985) *The Creative Computer*: Pelican Books, Harmondsworth.

Mitchell, Thomas (1982) Generalization as Search: *Artificial Intelligence,* **18**.

Popper, Karl (1959) *The Logic of Scientific Discovery*: Basic Books, N.Y.

Quinlan, John Ross (1979) Induction over Large Databases: Report HPP-79-14, Stanford University.

Quinlan, John Ross (1982) Semi-autonomous Acquisition of Pattern-based Knowledge: in Michie, Donald (ed.) *Introductory Readings in Expert Systems*: Gordon & Breach.

Quinqueton, Joel & Sallentin, Jean (1983) Algorithms for Learning Logical Formulas: *Proc. 8th IJCAI*, William Kaufmann, California.

Smith, Stephen F. (1983) Flexible Learning of Problem-Solving Heuristics through Adaptive Search: *Proc. 8th IJCAI*, William Kaufmann, California.

Winston, Patrick (1975) (ed.) *The Psychology of Computer Vision*: McGraw-Hill, New York.

Winston, Patrick (1984) *Artificial Intelligence* 2nd edition: Addison-Wesley, Massachusetts.

4

Evolutionary Learning Strategies

We have seen that some AI scientists take the human brain as a model when they try to design learning systems, but there is another natural model for self-improving systems — the process of evolution. It is certainly effective as a means of creating ever more advanced organisms, otherwise we would not be here discussing it. Admittedly it is slow; but it can be speeded up in computer simulation. Above all, it is relatively well understood — better, in many respects, than the inner workings of the human brain. It is simple enough for us to copy with some hope of success.

As a matter of fact this simplicity is partly illusory. Recent discoveries in biochemistry have smudged the stark clarities of the classic Darwinian/Mendelian synthesis. It is obvious that real-life genes have plenty of surprises still in store (Dawkins, 1978). Genetic engineering will complicate the picture still further. Nevertheless the broad outline of the theory remains valid: some organisms survive to breed, others do not; the heritable characteristics of the survivors proliferate. The idea of systems that improve their performance by an analogy (albeit a simplified one) with the evolutionary process is an attractive one; and it has produced some striking results.

The purpose of this chapter is to investigate an evolutionary, or Darwinian, approach to the problem of machine learning. We set this topic apart as a separate subfield in its own right because it has arisen outside mainstream AI and is only now being recognized as a legitimate AI technique, and also because of its distinctive nature.

4.1 THE EVOLUTION OF IDEAS

In an evolutionary learning scheme there is a population of structures which are treated as pseudo-organisms. Each of these structures (which we refer to as 'rules' for compatability with other writers) defines a potential solution to the problem at hand. They are also used to give rise to new structures (the 'offspring') in ways that mimic some of the features of biological reproduction (Holland, 1975).

Selection of which rules survive longest and have greatest likelihood of 'breeding' depends on their performance at the task in hand — survival of the fittest.

A typical genetic adaptation algorithm runs as follows.

(1) Generate an initial population of rules at random.
(2) Evaluate the rules and if the overall average is good enough halt and display the best of them.
(3) For each rule compute its selection probability $p=e/E$ where e is its individual score and E is the total score of all the rules.
(4) Generate the next population by selecting according to the selection probabilities and applying certain genetic operators. Repeat from step 2.

Each pass round the loop corresponds to a single generation.

The performance of such an abstract model of competition among organisms depends on a number of factors — the stucture of the rules (description language), the method of evaluation (the critic) and the precise nature of the genetic operators.

The most important genetic operators are crossover, inversion and mutation. Crossover is what happens when two rule structures 'mate' — chunks of genetic material are exchanged and combined. Inversion reorders the sequence of components in a rule: this brings together elements that were formerly far apart and separates items that were close together. The importance of inversion lies in its effects on later crossings. When rules are sliced up and recombined, neighbouring elements tend to stay together (as in real genetic material). To explore the space of potential rules thoroughly it is necessary sometimes to part closely linked items and bring distant ones together.

Finally mutation simply involves making a few random changes: a rule is 'zapped' or 'clobbered' in an unpredictable way. The role of mutation is much misunderstood. In genetic algorithms (as in nature) it is a 'background operator'. Its purpose is merely to ensure that the system does not get stuck at a local optimum. The failure of earlier attempts at simulated evolution (e.g. Fogel, Owens & Walsh, 1966) can be largely attributed to their over-reliance on mutation as the sole means of genetic change. In fact crossover is the primary means of generating new structures for testing. Inversion and mutation play ancillary roles.

Our discussion so far has been highly abstract. We may have a clear mental image of what it means for two rabbits or two dogs to mate and produce offspring. But what exactly do we mean when we talk about 'mating' or 'mutating' a rule? An informal example should help to clarify matters.

Below is a list of ten commandments, or rules, that should be familiar to most readers. They are expressed in simplified language for reasons that will become apparent.

Each rule has been put into a standard form

Generation 1

(1) Thou shalt not	have	other gods.
(2) Thou shalt not	make	graven images.
(3) Thou shalt not	take in vain	the name of God.
(4) Thou shalt	keep	the sabbath.
(5) Thou shalt	honour	thy father and mother.
(6) Thou shalt not	kill	anyone.
(7) Thou shalt not	commit adultery with	anyone.
(8) Thou shalt not	steal	other people's property.
(9) Thou shalt not	bear false witness	against thy neighbour.
(10) Thou shalt not	covet	thy neighbour's goods.

Prohibition/Exhortation + verbal group + object

so that the genetic operators can be applied without undue complication.

There are a number of criteria we might use to evaluate such rules. Without wishing to be drawn into profound moral judgements, let us say that the score obtained by a rule depends on how many people obey it. Some will command general assent; others will be disobeyed so frequently that they fall into disrepute.

With this yardstick we can imagine that, after one generation, rules 4, 9 and 10 score poorly. They are deleted and replaced by mating a pair of the surviving rules. For instance

(2) Thou shalt not	make	graven images.

and

(5) Thou shalt	honour	thy father and mother.

might produce as offspring

(2a) Thou shalt not	make	thy father and mother.
(5a) Thou shalt	honour	graven images.

among other possibilities. The next generation, therefore, might resemble the revised list below.

Generation 2

	(1) Thou shalt not	have	other gods.
(mut.)	(2) Thou shalt not	bake	raven images.
	(3) Thou shalt not	take in vain	the name of God.
(7 + 5)	(4) Thou shalt not	commit adultery with	thy father & mother.

(mut.)	(5) Thou shalt not	honour	thy father & mother.
	(6) Thou shalt not	kill	anyone.
	(7) Thou shalt not	commit adultery with	anyone.
	(8) Thou shalt not	steal	other people's property.
(6 + 8)	(9) Thou shalt not	kill	other people's property.
(5 + 2)	(10) Thou shalt	honour	graven images.

Rules 4, 9 and 10 from the first generation have been 'killed off' and replaced by descendants of the survivors. For example the new rule 10 is a combination of old rules 5 and 2. In addition, a couple of rules (2 and 5) have been subjected to mutations.

This illustration shows that the use of genetic operators imposes constraints on the form of the description language. Ideally it should consist of fixed-length, position-independent strings. Our rules have fixed length (always three components) but are not truly position independent. This restricts the use of inversion, since although

Other gods   thou shalt not   have

makes a kind of sense

Graven images   make   thou shalt

does not. Thus the syntax places restrictions on the rules that can be discovered. It is not clear whether

Thy father and mother   make   other people's property

ought to count as a well-formed rule or not.

However, we have pursued this example far enough. It gives an insight into the genetic operators in action. It also serves to highlight the relationship between genetic algorithms and the traditional 'Monte Carlo' methods as used in some branches of statistics and operational research. Both rely on controlled randomness, but there are important differences.

Genetic algorithms are in effect modified Monte-Carlo procedures. Monte Carlo methods are used routinely in operational research for problems that defy analytical solution. These are just the sort of problems that AI scientists wrestle with in different contexts, yet AI workers in general have made little effort to incorporate such techniques into their own work.

In a 'pure' Monte Carlo method, random solutions are generated for as long as there is time left, and the best solution found during the process is retained. Each trial generates a completely fresh potential solution, randomly, with no reference to what has gone before.

Fig. 4.1 — Baking images of ravens.

A pure Monte Carlo method is essentially blind search. A genetic algorithm, on the other hand, makes use of what it finds to direct further search. Specific patterns that contribute to good performance are preserved and propagated throughout the knowledge base (i.e. the population of rules). They are recombined in slightly different contexts. In effect the search is preferentially guided towards regions of the (multi-dimensional) problem space where good results have been found in the past. Unless the evaluation function is extraordinarily discontinuous, one would expect this to lead a reasonable search strategy. (Rada, 1984).

In fact, using the pure Monte Carlo technique as a baseline, we can usefully distinguish four levels of complexity:

(1) Pure Monte Carlo methods;
(2) Mutation-only methods;
(3) Basic genetic algorithms;
(4) The 'elitist' strategy.

Each of these four levels is characterized by a different anaser to the question: how is the next candidate to be chosen? Remember that learning can be viewed as a kind of search (Chapter 3). The next candidate is the next structure to be examined in the search through the rule-space. Method (1) simply generates a new structure on each trial, completely at random. It is a genuine 'trial and error' approach. Method (2) modifies existing structures to make new ones for testing. Thus new structures tend to resemble those that have succeeded in the past. Method (3) generates new structures from pairs of previously successful ones. This can be shown to be a more efficient search strategy than Method (2), since it has the effect of searching on more than one dimension of the problem space simultaneously.

There is therefore evidence that these correspond to levels of increasing efficiency. The 'elitist strategy' (Method (4)) is a variant on the evoultionary theme. It differs from the basic genetic algorithm in only one respect: the best rule never dies; it remains till supplanted by a better one. In the algorithm as outlined at the beginning of this section, the whole population is replaced at the end of each cycle. In the example of the ten command-ments, on the other hand, some rules were preserved from the first generation to the next.

It is interesting to speculate on the biological analogies. We offer the following tempting, but unproven, historical parallel:

(1) Primeval pre-organic chemistry;
(2) Asexual reproduction;
(3) Sexual reproduction;
(4) Artificial selection.

In this scheme the 'brave new world' of genetic engineering falls under heading (4). It is the sort of thing we have been doing to our plants and animals for a long time. We may shortly begin to practise it on human beings.

4.2 THE POKER-FACED MACHINE

One of the more interesting of practical evolutionary learning systems is LS-1, described by Smith (1980, 1984). This is a general-purpose learning system which can be adapted to a variety of tasks. It has been tested on a maze-walking problem and in the game of Draw Poker.

Its description language, KS-1, is based on the idea of production systems (Davis & King, 1977). Each rule consists of a variable number of fixed-length productions. The individual productions have the following format.

SV-patterns WM-patterns Message Operator

The SV-patterns are patterns that match state variables supplied from the environment. WM-patterns match patterns in the working memory. The message is deposited in working memory when the production is successfully triggered, i.e. when both kinds of patterns are matched. The operator carries out an output operation, i.e. does something in the task domain. The operator can be a NOOP, which does nothing, so some productions only have an internal effect. The patterns are expressed in a simple binary language consisting of the symbols 0, 1 and * of which the last is a 'don't care' field. Thus 001* is a pattern that would match a four-character string starting with two zeroes, followed by a one and ending with any other character.

This language forces the input to the system to be expressed as (or translated into) a binary state-vector (a representation we have met before). But notice that the number of productions in a single rule is not fixed. This means that the learning component is in effect generating little progams in a production-rule language. The programs can respond to inputs, leave messages for each other, and generate outputs. Message-passing increases the complexity of the system greatly because it permits productions to cooperate.

The critic employed by LS-1 has to be given some domain-dependent evaluation measures; but it also uses task-independent measures. It assesses structural properties of rules (such as the potential for intercommunication), dynamic properties of rules (derived from tracing execution of the production-rules) and the rule size. Although there is no limit on the number of productions in a rule, the LS-1 critic incorporates a bias towards conciseness. (This can conflict with the desire to have the best possible performance.)

LS-1 succeeded in a relatively challenging task — learning to play draw poker. In this game five cards are dealt to each player. Then both players alternately have the options of betting, calling or dropping. If a call is made each player may replace up to three cards in his hand with new cards from the deck. A drop terminates the current round. If a second call is made both hands are displayed and the player holding the higher ranking hand collects the money in the pot.

The state of the game is presented to LS-1 in terms of seven integer variables (which are in fact handled as one long bit-string). These are:

VDHAND	value of system's hand
POT	amount in the pot
LASTBET	size of the latest bet
POTBET	ratio of money in pot to last bet
ORPL	number of cards replaced by opponent
BLUFFO	measure of likelihood of bluffing opponent
OSTYLE	measure of opponent's conservatism in play.

LS-1 was pitted against a poker betting program hand-crafted by Waterman (1970) and judged to perform at the level of an experienced human player. No human would have had the patience to play against it long enough! There were four possible decisions for each play: Bet High, Bet Low, Call or Drop.

The objective of the program was to complete 10 consecutive rounds in complete agreement with Waterman's 'axioms' or poker. These axioms permitted the LS-1 critic to examine the record of play for any hand and deduce whether any mistakes had been made, taking into account both hands. The criterion of 10 successive rounds in agreement with the poker axioms was easily achieved. It was too easy, in fact. It turned out that Waterman's program was not suitable for long games of up to 40,000 hands. It tended to judge LS-1, incorrectly, as a very conservative player. This made it susceptible to bluffing. It had to be revised to make it a more formidable opponent.

After tuning the opponent, LS-1 played another 40,000 rounds or so of poker, consuming about 2 DEC-10 CPU hours, and at the end was capable of playing nine successful rounds in a row. (Smith does not reveal which player left the table with fuller pockets!) This, though not reaching the original criterion, was still an impressive level of performance. Its bet decisions agreed with those deduced from the axioms 82% of the time.

LS-1 performed creditably in two different domains, showing that a successful general-purpose genetic learning system is quite feasible. Its main drawback is the obscurity of the KS-1 description language. Nowhere in his thesis does Smith quote any of the knowledge gained by LS-1. This is because it would be unintelligible. In effect, LS-1 is a black-box method because the rules are not intended for public consumption. (See Chapter 2.) This is a problem with genetic algorithms in general. The requirements of the genetic operators (for rules that can be sliced up and stitched together with a minimum of fuss) tend to conflict with the requirement that acquired knowledge should be open to inspection. In nature it appears that there are 'punctuation' segments in the genetic code for precisely this reason: they ensure that cuts occur where they would not make nonsense of the genetic message (most of the time). But of course DNA was not designed for readability, and we are only beginning to understand its description language.

4.3 THE VOYAGE OF THE BEAGLE

BEAGLE (Biological Evolutionary Algorithm Generating Logical Expressions) is an evolutionary learning system that overcomes — to some extent — the problem of obscurity in the description language by representing rules as Boolean expressions. These are held internally as tree structures. Its objective is to learn discriminant rules by examing a database of examples, using a method termed 'Naturalistic Selection'.

4.3.1 The BEAGLE has landed

The original BEAGLE system (Forsyth, 1981) had two main modules, but the most recent version consists of six separate programs.

SEED	Selectively Extracts Example Data
ROOT	Rule-Oriented Optimization Tester
HERB	Heuristic Evolutionary Rule Breeder
STEM	Signature Table Evaluation Module
LEAF	Logical Evaluator And Forecaster
PLUM	Procedural Language Utilization Module

A diagram of how they link together appears as Fig. 4.2.

SEED is a simple data extraction program. It interfaces BEAGLE to external databases. It can read datafiles in a few simple formats, including comma-delimited or space-delimited ASCII files as produced by dBase II and other popular packages. It performs one or both of the following functions:

(1) splitting the database in two (random subsets);
(2) appending leading and/or lagging variables for time-series analyses.

The former is useful for making the important distinction between training and test data sets. The latter permits data which is chronologically ordered to be used in various forecasting tasks.

ROOT is merely a preliminary batch-tester for user-supplied rules. This allows the user to suggest initial hunches. (In almost all cases these are quickly superseded by superior machine-made rules.)

HERB is the main module: it actually generates new rules. It takes a datafile from SEED, a tag-file (describing the variables or fields) and an intial rule file as input (which normally comes from ROOT). It produces a new rule file as output. The initial rule file may be empty to start with, except for the 'target expression', which is what you want to predict. For instance, in a weather-forecasting example, a suitable target expression might be

$$((NEXTRAIN < 0.4) \ \& \ (NEXTSUN > 4.0)) \ \$$$

Fig. 4.2 — The BEAGLE has landed.

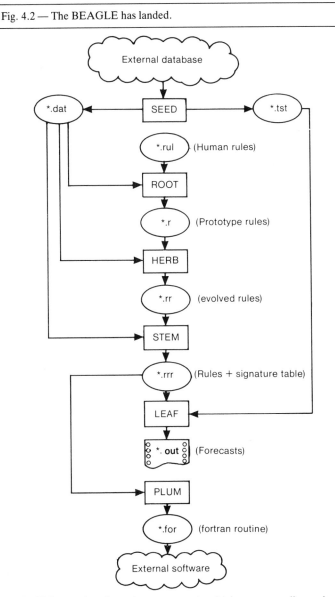

BEAGLE contains six main components which are generally run in sequence. SEED (Selectively Extracts Example Data) puts external data into a suitable format, and may append leading or lagging data-fields also. ROOT (Rule Oriented Optimization Tester) tests an initial batch of user-suggested rules. HERB (Heuristic Evolutionary Rule Breeder) generates decision rules by Naturalistic Selection. STEM (Signature Table Evaluation Module) makes a signature table from the rules produced by HERB. LEAF (Logical Evaluator And Forecaster) use STEM's output to do forecasting or classification.

Finally PLUM (Procedural Language Utility Maker) can be used to convent a BEAGLE rule-file into a language such as Pascal or Fortran. In this form the knowledge gained may be used in other software.

if we were interested in predicting fine days. This expression would be true when the following day's rainfall was below 0.4 (mm) and its sunshine was more than 4.0 (hours).

The rule language allows variable names (such as NEXTSUN) which refer to fields in the database, numeric constants (such as 4.0) and the following operators.

Logical

&	AND
|	Inclusive OR
!	NOT

Relational

=	Equals
< >	Does not equal
<	Less than
>	Greater than
≤	Less than or equal
≥	Greater than or equal

Arithmetic

+	Addition
−	Subtraction
*	Multiplication

These are combined into fully bracketed Boolean expressions, terminated by a dollar sign ($). There is no operator procedence, so brackets are mandatory. If necessary, numeric values are coerced to logical values by the convention that zero and negative numbers are false and numbers greater than zero are true. (Character string fields can be handled, by a kind of phonetic hashing, but the package is designed primarily for numeric data.)

Note that the target expression and the rules are encoded in the same language. This means there is no need for a special category field. BEAGLE can be used with whatever dependent variable seems appropriate or (as above) with a target that is the logical combination of dependent variables. For instance it is just as easy to try forecasting the wind as the rainfall or sunshine, provided the data is available.

HERB works by running through the following procedure, expressed here in 'pidgin pascal'. (This is in fact a simplified outline of the HERB main program.)

```
REPEAT
   mainloop := mainloop + 1;
```

```
    runs := 0;
    REPEAT
      runs := runs + 1;
      reset (datafile); (* start at beginning of data *)
      FOR nx := 1 to samples DO (* for every training instance *)
        (* Get the next data sample *)
        (* Try all the rules on it *)
        ;
      scoring;   (* evaluate new rules' performance *)
      culling;   (* get rid of sub-standard rules *)
      eugenics; (* mate the good ones *)
      mutation; (* make a few random changes *)
      tidying;   (* clean up the mess *)
      UNTIL (runs ≥ gens); (* enough generations *)
    savebest;    (* keep the top rule *)
    wipeout;     (* eliminate its variables from further use *)
    UNTIL (mainloop ≥ maxloops) OR (varsleft < 2);
    (* dump top rules on file *)
```

The main subprograms are explained in comments between '(*' and '*)' but there are one or two points that need further clarification.

Mating is achieved by picking out a random subtree (or subexpression) from each of two high-scoring rules and tying them together with a randomly chosen connective. Thus from the two parent rules

$$(\text{LASTWIND} > (\text{LASTRAIN} + 5.80))$$

and

$$((\text{RAINFALL} * 8.50) = \text{RAINFALL})$$

possible descendants could be

$$(\text{LASTWIND} > 8.50)$$
$$((\text{LASTRAIN} + 5.80) = \text{RAINFALL})$$

and so on. Note the rule ((RAINFALL * 8.50) = RAINFALL) can be true when RAINFALL=0. BEAGLE does not always find the simplest way to say what it means.

The scoring procedure rests ultimately on the Chi-squared statistic. That is to say, each rule can give a true or false result and the target expression can also yield a true or false result. Thus each joint outcome falls into one cell of a fourfold contingency table. The more this table departs from chance expectation, the better — i.e. the more effectively the target can be predicted from the rule value. In evaluating a rule the raw score, based on Chi-squared, is biased by subtracting the logarithm (or optionally the square root) of the rule's size to give a pressure towards short rules.

The tidying routine cleans up any solecisms introduced by the mutation procedure and performs a number of syntactic manipulations intended to simplify the rule and make it more comprehensible. Thus

$$(\text{RAINFALL} + -2.5)$$

would become

$$(\text{RAINFALL} - 2.5)$$

and

$$((10.75 + 99.05) \text{ \& } (\text{WINDGUST} < 30))$$

would be reduced to

$$(\text{WINDGUST} < 30)$$

since $10.75 + 99.05 = 109.80$ which counts as true in a logical context.

One point worth noting is that HERB contains two nested loops. The inner loop goes through a given number of generations in the manner of a conventional genetic algorithm, using the elitist strategy. At the end of this process the best rule found so far is retained and all the variables it uses are disqualified from further use. Then the process repeats. Thus several rules are generated for output, each one being the best that was found with the variables remaining. Earlier versions of BEAGLE just came up with a single 'best' rule. This was not found to be generally satisfactory. The newer system makes better use of information inherent in all the problem variables.

STEM takes the rules dumped by HERB and uses them to construct a signature table. (See Chapter 2.) Each rule is a predicate that can be in one of two states — true or false. Therefore with, say, four rules there are 16 possible states for the four rules in combination. Each of these 16 combinations defines a particular 'signature' (or 'fingerprint'). STEM re-examines the training data and counts the number of times each signature occurs; at the same time it accumulates the average value of the target expression for each signature. STEM will also optionally, drop the least useful rule — the one whose absence would least degrade its prediction score.

The revised rule-file (with signature table) produced by STEM is in a form that LEAF can use for forecasting. LEAF simply runs over a fresh data set (which uses the same variables as the training data, or at least all the variables mentioned in the rules) and estimates what the value of the target expression should be. It does this by evaluating all the rules and using them to point to a cell in the signature table. LEAF's output is sorted in descending order of the estimated target value. If the actual target value is known, LEAF also works out the success rate of the rules. In principle it could handle missing rule values by looking at all the cells corresponding to the values that are not missing, but it does not do so at present.

Finally PLUM realizes the objective of programming by example. It translates a BEAGLE rule-file into a Pascal procedure or Fortran subroutine. This means that once you have found a good decision rule with BEAGLE's help, you are free to export it into other software.

4.3.2   Empirical testing

BEAGLE has been tested in various domains — including categorizing cardiac patients, forecasting commodity prices, analyzing drilling data from North Sea boreholes and gambling. It is suitable for a wide range of diagnostic classificaiton tasks. Here we present some results from a medical and a meteorological trial.

In the medical example, it was used to find a set of rules that could discriminate heavy from light drinkers on the basis of some biochemical tests. The data used were for 345 men, measured on six variables. This data was kindly supplied by BUPA Medical Research Ltd. (See Appendix A.) The six variables were as follows.

MCV	Mean Corpuscular Volume
ALKPHOS	Alkaline Phosphotase
SGPT	Alamine Aminotransferase
SGOT	Aspartate Aminotransferase
GAMMAGT	Gamma-Glutamyl Transpeptidase
DRINKS	the number of half-pint-equivalents of alcoholic beverages drunk per day

By way of brief explanation, MCV measures the mean size of red blood cells; ALKPHOS is an enzyme created in the bone marrow and the liver whose level is known to change in women after the menopause; SGPT is an enzyme in the blood associated with liver function in so far as raised values are found when the liver is damaged; SGOT is another enzyme indicative of liver function whose value is raised by toxic hepatitis, malignancies and so on; GAMMAGT is a sensitive indicator of cellular liver damage used to assess alcohol abuse. Thus the first five variables are blood tests which are thought to be sensitive to liver or blood disorders arising from excessive alcohol consumption.

With the target expression (DRINKS < 7) after a run of 25 generations on a training set of 113 cases, BEAGLE found the following rules.

The numbers of following each rule correspond to the contingecy table as follows.

Target:	(DRINKS < 7)	
Rule 1:	((MCV $\geqslant$ 91) $\leqslant$ (120 $\geqslant$ GAMMAGT))	

	Target-True	Target-False
Rule-True	80	7
Rule-False	11	15

	(DRINKS < 7.00)\$		
((MCV ≥	91.00)	≤ (20.00 ≥ GAMMAGT))	
\$ 80	7	11	15
(SGPT ≥	44.83)		
\$ 85	14	5	8
(SGOT ≥	33.39)		
\$ 89	16	1	6
( ) \$			
	0.8053	113	
000	0.0000	4	
001	1.0000	4	
010	0.0000	1	
011	10.0000	17	
100	0.0000	1	
101	4.0000	4	
110	1.0000	1	
111	75.0000	81	

Here again HERB has not expressed it as we might like, even after the tidying procedure. We would probably prefer

$$((MCV < 91) \mid (GAMMAGT ≤ 20))$$

and in the long run it should be possible to get the system to reformulate rules to correspond to the (implicit) syntax we impose on arithmetical and logical expressions.

This rule set gave 87% correct classification on the 113 training cases. More significantly it was correct on 85% of the 232 test cases which it had not previously encountered. This compares favourably with a run of the well-known SPSS package, using its discriminant analysis module on the same training and test data. The SPSS linear discriminant functions achieved 77.5% success on unseen data. The signature-table format (and the rules themselves) allow for non-linear interactions between variables; and in this case it would seem to be an advantage.

A disadvantage, however, is illustrated here too. Only two of the eight cells in the signature table have a sample size running into double figures. This is a problem we mentioned in Chapter 3, in connection with ID3 decision trees. The table is in effect a sparse matrix. Really only two of the cells can be relied upon for prediction: the rest contain too few examples. For this reason LEAF flags forecasts based on small samples with a warning. It may prove better, however, simply to admit ignorance in these cases. What the system has really learnt here (from a training set that is smaller than desirable) is that if all three rules are true there is a 75/81 chance of the target being true, and if the first one is false and the other two true there is a 10/17 chance. In other cases it simply does not know. Even this one-sided knowledge could be useful for screening purposes. People in the all-Yes group are unlikely to have a drinking problem.

For the weather-forecasting test, BEAGLE was run on a training set of London readings for March, April and May of 1983 and 1984. It was then tested on the 90 days of March, April and May 1985 (excluding 1st March and 31st May on account of missing preceding and following data) together with 28 days from February 1984. The object of the excercise was to predict rain on the following day of more than 0.1mm. The rule set produced after a 32-generation run was as follows.

```
( NEXTRAIN > 0.1000)$
( RAINFALL > 0.00)
$       75        45        14        48
(( SUNSHINE < WINDMEAN) > (( LASTRAIN ≤ 0.300)
   + ( WINDGUST ≥ 45.00)))
$       50        18        39        75
(( PRESSURE − 997.00) ≤ MAXTEMP)
$       60        23        29        70
() $
                0.4890        182
000             6.0000         44
001             4.0000         10
010             2.0000          4
011             2.0000          4
100            13.0000         37
101            16.0000         23
110             8.0000         14
111            38.0000         46
```

Note that BEAGLE arranges for all the rules to point in the same direction, i.e. to be favourable to the target when true. To read the signature table you need to know that the first rule sets the first bit in the signature and the final rule sets the last bit. So the signature 011 points to cases where rule 1 was false but rules 2 and 3 were true.

Sixteen variables were used in this example.

DATE	The date
MINTEMP	Minimum temperature in degrees Celsius
MAXTEMP	Maximum temperature in degrees Celsius
MORNDAMP	Humidity % at 0600 hours
EVEDAMP	Humidity % at 1500 hours
RAINFALL	Rainfall in millimetres
WINDMEAN	Average wind speed in knots
WINDGUST	Maximum wind gust in knots
SUNSHINE	Hours of sunshine
PRESSURE	Atmospheric Pressure in millibars at 1800 hours (sometimes 1900 hours)

LASTSUN   Previous day's SUNSHINE
NEXTSUN   Following day's SUNSHINE
LASTRAIN   Previous day's RAINFALL
NEXTRAIN   Following day's RAINFALL
LASTWIND   Previous day's WINDMEAN
NEXTWIND   Following day's WINDMEAN

All data are London readings. A single example, from May-85, is

'30-MAY',   7.5,18.6,70,24,   0.0,13.2,29,15.5,1027,15.211.9,   0.0,
0.0,10.6,12.7

which, as it happens, was the sunniest May day in central London since
records began in 1929.

On the unknown data from spring of 1985 the success rate was 68%,
which is quite respectable for an amateur. Chance expectation would be
close to 50%. (A LEAF printout is shown in Appendix B.) Britain is
positioned at the edge of a continent and an ocean, lying in the track of
Atlantic depressions. In consequence, the weather of the British Isles is
notoriously upredictable. The Meteorological Office claims to get 80% of its
forecasts right; but these require enormous computing resources, and are
usually couched in rather vague terms. If you require specific predictions,
such as whether there will be more than 6 hours of sunshine tomorrow in a
particular location, the success rate falls (and the cost rises!).

In fact BEAGLE's performance on unknown data was better than it
appears. By ignoring the forecasts that LEAF flagged as based on too small a
sample in the signature table, the overall success rate rises to 65/92 or
70.65%. (with 26 unknowns). This uses only the four groups with the biggest
samples. Whether this conservative strategy confers any practical benefit
depends on your application; but in any case it is useful that the system can
confess when it is uncertain. If you must forecast the weather every day, you
just have to make the best prediction you can. But if your task is picking
horses to win races or buying shares when they are likely to go up, you may
be able to afford to wait for a confident forecast — and then strike!

The results look even better whey you add up the rainfall for the 37 days
when BEAGLE was confident of rain (75.8mm in total) and the 55 days
when it confidently forecase a dry day (22.8mm). For the former the average
daily rainfall was 2.0486mm, while for the latter it was 0.4145mm. Clearly it
is on to something.

But this is starting to sound like special pleading. Suffice it to say that
there is evidence that combining on evolutionary learning strategy with a
signature table works quite well.

(Commercial versions of the BEAGLE package are available for VAX
minicomputers and for PC-compatible microcomputers from Warm Boot
Ltd.)

4.4 CONCLUSIONS

We have used the term Naturalistic Selection to describe a variety of methods that draw on evolutionary principles. This covers systems we have not described here (see Lenat, 1983, for example). Naturalistic Selection is no panacea, but it is a robust and practical technique in cases where there is a very large search space. If your problem has

(1) information structures that encode potential solutions,
(2) a way of evaluating those structures,
(3) formal means of chopping up and re-splicing those structures without creating nonsense rules,
(4) no obvious algorithmic solution.

then you would be well advised to consider an evolutionary learning scheme. After all, there are not many computing techniques that have proved their worth over 3 billion years of field testing.

4.5 REFERENCES

Davis, R. & King, J. (1977) An Overview of Production Systems: in Elcock & Michie (eds.) *Machine Intelligence, 8:* Ellis Horwood, Chichester.

Dawkins, Richard (1978) *The Selfish Gene:* Granada, St. Albans.

Fogel, Owens & Walsh (1966) *Artificial Intelligence through Simulated Evolution:* Wiley.

Forsyth, Richard (1981) BEAGLE: A Darwinian Approach to Pattern Recognition: *Kybernetes* **10.**

Holland, John (1975) *Adaptation in Natural and Artificial Systems:* University of Michigan Press.

Lenat, Douglas (1983) The Role of Heuristics in Learning by Discover: in Michalski *et al.* (eds.) *Machine Learning:* Tioga Press.

Rada, Roy (1984) Automating Knowledge Acquistion: in Forsyth, R. S. (ed.) *Expert Systems, Principles and Case Studies:* Chapman & Hall, London.

Smith, Stephen F. (1980) A Learning System Based on Genetic Adaptive Algorithms: PhD Thesis, Dept. Computer Science, University of Pittsburgh.

Smith, Stephen F. (1984) Adaptive Learning Systems: in Forsyth, R. S. (ed.) *Expert Systems: Principles and Case Studies:* Chapman & Hall, London.

Waterman, D. A. (1970) Generalization Learning Techniques for Automating the Learning of Heuristics: *Artificial Intelligence,* **1.**

5

Towards the learning machine

In Chapter 1 we identified four key components of any learning system —
the Performer, the Learner, the Rules and the Critic. The performer is
necessarily specific to a given task, but the other three can and should be
largely domain-independent. We have looked at a number of learning
algorithms (Learners) employing a variety of description languages (Rules).
We have been less forthcoming about the evaluation functions used (Critics)
because the precise form of evaluation depends on the aim of the learning
exercise and is thus at the discretion of the user. However, all learning
systems must have some kind of performance measure and this nearly
always gives some weight to features of the rules other than their effectiveness at the chosen task — e.g. brevity or structural simplicity.

In this chapter we attempt to draw some of the disparate threads together
so that the reader with a practical orientation can gain some advice on how to
design a workable learning system (and how not to).

5.1 ASPECTS OF MACHINE LEARNING

Machine learning is potentially applicable to a bewildering diversity of tasks.
This means that there are many ways of looking at the problem, each
perspective emphasizing some aspects of the overall process at the expense
of others. For example

Automatic Programming
Artistic Creativity
Data Compression
Knowledge Synthesis
Optimization
Search
Theory Formation

are all facets of machine learning.

5.1.1 Automatic programming

The objective of automatic programming is for the computer to write its own programs. Typically it is given examples of input–output pairings and has to synthesize a program that will produce the appropriate output for every input. In one sense Smith's LS-1 (Chapter 4) is an automatic programming system. If the description language is a programming language then learning descriptions in that language is a kind of automatic programming.

Automatic programming is a very difficult problem. One reason for this is that we expect our programs to give the right answers under all conditions. (They may not, but we still expect it.) This means that there is no place for noise in the system.

5.1.2 Learning as creativity

The association between learning and creativity is also very strong. Very often learning, in people, is a creative act: we discover how to tie our shoelaces or draw a picture of a cat. We may think we have done something original, but it is not called creativity either because the subject matter is too mundane or because someone else has made the discovery already, or both. Nevertheless the two activities are very closely related. Learning is creativity at second hand. Conversely, creativity is learning something for the first time ever.

5.1.3 Data compression

Data compression is normally an unintended by-product of machine learning simply because the rules learned are typically much shorter than the training data. Yet they can be used to reconstruct the important properties of that training data. Sometimes, however, data comprssion is a major objective. Indeed many approaches based on signature tables are best viewed as attempts to reduce a large collection of examples to a compact tabular format.

5.1.4 Knowledge synthesis

Designers of expert systems tend to think of machine learning in terms of synthesizing knowledge. For them it is a short-cut on the long and tortuous road towards obtaining knowledge from a human expert. Currently such knowledge has to be elicited, codified and checked by a knowledge engineer. This involves much human labour. In future much of it may be done by machine.

This is an approach we have stressed in the present work, but it is only one way of looking at the subject.

5.1.5 Learning as optimization

Machine learning can also be seen as a kind of optimization. This is particularly clear in parameter-adjustment systems (like the Perceptron) where the knowledge is expressed as a linear function of some sort. Here the objective is to find a set of parameters or coefficients. When the expression is a simple one this can be achieved by conventional optimization techniques; but a complex expression may not yield to conventional optimization techniques. In such a case, a search is required.

5.1.6   Learning by searching
The search space in a parameter-optimization problem is the set of all possible parameter combinations. Since this space is enormous, efficient heuristics have to be used to explore that space. This is the point we emphasized in Chapter 3, where we considered learning as a search process.

5.1.7   Computer science and computerized science
Finally, the search for new knowledge can be regarded as a process of theory formulation. This is exemplified in those systems that base their methods on induction as practised by the scientific community, past and present (e.g. Bacon the man, Chapter 1, and Bacon the program, Chapter 3).

In the long run this may prove the most significant aspect of machine learning. Scientists who are quite willing to accept the computer as a workhorse for calculations may have reservations about its role as a fellow voyager on the great ocean of truth — especially if it sails rapidly over the horizon of human comprehension. It is bad enough for a machine to make scientific discoveries that nobody ever thought of: that has already happened to a limited extent. But in due course computers may well discover facts that are literally beyond our understanding. This could be rather humiliating. (In the physics of subatomic particles we have almost reached this sorry state of affairs without much help from the computer.)

This then is the long-term outlook for machine learning: the automation of science itself. It is both a promise and a threat.

5.2   CREATIVE COMPUTERS

The automation of scientific discovery may seem a distant prospect, but the first steps have already been taken. One of the pioneers in this field is Doug Lenat of Stanford University, who devised the Eurisko program (Lenat, 1982).

Eurisko is a discovery program which we have already mentioned briefly. It has been applied in several domains ranging from a naval wargame to the design of VLSI (Very Large Scale Integration) circuits. It begins with a collection of heuristic rules and concepts and applies them to the chosen domain. Its novelty lies in the fact that it can modify its own heuristics, which are expressed like everything else in the system as frame-like data structures. This gives the system great power, since it can adapt and specialize its general rules to deal with new situations.

It has made one discovery for which a patent was subsequently granted. This was a new design for a three-dimensional logic circuit (a NAND/OR gate), which nobody in Silicon Valley — or anywhere else — had thought of. Yet it was generated by the application of a single rule.

When Eurisko was applied to VLSI design it already had a heuristic rule, carried over from previous tasks, that said, in effect: if a concept is interesting, try to make it more symmetrical. Applied to a two-dimensional device it led to a more symmetrical version of that device — which has recently been successfully fabricated. This three-dimensional device can be packed more densely, thus offering greater capacity.

Fig. 5.1 — 2D and 3D VLSI gates.

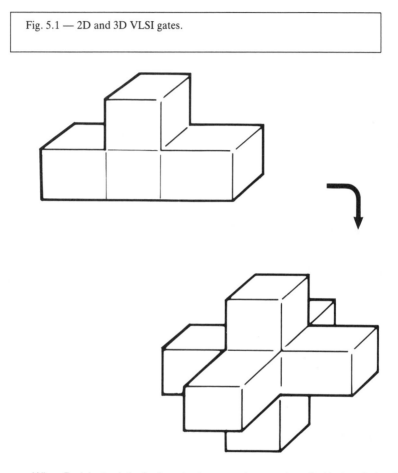

When Eurisko took the logic-gate structure above and applied its heuristic rule about symmetry, it transformed it into a new 3-dimensional structure below. Subsequently a patent was granted for a device based on the lower design, so it represents a genuine non-trivial discovery.

Creativity is seen as the pinnacle of human intelligence, and shrouded in mysterious explanations involving intuition and insight; but Eurisko should give us pause for thought. Here is an example of a genuine discovery resulting from the application of a single rule. Perhaps scientists, as scientists, behave in ways that are simpler than previously thought. They take an existing concept and give it a tweak; or take two old concepts and find a way of joining them. In effect they say to themselves such things as the following.

Let's try inverting that function.
I wonder what happens in extreme cases.
Surely this design can be made more symmetrical?
These two functions look interesting, can we link them?

These are the sort of operations that Eurisko can carry out. They are also the kind of operations that have been identified as fundamental to scientific creativity by Koestler (1964) and others.

The creative computer is closer than many people realize.

5.3 PROBLEMS OF MACHINE LEARNING

This brings us to a consideration of the problems of machine learning. For the present the main problem is getting it to work at all; but in the longer term one can envisage that the chief problem may not be failure but success — at least success of a certain kind.

Learning can be a dangerous activity, as the story of the Tree of Knowledge illustrated. Inductively derived knowledge can never be proved, which is why (as we saw in Chapter 1) it has always cause disquiet among philosophers. Yet computerized learning systems indulge in rampant inductionism. This is bound to introduce uncertainties. The trouble is that we respect computer solutions too much. In many cases we are overawed by printout, as if it were the word of God carved in stone.

Suppose a computer system has learned how to identify early signs of leukaemia (using, let us say, standard biochemical tests). Your eldest child is sorted into a high-risk group, and the doctors recommend a course of preventive therapy which includes a potentially hazardous bone-marrow transfusion. Who is in a position to evaluate the risks? Probably neither you nor your doctor, unless the computer-generated rules are more explicit than anything we have seen so far.

Then again, suppose your younger child slips through the screening tests, but later develops the disease. Is the doctor to blame? Is the programmer to blame? Is it anyone's fault? Who, after all, will dare to countermand the computer, even when it is wrong?

Dilemmas like these make it likely that we shall have to certify and ratify computer-produced knowledge. In medicine (and some other fields) decision-rules generated by computers may have to be scrutinized and passed by a standards board before being released for general use, rather as drugs have to be clinically tested. The knowledge, even when released, may need to carry a grading certificate which states the circumstances in which it can safely be used.

The more efficient computers become at inducing new knowledge, the more widely that knowledge will be applied, even in matters of life and death. It is essential that such knowledge be open to inspection. This means that designers of learning systems have a public duty to use comprehensible description languages — even if that means sacrificing performance. Otherwise we run the risk of generating truly 'unknowable knowledge'. It is quite easy to think of codes that are effective in guiding a machine's decision making but which are virtually incomprehensible to people. Binary machine code is a good example.

But even if the knowledge generated by the next generation of learning systems is intelligible to people, there is no guarantee that they are going to like it when they see it, nor even that the people to whom it matters will be allowed to see it at all. Suppose that a large company applied an inductive rule-finder to an archive of data on past and present employees, and came up with a rule that said in plain English: do not hire any coloured people?

We are alrady familiar with abuses of credit-rating data-processing systems and the like. The advent of effective machine learning will broaden the scope for such abuses. The problem becomes particularly acute in military applications.

We can easily imagine systems that learn to recognize submarines from sonar signals or aircraft from radar images. It is not too far-fetched to imagine a roving robot with a machine-gun that could be taught how to distinguish English speakers from Russian speakers. We do not have to use our imaginations at all to realize what such machines will do when you open your mouth. So-called 'smart weapons' pose frightening ethical problems for all AI workers, not just those concerned with machine learning. But, as we have argued, learning is fundamental to intelligence; so the problems are particularly severe in this area. Setting loose on the battlefield weapons that are able to learn may be one of the biggest mistakes mankind has ever made. It could also be one of the last.

5.4   THE WAY AHEAD

In any field of human endeavour it is wise to be aware of potential long-term hazards, in order to be better equipped to combat them when the time comes. Machine learning is no exception, although some AI researchers exclude questions of morality from their work (despite the example of physicists and the atomic bomb). That is why we have raised such issues here.

However, the gloom of undiluted pessimism has little value, so let us end this part of the book on a more positive and more practical note, with some advice.

If you wish to build a learning system of your own, here are some hints and tips. They have to be rather generalized, but should still prove a useful starting point for your own researches

Aims

(1) If the purpose of the project is morally reprehensible (e.g. killing civilians), stop right there.

(1) If the purpose of the project is morally reprehensible (e.g. killing civilians), stop right there.

Description language

(2) Ensure that the description language is capable of expressing the distinctions that will be needed. For instance, if numeric comparisons are required, do not be satisfied with a simple string-matching language.

(3) Try to make the format of the rules as legible as possible for people. Vectors of floating-point numbers are particularly poor in this respect.

Learner

(4) Choose the simplest algorithm you can get away with. There are plenty to choose from in this book. Others can be looked up via the Bibliography.

(5) If you intend to devise a new method of your own, look closely first at natural models (e.g. genetics, the brain, the immune system, science as a social phenomenon, etc.) before designing your alorithms.

Critic

(6) Think hard about the criteria for differentiating successful from unsuccesful trials. If you want the system to learn multiple cooperating rules (as in automatic programming), the problem of credit assignment is especially hard. One possible solution, not fully exploited, is money (computer-based credit, of course, not hard cash). Each rule is rewarded for contributing to successes and penalized for contributing to failures. Rules have to pay each other for services renderd, such as providing information. A quasi-economic model along these lines — the 'bucket-brigade algorithm' — has been propsed by John Holland at the University of Michigan (see Lindsay, 1985). But always remember: computers give you what you ask for, not what you want; and machine learning is no exception.

(7) Make sure the evaluation function is modifiable, so that you can vary the weights (e.g. between false positives and false negatives) if necessary; and keep the option of evaluating the rules partly on structural criteria (such as brevity) as well as performance in the task domain. You never know exactly how to evaluate what you want till you see what you get.

General

(8) As far as possible, only ask the machine to learn what it nearly knows already. Machine learning works best when it is tuning or refining existing knowledge. To put it another way: you will get best results by selecting appropriate input variables, by presenting carefully chosen training examples and by fitting the description language to the task in hand. Natural language rules will look different from computer-vision rules. It is not 'cheating' to reduce the search space to manageable proportions before letting the learning program wander round it: it is good sense. The machine's task is then merely to home in on the precise behaviour required (Forsyth & Naylor, 1985).

But the most important advice of all is to give it a try. Machine learning, as we have attempted to show, is not a black art; and there are few fields within computing where it cannot profitably be applied. A number of important ones spring to mind:

Medical diagnosis
Predicting earthquakes
Scientific gambling
Mineral exploration
Game playing
Image recognition
Robotics
Signature verification
Weather forecasting
Intelligent information retrieval.

A full list would occupy too much paper, because learning is the key to intelligence and intelligence is the key to the next generation of software. As in nature, so in programming, the slogan is: adapt or die. You are encouraged to think of ways of making your own programs more adaptable, perhaps using techniques outlined in this book.

With these recommendations the general introduction to our book is finished. In Part 2 we try to practise what we preach by focusing on the last item in the above list — intelligent information retrieval. This complements our wide-ranging survey by delving more deeply into a single problem domain and showing how machine learning methods fit into an overall problem-solving strategy.

5.5 REFERENCES

Forsyth, Richard & Naylor, Chris (1985) *The Hitch-hiker's Guide to Artificial Intelligence*: Methuen, London.
Koestler, Arthur (1964) *The Act of Creation*: Hutchinson (Pan Books), London.
Lenat, Douglas (1982) 'The Nature of Heuristics': *Artificial Intelligence*. **19**.
Lindsay, Robert (1985) 'Artificial Intelligence Research at the University of Michigan': *AI Magazine,* **6**, Summer.

Part 2

Machine Learning in Information Retrieval
Roy Rada

6

Introduction

6.1 INFORMATION RETRIEVAL SYSTEMS AND ARTIFICIAL INTELLIGENCE

The growth of technology is leading mankind to an increased awareness of the need for more intelligent document retrieval systems. Any collection of information which can be retrieved according to its content description can be considered a document. More abstractly, knowledge which has been recorded so that it can be used later without the need to redevelop the knowledge is knowledge in a document (Bar-Hillel, 1964).

The amount of information available in document rather than database form is growing quickly. There are over 300 different document retrieval services to which individuals can subscribe. Document retrieval systems are based on much more subtle and fuzzy information than in data base retrieval systems. The relations among data in a data base are more readily delineated than the relations among concepts in documents.

Advances in technology make the increase in computer documents and the sharing of those documents a major issue. Some of the standard ways of dealing with information, such as filing different documents in different colored folders on certain shelves in the office, are not appropriate for computer-stored and disseminated information. While robust natural language processing capabilities of the computer might solve many document storage and retrieval problems, it seems that we must solve certain important parts of the document problem before we solve the natural language processing problem. To quote Maron and Kuhns (1960):

> It appears that as a first step in the direction of the automatic processing of ordinary language ... the problems of information identification and retrieval must be met and dealt with successfully. We therefore turn our attention to the problems of mechanizing a library.

People may not be able to effectively create and maintain by hand all the structures and functions needed for intelligent information retrieval systems. Rather, various forms of learning by computer may be critical in the successful growth of information retrieval systems. The information retrieval problem cuts across many boundaries in artificial intelligence but clearly depends on large and evolving knowledge bases. To create and maintain these knowledge bases would seem to require machine help — such as from automatic knowledge refinement tools.

Work in intelligent document storage and retrieval involves study of representation, reasoning, and learning. Queries and documents have to be represented, and a reasoning strategy must be able to match the representation of a query to that of the relevant documents. Given the vast amount of knowledge that must be put into a computer system in order that the representation and reasoning problems can be solved, we want to use machine learning techniques to help develop this knowledge. Furthermore, the knowledge once developed cannot afford to stay static. New documents and queries continually appear and proper handling of them will require an adaptive information retrieval system.

6.2 PREVIEW

The intricate interconnections among representation, reasoning, and learning must be appreciated for significant developments in any one of them to occur. These chapters on Learning in Information Retrieval (IR) focus on the relationships that should exist between learning systems on the one hand and the representation and reasoning of IR systems on the other. We will both try to stress the role of

(1) sound, scientific experiments in advancing the science of intelligent information retrieval and
(2) gradualness in the changing of representation and reasoning.

The chapters are organized into two main sections: Existing Work and Case Study. The first reviews what has been done by various researchers, and the second describes a particular project done by the research group with which this author is affiliated. The Existing Work section contains four chapters:

> Ch. 7.   The Language of IR
> Ch. 8.   Theme for Machine Learning and IR
> Ch. 9.   Knowledge-sparse Learning
> Ch. 10. Knowledge-rich Learning.

In Chapter 7 the IR problem is flowcharted as a parsing and matching process through which documents and queries pass. The main approaches to representation and reasoning in IR are discussed. Chapter 8 argues for the role of gradualness and for the attractiveness of intelligent information retrieval as a problem that facilitates good experimentation. Learning that does not require elaborate representation or reasoning is considered in Chapter 9 'Knowledge-sparse Learning', and learning that relies on knowledge bases is studied in Chapter 10.

The second section called Case Study has also four chapters whose titles are:

Ch. 11. The MEDLARS System
Ch. 12. Matcher
Ch. 13. Adding an Edge
Ch. 14. Indexer and Additional Terms.

The case study is performed with the resources of one of the world's most famous IR systems — MEDLARS. Chapter 11 reveiws the features of MEDLARS as they pertain to our experiments in Learning for Improved Retrieval. Our particular emphasis has been on automatically building a classification structure (or knowledge base) and to that end we need, among other things, tools for evaluating a classification structure. Our first experiments used a matcher between documents and queries as a tool for evaluating the classification structure. The surprising power of this tool is presented in Chapter 12. Chapter 13 describes our work in adding edges to one knowledge base that were found in another knowledge base. As we found that adding edges was trickier than adding nodes and that 'matcher' wasn't as sensitive as we would like to adding terms, we started to develop other tools for evaluating a classification structure. The tool discussed in Chapter 14 is a simple automatic indexer. Also presented in Chapter 14 are the results of experiments in adding terms to the classification structure.

6.3   POSTVIEW

The aim of this part of the book is to complement Part 1 by presenting an extended case study. This shows how — in the particular field of IR — learning algorithms can be used in the service of improved information processing.

6.3.1   Description languages

Our concern with representation ties in with the emphasis placed on the description language in Chapters 1 and 3; and is especially relevant to the trade-off between simplicity and expressiveness. In information retrieval the problem of representation looms large. We are handling great volumes of structured information, and we wish to match one set of information structures (user queries) against another (stored documents). Problems of representation arise from three sources: the query, the document and the learning mechanism that attempts to improve the matching between them. Inevitably many of the simpler structures described in Part 1 (e.g. weighting vectors and discrimination trees) prove inadequate in this more demanding context. Nevertheless, the alert reader will notice that analogues to many of the formalisms presented in the first half of the book do occur within our domain. For example, the weighting methods used in some word-frequency IR systems (section 7.1.2) resemble the feature vectors of a typical pattern recognizer. (See also Chapter 9.)

6.3.2 The Critic

As in all learning systems, the role of what we have termed the critic is paramount. Learning without evaluative feedback (knowledge of results) is problematic for people and impossible for machines. But in IR there is no standard measure of performance. Is it better to increase the retrieval of relevant items at the expense of including a larger number of irrelevant ones? This is primarily a matter of the user's intentions, and so the issue cannot be settled once and for all. Such unresolved questions make the task of the critic far harder than in most of the systems discussed so far, where success and failure could usually be judged in clear-cut terms. Indeed progress in the assessment of IR strategies is a precondition for better IR learning systems. (See section 8.2.2.)

6.3.3 Gradualness

We have found the concept of gradualness important in the application of learning strategies to IR subfields (see section 8.1.4). This is a reminder that learning is a search process, as we saw in Chapter 3. A small step in the search space — e.g. from one rule to a closely similar one — should produce only a small change in evaluation. If there are major discontinuities, so that similar rule structures have very different values, no heuristic search algorithm will perform effectively. Thus it is necessary to choose a problem in which gradualness as defined in section 8.1.4 does exist, or to reformulate the problem in such a way that it does. Section 8.2 can be seen in this light — an attempt to ensure gradualness in the search space.

6.4 EXERCISE

Make an outline of a book about Intelligent Information Retrieval. Your book may be one of two types:

(1) It can sketch an experiment that you would do. This would be like a monograph of one scientist's work. You can view this as a first pass at a project proposal.
(2) Find an AI (or IR) book, copy part of its outline, and amend it in a way that tailors the work for the topic of Intelligent Information Retrieval.

Don't spend more than 40 minutes in the course of producing a short hand-written outline which fills about a page.

One particularly intriguing answer to the above exercise provided by Marlene Peterson shows the role of images in intelligent information retrieval. She also draws a distinction between 'documents' whose structure is poorly understood, such as natural language and images, and 'documents' whose structure is well understood, such as databases. A sketch of her outline follows:

Review of Existing Work
  Introduction
  Traditional Techniques
    Non-Structured Knowledge Systems
      Text
      Images
    Structured Knowledge Systems
  AI Issues in IR
    Techniques
    Query Languages
    Inference Rules
  Other Implementation Considerations
    User Interface
    Commercial Issues
    Development Languages
    Hardware Performance
Case Study
  Navy Technical Information System
  Representation
    Text
    Databases
    Images
  Interface
  Inference Engine
  Design and Development
  Implementation and Evaluation

6.5 REFERENCES

Bar-Hillel, Yehoshua (1964) in *Language and Information: Selected Essays on their theory and application,* Addison-Wesley, Reading, MA.

Maron. M. E. & Kuhns, J. L. (1960) 'On Relevance, Probabalistic Indexing, and Information Retrieval', *Jr Assoc. Computing Mach,* **3**, pp. 216–244.

Part 2A
EXISTING WORK

7

The language of information retrieval

Document retrieval is the process of providing an inquirer with references to information or documents that will satisfy her information need. The central problem is that the subject of a document may be described in many different ways, as may queries. A dictionary definition of representation says that a representation 'symbolizes' something else. In document retrieval we have representations for documents and queries, both of which usually, substantially simplify the document or query.

A document—the term applies equally well to books, journal articles, mail, or any such textual material—may be arbitrarily long or short. Likewise, queries can be of many types. We don't need to stretch our imagination much to realize that document retrieval does not necessarily deal with 'documents' in the usual sense. Any collection of information stored in the computer that might be retrieved by content description falls under the purview of the broad connotation of document.

From a process point of view intelligent information retrieval can be seen as a combination of parsing and matching (see Fig. 7.1). Parsing transforms a document or a query into something more canonical than natural language. Matching takes that parsed form and assesses the extent to which a document would satisfy a query.

Man and information have gone a long way together. It is the ability of humans to chronicle their experience and share it with future generations that largely distinguished people from other animals. Storing and retrieving this information has been a problem which has typically been solved by the development of various indexing or cataloging schemes. Thousands of years ago there already existed indexing schemes to documents. The average adult in a modern society has some method of storing and retrieving documents such as income tax forms and automobile insurance—even though this method might be as simple as one that keeps income tax in the green folder and automobile insurance in the red folder.

In the early stages of computerized IR, documents were hand-coded into terms from a specially selected set. The MEDLARS system which was developed in the 1960s at the National Library of Medicine is an excellent example of a system which depends on human coding into a special language. As computers have become more powerful and available, strategies have become popular that depend less on human indexing. In the 1970s methods of classifying documents by word-frequency were much explored. In the 1980s many of the massive IR systems such as LEXIS depend on string-searching. Negligible pre-processing of documents is done, and queries are posed as strings of characters which are matched against strings in documents. Documents which contain the string are returned to the querist. One ironic feature of this history of movement from systems like MEDLARS to those like LEXIS is that while the technology has advanced the conceptual sophistication of the indexing and retrieval strategy has gone backward. What has gone forward with the technology is the amount of literature that can be obtained in a flash from anywhere that a computer terminal can run.

7.1 NOT REQUIRING HUMAN INDEXING

7.1.1 String-searching systems

7.1.1.1 Operation

A string-searching system is one which allows the searcher to type an arbitrary string of characters into the information retrieval system and which returns citations to or actual copies of all the documents that contain that string. Automatic full-text, string-searching retrieval is on its surface disarmingly simple. It means storing the full text of all documents in the document collection on a computer so that every word can be located. When a person wants information, the computer is instructed to search for all documents containing certain word or string combinations. This approach is attractive because it:

(1) takes advantage of modern digital technology, and
(2) it reduces the load on human indexers of documents.

Since the computational feasibility of full-text string-search is limited to small textual databases at the moment, most approaches that are oriented

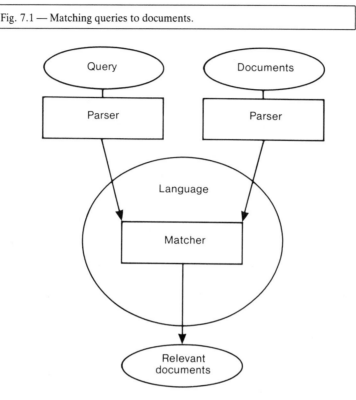

Fig. 7.1 — Matching queries to documents.

towards the string-search philosophy do, in fact, use rather sophisticated strategies of indexing documents by all the words in the documents and reconstructing strings based on those words. Even for microcomputers software has been written which allows rather robust information retrieval classification and retrieval based on string-search strategies (Group L Corporation, 1985). At the main-frame end of the spectrum many products are in daily use and we will discuss one of the most successful ones, namely the IBM STAIRS product.

STAIRS is a *storage* and *information retrieval system* which is a program product of the IBM Corporation. Whereas STAIRS is itself available through IBM, no textual data bases are made available by IBM. An institution that wants to use STAIRS acquires it from IBM but provides the text and other build-up steps itself. STAIRS includes:

(1) utility programs for textual data base creation and maintenance, and
(2) utility programs for on-line query and retrieval generation.

One of the larger examples of the use of a system like STAIRS is provided by BRS Information Technologies. BRS is a commercially available system operating on about 40 textual data bases.

The STAIRS retrieval system uses the free text of documents. The location information for each term is critical. Documents are found using the

SEARCH command which has a variety of forms. A SEARCH command normally consists of a term followed by an operator and another term. Legitimate search statements include

memory
memory and sleep
memory or sleep
memory not sleep
memory adj sleep
memory with sleep
memory same sleep

Various combinations of these operators can be used in one search statement, such as ((memory and sleep) or dreams). The 'and' and 'or' have their typical meaning. 'Adj' means that two terms must be adjacent in the text. 'With' means that two terms must appear in the same sentence. 'Same' means that two terms must appear in the same paragraph.

Another feature of STAIRS is its ability to rank retrieved documents. Once a document set has been selected with the SEARCH command, a ranking can be obtained by specifying various formulas for terms that depend on the frequency of occurrence of terms.

7.1.1.2 Assessment

In a pioneering assessment of full-text string-search, Swanson concluded that such searching by computer was significantly better than conventional retrieval using human subject indexing (Swanson, 1960). Salton (Salton, 1970) has also reported optimistically on string-searching. More recent evidence, however, suggests that string-searching is only effective on small textual databases (Swanson's and Salton's previously mentioned studies used less than 750 documents). A research project by Blair and Maron (Blair & Maron, 1985) shows that string-search behaves poorly when the document space is of substantial size.

Blair and Maron studied the performance of a STAIRS system that had bee loaded with 40,000 documents totalling about 350,000 pages of hard-copy text. The content of the documents concerned a large corporate law suit. Several lawyers and para-legals worked with the information retrieval system over many months and their satisfaction with the performance of the system was assessed. It was determined that the searchers wanted about 75% recall. Searching was continued until the searchers said they were satisfied. Subsequent careful analysis by Blair and Maron of the recall and precision which was actually obtained by the system showed dismal failure. Recall was only about 20%. Precision was close to 80%.

Why was recall so low and why did the searchers believe they were getting $\frac{3}{4}$ or better recall when in fact they only obtained $\frac{1}{5}$ of what they wanted? Full-text string-search is difficult to use to retrieve documents by subject because its design is based on the assumption that it is a simple matter for users to foresee the exact words and phrases that will be used by authors. One needs to find the phrases that characterize exactly the documents one wants. This has never been shown to be possible on large textual databases. It is very difficult for users to predict the exact words that are used in relevant documents.

If one allows free-form English (or whatever the natural language of the users is) to be entered for queries, what kinds of problems can occur (Sudarshan, 1979).

(1) The synonym problem: If the query term has synonyms, a searcher and a document author may use different terms to characterize the same concept. For example, 'acoustic measurement' and 'sound measurement' mean the same thing.

(2) The homonym problem: There are some words which look identical but have entirely different meanings. The word 'tank', for instance, can mean either container or armored vehicle.

(3) The syntactic problem: This is caused by using improper word order, such as 'diamond grinding' versus 'grinding diamond'.

(4) The spelling problem: The same word will sometimes be spelt in different ways. For example, 'gauges' and 'gages' may mean the same thing.

In the Blair and Maron (Blair & Maron, 1985) study one of the queries concerned an accident that had occurred and had become the subject of litigation. The lawyers wanted all the documents pertaining to this accident and posed queries that contained the word 'accident' in combination with a wide variety of other relevant terms. Subsequent study of the database found that many relevant documents did not refer to the accident as such. Instead, those who had written documents arguing against a guilty charge on the accident tended to refer to the accident as an 'unfortunate situation' or 'event'. Sometimes relevant documents dealt with technical aspects of the accident without mentioning the accident directly. Depending on the perspective of the author, references to the accident took far different forms than the searchers had anticipated. Maron and Blair conclude that manually-indexed documents are the key to successful document retrieval systems for large-scale textual databases.

7.1.2 Word frequency systems

The most obvious place where appropriate content identifiers might be found is the documents themselves. Extracting all the words from a document and using them to charcterize documents places an enormous burden on the searcher of estimating how the writer of the document chose to express the concepts which the searcher is seeking. Accordingly, one looks for strategies of determining from the words what are the important concepts.

If all words were to occur with equal frequencies, it might be impossible to distinguish the main concepts of a document from the frequency of occurrence of words. In fact, words occur in text unevenly. Luhn (Luhn,

1958) was an early pioneer in information retrieval who noted that fre-
quiences of words can give meaningful indications of the concepts in
documents. Zipf (Zipf, 1949) argued that

$$frequency \times rank \approx constant,$$

where the rank of a word is 1 for the most frequent word.

The basic strategy for indexing words by frequency is to first count the
frequency with which each word in the document occurs. Then

(1) the very low frequency words can be excluded as being not much on the
     writer's mind, and
(2) the very high frequency words can be discarded on the grounds that they
     are almost always insignificant.

To improve the value of such frequency assessments of content many
techniques have been elaborated. Some of the key concepts are:

(1) The document space which is all the documents which can be obtained
     from the information retrieval system in question.
(2) Word discrimination value which gives the extent to which a given word
     makes the documents in the document space seem more or less similar.
     This can be completely defined by a formula which relies on word
     frequencies.
(3) Thesaurus classes are groups of words that are related by broader,
     narrower, and synonym relations. Thesaurus classes may be defined by
     hand, semi-automatically, or automatically.
(4) Phrases can be generated by computer based on the co-occurrence of
     high-frequency words. For instance, 'computer' and 'programs' are two
     words which tend to occur with very high frequency in a document about
     'computer programs'.

A good method for automatic indexing by word-frequency is well-
summarized as follows (Salton & McGill, 1983).

(1) Starting with documents, remove common high-frequency words and
     generate word stems by removing common suffixes from the remaining
     words.
(2) Compute the discrimination value of each word. Generate phrases for
     high-frequency nondiscriminators and assemble low-frequency nondis-
     criminators into thesaurus classes.
(3) Compute a weighting factor for each remaining single word, phrase, and
     thesaurus class, using for example discrimination value.
(4) Assign to each document the weighted term vector that results from step
     (3).

Assume that all the words of a given language are stored in a vector V.
Any query or document might be represented by a vector of the length of V
but where each word is replaced by a number between 0 and 1. Each number
or weight testifies to the extent to which the corresponding word from V
characterizes the query or document at issue.

In an IR system a document is returned to a query when the similarity between the document and query is over some threshold. One popular similarity measure between a document and a query is the cosine function (Salton & McGill, 1983):

$$\text{cosine (document, query)} = \frac{\sum_{k=1}^{m}(\text{doc}_k \times \text{qu}_k)}{\left[\sum_{k=1}^{m}(\text{doc}_k)^2 \times \sum_{k=1}^{m}(\text{qu}_k)^2\right]^{0.5}}$$

where doc_k refers to the weight on the kth term of the language for this document and qu_k has the corresponding meaning for the query. All documents whose cosine (document, query) value are greater than some threshold are considered relevant to the query and retrieved.

Many have realized that the word-frequency approach ignores some of the wealth of knowledge that people have. As long ago as 1963 an abstract to a paper by Salton said (Salton, 1963).

> These systems are wholly successful because both the sentence structure and the semantic relations between words are normally disregarded. An attempt is made in the present study to overcome the limitations of the strictly quantitative methods by presenting two systems for automatic document retrieval which are based on hierarchical storage arrangements as well as the usual frequency counts and association measures. The first one utilizes a hierarchical arrangement similar to a library classification schedule, including lists of synonyms or related words, and cross-references. The second uses, in addition, a simplified form of syntactic analysis, thus making it possible to represent the syntactic dependency structure between individual words.

In the conclusion to his paper Salton noted that while computational costs were clearly different for the purely statistical versus hierarchical and syntactic approaches, the differences in pay-off in user satisfaction were not yet understood. Twenty years later Salton concludes that the extra computational and design costs of the more complex systems do not merit their inclusion in the word-frequency based systems (Salton & McGill, 1983). He finds the performance of the statistically-based systems to be so impressive that more is not needed to satisfy important existing needs. Nevertheless, word-frequency based indexing and retrieval have not been particularly successful on the market place, and library scientists now often talk about concept theory and semantic analysis. There is much enthusiasm about the role that artificial intelligence techniques might play in information retrieval systems.

7.2　REQUIRING HUMAN INDEXING

If the language of queries and documents is not unified at some point, a match can not be made between queries and documents. We do not have computer systems capable of processing natural language in its unconstrained form. People do not exist who know intimately all the documents that are available and understand arbitrary queries. For successful information retrieval it is necessary to have documents indexed and for querists to phrase their requests in a form that can be mapped into the indexing language. In this book indexing typically refers to the process by which a person or computer reads a documents and assigns certain classifying information to it. While this abstraction of the document could also apply to the abstraction of queries, we will usually be referring to document abstraction when we use the term indexing.

To lessen the constraints that one would put on indexers of documents and querists, the language of indexing and queries might be individual words from natural language. A document would be characterized by a set of words all of which applied to the document. In IR, queries are often represented as words connected by three special operators, namely intersection $\cap$, union $\cup$, and complement —. Say we had three documents indexed, respectively, as {boy, dog}, {dog, football}, and {boy, football}. Then a query for boy $\cap$ dog retrieves exactly the document {boy, dog}, while a query for boy $\cup$ dog returns all three documents. The same problems that we discussed for string-search systems occur, however, here also. Namely, a querist that asks for boy $\cap$ hound would probably want the document {boy, dog} but wouldn't get it. To solve this problem we need a thesaurus or classification structure which notes that hound is closely related to dog. Then either the retrieval system or the querist can translate the query for boy $\cap$ hound into one for boy $\cap$ dog.

7.2.1　Ordering systems

The language for classification of documents can take several forms of which the hierarchical is one of the more popular. The hierarchical classification structure is a graph in which terms are nodes and relations among terms indicate 'broader than' and 'narrower than'. Schemes like the Dewey Decimal Classification, the Universal Decimal Classification, and the Library of Congress Classification were designed for the storage of books on shelves where one book must occupy exactly one place. The use of these schemes has lead to some views of hierarchy which are not appropriate for computerized storage and retrieval of documents (Soergel, 1972). Hierarchies need not be straightjackets into which the universe of knowledge fits, but are rather a guide to the generally conceived 'is-a' relations which connect terms (Brachman, 1983). One term A is 'broader than' another term B, whenever B is an instance of A or a part of A. The 'narrower than' relation is the inverse of 'broader than'.

Given a set of concepts, one arcane approach to hierarchy building is to subdivide this set into mutually exclusive groups, and to continue in this fashion until no more subdivisions can be made. If a concept might fit into several places an arbitrary decision is made to place it in exactly one of those places. This approach of 'mutually exclusive groups' imposes many unnecessary constraints and a more natural approach is to allow each term to point to both many broader and many narrower terms.

We have used terms like 'thesaurus' and 'classification structure' freely, but their definitions are fuzzy. From a computer scientist's perspective both terms might mean the same thing, but from a librarian's view they have traditionally had different meanings. To a librarian a classification structure is a linear listing of terms that depicts the hierarchical structure (Litoukhin, 1980). For instance, a classification structure would show the terms 'disease', 'joint disease', and 'arthritis' one after the other on the page, perhaps with indentations to indicate parent-child or 'x contains y' relationships.

```
disease
        joint disease
               arthritis
```

Typically, these classification structures include numeric indicators of hierarchical position, as in:

```
1.  disease
      1.1  joint disease
              1.1.1  arthritis
```

While a thesaurus in the lay use of the word usually suggests an alphabetically sorted list of keywords with attached synonyms, in the library science field this is often expanded to include some indication of *broader than* or *parent* terms and *narrower than* or *child* terms. In *Roget's Thesaurus* (Roget, 1977) the word structure has as a broader term 'general form' and many synonyms such as 'construction', 'frame', and 'shape'. *Roget's Thesaurus* gives several levels of 'is-a' so that, for instance, 'general form' is a child of 'form' which is, in turn, a child of 'space', but synonyms are only given for the terms which have no children. From a thesaurus where each term points to its conceptual parents and children, a computer program can readily generate a classification structure. Furthermore, a classification structure could incorporate with each entry a list of synonyms, and in that case a computer could generate a thesaurus from a classification structure.

To give an example of a listing from a thesaurus that is used in an IR system, in Fig.7.2, we have copied a portion of a randomly selected page from the *Annotated Alphabetical MeSH* (Medical Subject Headings, 1984). Our copy was actually taken from the computer version which we have stored on our disk. The computer version was transformed so that code numbers like 273 and 277 were replaced by what they represent, in this case, 'MeSH Number' and 'Backward Cross-Reference', respectively.

Fig. 7.2 — Portion of annotated alphabetical MeSH.

MeSH Term
    EGGS
Annotation
    differentiate from OVUM; eggs as food (chicken, duck, quail,
    etc. eggs); fish roe & reptile eggs go here
MeSH Tree Number
    J1.341.322
Backward Cross-Reference
    POULTRY PRODUCTS
MED66Postings
    658

MeSH Term
    EGO
Online Note
    to search SELF use EGO back thru 1975 & SELF CONCEPT
    1966–68
MeSH Scope Notes
    The conscious portion of the personality structure which serves
    to mediate between the demands of the primitive instinctual
    drives, (the id), of internalized parental and social prohibitions
    or the conscience, (the superego), and of reality.
Annotation
    no qualif; egocentrism: index DEFENSE MECHANISMS
Previous Indexing
    Mechanisms (66–67), Personality (66–67), Psychoanalytic The-
    ory (66–67)
MeSH Tree Numbers
    F1.752.747.189, F2.739.794.206
Backward Cross-References
    SELF, REALITY TESTING
MED66 Postings
    618

'MED66 Postings' means the number of times that the term was used to index documents on MEDLARS prior to 1966. There are similar postings for a handful of other periods of time, as well as a number of other categories of information in the thesaurus which we have elected to ignore for now.

As computers become more common in library work, the difference between an alphabetically sorted list and a list sorted by hierarchical position becomes less critical, and a thesaurus and a classification structure are more likely to be viewed as different representations of the same information. To quote Dahlberg (Dahlberg, 1980). 'It is irrelevant to distinguish between classification system and thesaurus because the development of classification theory has long incorporated the thesaurus method of recognizing and indicating concept relationships and modern thesaurus theory has adopted classification methods'. Another term 'Ordering System' has risen to popularity as a combination of thesaurus and classification system. An ordering system is 'any instrument for the organization, description, and retrieval of knowledge which consists of verbal or notational expressions for concepts and their relationships and which displays these elements in an ordered way, as a classification system, a thesaurus, a subject heading list or similar device' (Dahlberg, 1983). What people from the library science field call an ordering system is similar to what people from the artificial intelligence field call a knowledge base.

7.2.2   Preserved context systems

One popular method of automatically generating a simple kind of index for a set of documents is to list each term followed by a few of the words that occur in that word's immediate context. Such an index is called a key-word-in-context (KWIC) index. A substantial extension of the KWIC approach has been taken in the PRECIS effort, although the index is no longer automatically generated by the computer. The name PRECIS is an acroynm for Preserved Context Index System, and is intended to convey the idea of context dependency as well as the fact that a summarization of the subject—a kind of precis—is offered to the user (Austin, 1984).

PRECIS is employed by the *British National Bibliography* Library System for the classification of books. It employs a more sophisticated knowledge representation of documents than the set of keywords used by systems like MEDLARS. It was designed with the computer in mind but is largely a manual system both for indexing and retrieval. The British National Library publishes the results of the indexing in a document which is then used by querists.

Initially, an indexer scans a document looking for those terms which he regards as essential to a verbal expression of its subject content. He next considers the role which each of these terms plays in the subject as a whole. The relation between terms in the classification of the document is restricted to a set of relations, 5 of which are given here (Austin, 1972):

(0) Key system
(1) Active concept
(2) Effect
(3) Study region
(4) Viewpoint

If we were indexing a document about 'The management of railways in France', we would begin by breaking the subject into 'France', 'management', and 'railways'. We would then check each of these terms against the set of relationships and decide under what relations to place each of the 3 terms. In this example we recognize 'management' as the activity concept (relation 1). The use of the activity code calls for the name of the entity on which the action has been performed which is 'railways'. Railways would be stored in slot 0 'key system'. The locality 'France' could be assigned to the 'study region' relation.

The published version of the indexing loses some of the information that is obtained in the index but does show an entry for each term of the index. The above example of an index, when inversely ordered by the number of the relation, is: France, management, railways. In the published index this might appear in three places with the following type of scheme:

railways
      management, France

management, railways
     France

France, management, railways.

Each term is associated with all the other terms in the index, but the ordering is designed so that one can always deduce the original ordering, which in the case of our example is 'France, management, railways'.

Up to now we have concentrated on the organization of words according to their special relations in PRECIS. However, no matter how well an index has been constructed, we can never guarantee that a user is going to enter the retrieval system with just those terms which an indexer has selected. PRECIS handles this by providing a large thesaurus that corresponds to the terminology used in the index.

A PRECIS index is therefore the product of two different but interdependent teams. The first team is concerned with organizing key terms from a document into strings based on a small set of relations, like 'active concept' and 'key system'. The second team builds a thesaurus. Between them, these two teams create the index system—one team's product expresses a summary statement of the subject at any level of specificity, and the other team's product guides the user to an appropriate entry word from other terms which share an element of common meaning.

Schabas compared the performance of two retrieval systems where one used documents indexed under the Library of Congress Subject Headings (LCSH) and the other used documents indexed under the British Library's PRECIS scheme (Schabas, 1982). Performance was also compared for queries about social science topics and queries about pure/applied science. The users seemed equally satisfied with LCSH and PRECIS for queries in the pure/applied sciences but felt that PRECIS allowed substantially more good documents to be retrieved in the social sciences than did LCSH. Since PRECIS is more flexible than LCSH, the improved recall with PRECIS is not surprising. The explanation for the difference between the social and pure/applied sciences may rest on the 'soft' versus 'hard' nature, respectively, of the vocabularies. In the social sciences more so than in the pure/applied sciences (Schabas, 1982):

(1) terms tend to be used less precisely, new terms keep emerging, and several terms often overlap in meaning, and
(2) the focus tends to be more interdisciplinary and to bring together more concepts in ways which cannot be as well anticipated in a controlled vocabulary like LCSH.

Communication within science/technology is usually confined to a highly specialized area. As descriptors in the science/technology arena are required to denote a concept or object precisely, these descriptors tend to have fewer synonyms (Kim, 1982).

A number of PRECIS-like systems have been devised. The Nested Phrase Indexing System (NEPHIS) allows a sequence of words to be used to index a document and only a few special connector symbols are defined. In NEPHIS the symbols ' < ' and ' > ' isolate phrases and in conjunction with a '?' say that one phrase is connected to an immediately preceding or following phrase (Farradane, 1977). In Farradane's Relational Indexing System a two-dimensional graph with words as nodes and edges as relations is first constructed and then is transformed into a permuted alphabetical index.

7.3   THE NEW AI APPROACH

The advantage to the string-search approach to IR is that the human indexers are unnecessary and the number and type of documents that can be stored for search are much greater than when humans must index each document. With string-search the computer and the searchers do all the work. The disadvantage to the string-search approach is that the searchers have to second guess the authors of the documents. The artificial intelligence efforts in IR would partially automate the indexing and searching of text so that more documents could be made available to more people.

The artificial intelligence approach to information retrieval focuses on the development of sophisticated knowledge bases or ordering systems that interact with queries and documents. AI researchers study the organization of the text they are storing and attempt to gain access to it via its meaning rather than just its form. This approach is attractive since searchers are typically looking for a certain meaning rather than a certain word.

Some work in Natural Language Processing has led to front-ends for databases. (The information in a database is organized in a less complicated way than the information in a knowledge base). The Natural Language front-ends to databases partially understand a user's query and are able to access that part of the database that is relevant to the query (Waltz, 1978). There has been some success by workers at New York University (NYU) in translating textual material into database form for subsequent retrieval by database interfaces. The NYU team (Grischman & Hirschman, 1978) uses syntactic rules for automatically analysing the contents of medical records and producing a normalized, database form.

Schank's group (Schank, Kolodner & DeJong, 1981) has developed over the years a hierarchy of models for dealing with language and memory. Conceptual primitives are used to capture meaning in sentences and parsers exist to take sentences into conceptual dependency diagrams. The meaning of a short story is conveniently represented in a script. Scripts are organized at a higher level by Memory Organization Packets. For discussion of learning within the context of Memory Organization Packets see Chapter 10, entitled 'Knowledge-Rich Learning'.

7.4   EXERCISE

Imagine an IR system which allows access to parts of this chapter. What language would you use? Produce two queries such that each would retrieve a part of this chapter (define part any way you want). If the language were the 'table of contents' for this chapter, and the query were 'give me everything about thesaurus', then the search would lead to poor recall. String-search would work better for this particular example. If your result resembles that of this example, relate the analysis to Blair and Maron's conclusions (Blair & Maron, 1985). (This exercise could take days, but you should only put 80 minutes into it. In other words, sketch a very simple system, make a few quick trials, and write a few notes on paper).

Answers by two people to the above exercise will be sketched. The first is from Hafedh Mili and the second from Joseph Maline.

Hafedh Mili
First the chapter must be divided into 'documents' which are retrievable. Using the table of contents as an index language leads to the problem for search that the terms have little meaning out-of-context. For instance, the subtitle of 'Assessment' is too vague alone but in the context of the hierarchy means 'assessment of string-search methodologies'. Indexing based on word frequency might work. For the query 'automatic indexing' the word indexing is not helpful since it is used too frequently. The word automatic, however, occurs twice and might be a good guide. String searching tested on several queries gave about 50 percent recall and 50 percent precision, which is below what one would like of an IR system. Mili concludes some more sophisticated indexing and matching might be appropriate.

Joseph Maline
The chapter is broken into parts each of which is then characterized by subject/verb pairs. Queries are posed as subject/verb pairs. Analysis of the performance of queries in this format showed that verbs do not seem to lend themselves to as good recall as subjects.

7.5   REFERENCES

Austin, Derek (1972) The PRECIS System for Computer-Generated Indexes and its Use in the British National Bibliography, in *Subject Retrieval in the Seventies*, T. Wilson (ed.), pp. 99–115, Greenwood Publishing Co, Westport, CT.

Austin, Derek (1984) *PRECIS: A Manual of Concept Analysis and Subject Indexing*, British Library, London.

Blair, David & Maron, M. E. (1985), An Evaluation of Retrieval Effectiveness for a Full-Text Document-Retrieval System, in *Communications of the ACM*, **28**, 3, pp. 289–299, March.

Brachman, Ronald (1983) What IS-A Is and Isn't: An Analysis of Taxonomic Links in Semantic Networks, in *Computer* **16**, 10, pp. 30–36.

Dahlberg, Ingetraut (1980) The Broad System of Ordering as a Basis for an Integrated Social Sciences Thesaurus, *Intern Classif*, **7**, 2, pp. 66–72.

Dahlberg, Ingetraut (1983) Conceptual Compatibility of Ordering Systems, *Intern Classif*, **10**, 1, pp. 5–8.

Farradane, Jason (1977) A Comparison of Some Computer Produced Permuted Alphabetical Subject Indexes, *Intern Classif*, **4**, 2, pp. 94–101.

Grishman, R. & Hirschman, L. (1978) Question Answering from Natural Language Medical Data Bases, *Artificial Intelligence*, **11**, pp. 25–43.

Group L Corporation (1985), *TEXTBANK Users Manual*, 481 Carlisle Drive, Herndon, VA.

Kim, Chai (1982) Retrieval Language of Social Sciences and Natural Sciences: A Statistical Investigation, *Jr Amer Soc Inform Sc*, pp. 3–6.

Litoukhin, J. Toward an Integrated Thesaurus of the Social Sciences, *Intern Classif*, **7**, 2, pp. 56–59.

Luhn, H. P. (1958) The Automatic Creation of Literature Abstracts, *IBM Jr Res Devel*, **2**, 2, pp. 159–165.

Roget, Peter (1977) *Roget's International Thesaurus*, Thomas Crowell, New York.

Salton, Gerard (1963) Some Hierarchical Models for Automatic Document Retrieval, *American Documentation*, **14**, 3, pp. 213–222.

Salton, Gerard (1970) Automatic Text Analysis, *Science*, **168**, pp. 335–343.

Salton, Gerard & McGill, Michael (1983) *Introduction to Modern Information Retrieval*, McGraw-Hill, New York.

Schabas, Ann (1982) Postcoordinate Retrieval: A Comparison of Two Indexing Languages, *Jr Amer Soc Inform Sc*, pp. 32–37.

Schank, Roger, Kolodner, Janet & DeJong, Gerald (1981) Conceptual Information Retrieval, in *Information Retrieval Research*, ed. P. W. Williams, pp. 94–116, Butterworths, London.

Medical Subject Headings Section, (1984) *Medical Subject Headings, Annotated Alphabetical List*, 1985, National Library of Medicine, Bethesda, MD. Publication PB84-223156.

Soergel, Dagobert (1972) A General Model for Indexing Languages: the Basis for Compatibility and Integration, in *Subject Retrieval in the Seventies*, T. Wilson (ed.), pp. 36–61, Greenwood Publishing Co, Westport, CT.

Sudarshan, B. (1979) Development of Reference Retrieval System with Simultaneous Building of Thesaurus, *Lib Sc*, **16**, 3, pp. 77–83.

Swanson, D. G. (1960) Searching Natural Language Text by Computer, *Science*, **132**, pp. 1099–1104.

Waltz, David (1978) An English Language Question Answering System for a Large Relational Database, *Communications of ACM*, **21**, pp. 526–539.

Zipf, G. K. (1949) *Human Behavior and the Principle of Least Effort*, Addison Wesley, Reading, MA.

8

A Theme for Machine Learning in Information Retrieval

8.1 THE ROLE OF LEARNING

8.1.1 Representation, Reasoning, and Learning

In order to handle the burgeoning information of the electronic age new sciences and technologies are needed. The cornerstones of work for this new age are representation, reasoning, and learning. We need more sophisticated information processing as in:

(1) Many terms intricately related—*machine representation of a knowledge base (kb)*
(2) Getting information from kb—*machine reasoning*
(3) Augmenting kb—*machine learning*

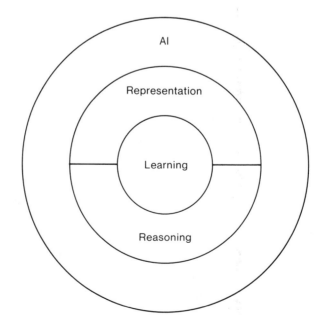

Both the structure and content of the knowledge base (kb) have to do with knowledge representation. How this knowledge is used is machine reasoning. Through time intelligent systems have to change. The transition is controlled by learning and takes a form of representation and reasoning at time t and moves it to another more adapted form for the environment at time $t + 1$:

$$\text{representation}_t + \text{reasoning}_t \rightarrow \text{representation}_{t+1} + \text{reasoning}_{t+1}$$

Without adaptability in the machine, the ability of the machine to help us solve our information problems would be severely limited. Ultimately, we must also design systems whose learning component is itself modifiable through time. We can view the learning box as itself consisting of representation and reasoning components. These compoennts of the learner are examined and changed by another learner, which itself can be seen as composed of representation and reasoning parts.

8.1.2   Famous studies

Two basic strategies for a machine learning research experiment are

(1) start with almost no information (the bottom-up approach) and test what can be discovered, or
(2) take an almost perfectly working system, remove some small part of it, and investigate ways to automatically replace that lost information (the top-down approach).

The first of these two was popular early in the days of artificial intelligence. But all the major successes have depended on the development of extensive representation and reasoning systems which then underwent small changes as they were slightly improved in the performance of a task at which people were already good.

An excellent example of the old 'tabula rasa' approach comes in *Artificial Intelligence through Simulated Evolution* (Fogel, Owens & Walsh, 1966). The authors of that book created arbitrary finite state automata (fsa) which defined certain input-output behaviors. The experimenters also chose input-output sequences that they defined as desirable. The fsa then underwent a reproduction with random mutation and selection of the fit process. This strategy was effective in only very limited contexts. The representational system here is fsa. The reasoning is accomplished by state transitions in the fsa. The learning depends on a mutation operator.

Samuel's checker player (Samuel, 1959) represented information by storing histories of many famous games and employing a weighted, linear function to characterize important features of a board position. The function had about 16 feature detectors or predicates which responded to such aspects of the board as 'white has more pieces than black' or 'white has center control'. Weights in front of each predicate that were true for a given position would be summed. Of the positions which the computer might assume in the next move that which led to the highest score would be given high priority. Other reasoning strategies were also used in the process of selecting moves. Learning occurred through experience both by acquiring new histories of checker games and by automatically adjusting weights on the linear threshold function. The adjustment of weights was similar to that used in the perceptron learning algorithm (Minsky & Papert, 1969). The careful selection of information in the representations for Samuel's checker player was the key to its success. Samuel's later attempts to decompose the feature detectors of the threshold function and to have the machine learn to compose good feature detectors were largely unsuccessful (Samuel, 1967).

One of the early stimulants of the 'expert systems' explosion was Edward Shortliffe's work with MYCIN (Shortliffe, 1976). MYCIN employed a few hundred if-then rules about meningitis and bacteremia in order to deduce the proper treatment for a patient who presented with signs of either of those diseases. Claims were made that the rule-based approach to encoding knowledge was ideal for many problems, and the Japanese have initiated massive AI experiments based, in part, on production rule representations (Chikayama, 1983). The reasoning with if-then rules can be forward or backward chained and has a number of attractive computational and cognitive properties. One of these cognitive properties is the ease with which traces of fired rules can be used to explain why a decsion was reached. Many extensions have been made to MYCIN and one, in particular, has focused on learning or knowledge acquisition (Buchanan & Shortliffe, 1984). Davis's work on TEIRESIAS allowed an expert to interact with MYCIN and introduce amendments to rules as explanations of existing behaviour of the system might point to weaknesses in the rules (Davis, 1982).

8.1.3   Criteria of intelligence

The standard criterion for success of an artificial intelligence program is that the program behaves like people. Turing (Turing, 1963) argued that a machine would be intelligent when a person communicating via a teletype-writer could not distinguish the responses of a person from those of the machine. This criterion clealy puts a heavy anthropomorphic bias on the types of machines that are produced. At times, a view of intelligence that is independent of its manifestation in people might allow new insights into ways to build machines that creatively help people. An intelligent system should learn and Simon (1983) says that learning occurs when a system changes so as to more effectively perform tasks. What is the system, what are the tasks, when has performance improved? We propose a framework or model in which the degree of *influence* that a system manifests is the degree to which it is intelligent.

An organism can exert influence in several ways:

(1) remaining alive;
(2) begetting offspring;
(3) communicating with others;
(4) creating a machine that has *influence*.

8.1.3.1   An abstract system

To get a simple handle on *influence* we define a primitive system called INFLU.

(1) *Entities* (Zeigler, 1984) are the basic structures and in INFLU they are space, reward, active cells, inactive cells, and noise.

(2) A *model* describes the relations among the entities and in INFLU depicts an abstract evolution system.

(3) *Parameters* are features of the model that are manipulated by the experimenter; for INFLU the parameters are the programs with which the active cells are initialized.

(4) The *variables* are the features of the system that the experimenter observes to note the effect of different parameter settings. In INFLU the variable is a composite measure called *influence*.

The standard of *influence* should not be dependent on humans having to define individual tasks and having to assess the system's performance on those tasks. Instead, organisms or sets of cells in the system should compete and cooperate with one another and in the dynamics of this interaction over time the system can manifest *influence*.

Reproduction-with-change plus selection-of-the-fit are fundamental to *influence*. Accordingly, each primitive organism, called a cell, in the system is capable of copying or generating part or all of itself. Each cell consumes energy or reward. To become more complex a cell must form connections with other cells that are willing to share reward. There is some level of noise in the system.

To make precise the notion of *influence* assume that each cell is described by a set of bit strings and each bit can be assigned a unique tag. When a string is copied, all the tags associated with its bits are also copied. Some subset of tags should monotonically increase in number as evolution or *influence* proceeds. One way to formalize this increase requires that there be a subset of bits whose tags represent less than half of those in the population but later those tags and their copies represent more than half of the tags in the system. In other words, at any time t there must exist a subset s_t of the set S_t of bits describing active cells, such that

(i) Less than half of the bits in S_t are in s_t. In other words,

$$\frac{|s_t|}{|S_t|} < 0.5.$$

(ii) There exists a time t' greater than t for which the *influence* of s at t' dominates the system.

The *influence* of s_t at t' is the set of all bits whose tags trace back to the tags of s_t. Call this S_t *influence* at t' $s_{t'}$. The criterion of *influence* requires that there exists a t' such that

$$\frac{|s_{t'}|}{|S_{t'}|} > 0.5.$$

The extent of *influence* is equal to scalar j such that for all t'' between t' and $t' + j$

$$\frac{|s_{t''}|}{|S_{t''}|} > 0.5.$$

Influence like intelligence is not a yes—no measure. There are degrees of *influence*, and the notion here advanced is that the more *influence* a system has the more we would be impressed with that system's intelligence.

A trivial case of *influence* is easily described. Suppose that the set of active cells consists of 3 cells A, B, and C, each of the same size (i.e., the same number of bits in its program). A and B now die, and C is transformed into 3 cells. These 3 offspring of C behave like the original A, B, and C; namely, 2 of the 3 die, while the third again produces 3 cells. In the absence of noise the following obtain:

(i)   At any time t there exists a cell C that represents $\frac{1}{3}$ of the system's bits.
(ii) For all times after t, the descendants of C occupy all of the population.
(iii) This process repeats until noise hits the control of C.

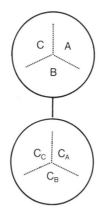

8.1.3.2 *Analysis of influence in systems*

In experiments performed in INFLU each active cell had a number of processors and a memory with load, store, add, and jump-on-negative instructions (Rada, 1981). The programs of each cell were designed to facilitate simple exchanges among cells. On simulation of the model, the population of cells quickly degenerated to a stable state. Modifications to each cell's program were then introduced so that the cell was less likely to lose its ability to send information to other cells. This was achieved by introducing redundancy, i.e. the cell had multiple copies of those portions of its code that were most precious. This redundancy allowed the system a little *influence*.

One focus of the experiments was the method by which cells produced offspring. Crossover is a more powerful method of introducing variation to a population than is point mutation (Holland, 1975). In this author's experiments crossover did not bestow significant *influence*. The difficulty is that crossover requires certain properties of the strings on which it operates, and those properties are very difficult to obtain. One essential property is that arbitrary substrings should have meaning (Bethke, 1980).

8.1.4 Gradualness

We must ask ourselves how it is that systems can be designed which endlessly improve themselves. What allows a given representation and reasoning system to be amenable to improvement from a given learning system. One argument advanced in this chapter is that small changes in a representation should tend to correspond to small changes in the meaning that the reasoner obtains from that representation.

What are necessary and sufficient conditions for intelligence? An organisms's intelligence depends on its performance relative to other organisms. The organism generates trials; the trials are evaluated by the environment; and the organism adjusts its next trial. We assume that a generate-and-test mechanism is necessary in an intelligent system.

Generate + test are clearly not sufficient conditions for intelligence. In a system with noisy regularity, an organism that is to succeed must be able to make low-risk trials. A small change in the code should lead to a small change in the input–output behavior manifested by the code. Gradualness also means that the range of behaviors searched by the small changes in structure well covers the small changes in function that are possible.

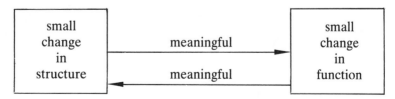

One way to show the importance of gradualness is through probabilities. Suppose that you are told that there is a pot of gold near you. You need to walk down the street and at some point make a turn. Continuing in that fashion after the third turn, if your choices are correct, you will have found the gold. Assume that with each turn you make the probability of its being the correct one is $\frac{1}{3}$. The probability of reaching the gold after 3 turns is 3^{-3} or $\frac{1}{27}$ and on the average you would need 13.5 trials to get the gold. If, on the other hand, you get feedback after each turn as to whether you are on the right path or not, then on the average after 1.5 turns, the first turn will be correct. Starting from the first correct turn, the second correct turn will also have been made with another 1.5 turns on the average. So that with continual feedback, the average number of trials is 3×1.5 or 4.5. This continual feedback allows small changes in the path to correspond to small changes in its value, and gradualness leads to a more quickly successful gold hunt. Note that these arguments are loose and don't take into account many of the details of a real situation.

Conrad gives a biological argument for gradualness that accounts for many, real details (Conrad, 1983). The argument applies directly to the evolution of proteins but can be readily extended to the development of organisms. Quoting from Conrad (Conrad, 1979).

> Suppose that a population carries protein S_0, That S_m is the genetically closest protein of higher fitness, that M independent genetic changes are required to jump from S_0 to S_m, and that all intermediate protein forms are unfit. Then the average number of generations required for the appearance of S_m is given by
>
> $$\tau_{0,m}^m = \frac{20^m}{N_0 p^m (1-p)^{(n-m)}}$$
>
> where m indicates the number of required simultaneous genetic events, N_0 is the initial population size, n is the length of the protein, p is the mutation probability, the factor 20 enters because the $n - m$ remaining amino acids must not change . . . Alternatively, suppose that of the $m!$ possible ways in which S_0 can change into S_m by single changes in amino acid sequence, there is at least one for which every protein species in the sequence has at least slightly increased fitness. The average required number of generations is now given by
>
> $$\tau_{0,m}^1 = \frac{20^m}{N_0 p (1-p)^{(n-1)}} + (m-1)D$$
>
> where the delay time D is the number of generations which it requires for the population to grow to the same size as the old population.

For a protein of length 300, a mutation rate of $p = 10^{-8}$, and a step length of $m = 3$, the advantage is of the order 10^{18} (assuming $D = 1000$ and $N_0 = 10^6$).

The artificial intelligence literature addresses the role of gradualness in *influence* or intelligence. When a program successfully learns, the predictability or regularity in the problem space has been captured. Carbonell (Carbonell, 1983) argues that the key to learning by analogy is a similarity metric that retrieves solutions of previously-solved problems that closely resemble the present problem. Philosophy also provides evidence of the role of gradualness in problem solving. New theories of science evidently arise from combinations of good parts of earlier theories (Darden, 1982).

Ernst and Newll's General Problem Solver (Ernst & Newell, 1969) solved problems by creating subgoals when the step from initial state to goal state was too big. Subgoaling is a way to achieve gradualness in a search space. Rosenbloom (Rosenbloom *et al.*, 1984) has been emphasizing the role that knowledge can play in guiding the choice of subgoals. Pearl (Pearl, 1983) argues that problems are solved by consulting simplified models of the problem. The key to the applicability of these simplified models is the decomposability of the problem. Decomposability means in part that all subgoals can be solved independently. Pearl tries to discover the decomposability or gradualness of a problem by constructing models of the problem and manipulating parameters or constraints.

8.2   A METHODOLOGICAL APPROACH TO LEARNING EXPERIMENTS

Work in machine learning has had a long and not altogether distinguished history. Early in the history of computing the importance of automatic learning was appreciated. In the mid-1950s much work was done with perceptrons. Numerical weights on a perceptron can be readily adjusted so that the preceptron learns to correctly classify certain classes of patterns (See Chapter 2). Minsky and Papert's (Minsky & Papert, 1969) monumental work on the limitations of perceptrons showed that only linearly separable classes of patterns could be distinguished by perceptrons. This limitation was enough to mark the end of major work with perceptrons. The birth of interest in expert systems has caused a new burst of interest in learning. Some early, highly-publicized work by Douglas Lenat (Lenat, 1982) was subsequently attacked for claiming results that were not experimentally repeatable (Ritchie & Hanna, 1984). In general the field of machine learning, or artificial intelligence more broadly, has been guilty of perpetrating a large number of results that do not stand the normal tests of scientific quality. Experiments in machine learning should be repeatable. To facilitate the spread of the science it is necessary that hypotheses be clearly stated and that the methods of testing the hypotheses can be employed by other research groups. In other words, other scientists have to be able to straightforwardly be able to repeat the experiment that is reported and verify that the results are correct.

8.2.1 Environments suitable to learning experiments

It seems to be the nature of Artificial Intelligence (AI) that it deals with problems which have escaped ready mathematical characterization. AI is concerned with complex, real-world problems that require knowledge and reasoning that no one has been able to succintly capture. It seems part and parcel of the domain that tangled hierarchies of information are traversed by many heuristics in ways that depend on the organism in question and the environment in which that organism has been raised. Accordingly, experiments in AI are *not* usually done on small bodies of information with simple strategies that are evaluated by a few clear-cut criteria. Experiments about intelligence tend to rely on large amounts of computer-stored information and to require extensive man-machine interaction.

Just as the computer age has forced machine learning to the forefront. So the computer age offers the experimental framework in which learning experiments can be done. Look to where computers are being used in daily practice (Rada, 1983). See what kinds of information are stored and retrieved. Imagine ways that the humans who interact with the system could be better satisfied. Inevitably more knowledge in the machine would be helpful but ways to get that knowledge into the machine are painful unless the machine can help in the process. When a massive computer system is part of an intensive man-machine dialogue, one has the scenario for a good machine learning experiment.

The field of medical AI offers many good examples of the importance of choosing a domain in which people routinely depend on the computer for results. The MYCIN project (Shortliffe, 1976) was heralded as proof that computers could behave like human experts. But the test of MYCIN has been hampered by the inability of anyone to get the program to be regularly used. MYCIN diagnoses and treats certain infectious diseases after the user has entered a set of data. The program is unable to handle other diseases and is fairly rigid in the input that it will accept. Accordingly, physicians do not find it cost-effective to use MYCIN. On the other hand, programs which make small decisions about pathology laboratory data are routinely used. Currently, the developers of MYCIN are focusing their energies on the design of a kind of hospital information system which would encourage physicians to use the computer (Buchanan & Shortliffe, 1984). Only in that context of a routinely-used computer system are the researchers interested in testing new ideas in AI.

Information retrieval systems offer excellent opportunities for researchers in AI. Modern Information Retrieval (IR) systems are dependent on computers. Users often could not retrieve the documents they want unless the computer served as an intermediary. Furthermore, there is clearly room for improvement in the quality of the interaction between person and computer in IR. Here AI has its opportunity.

A typical IR system is continually bombarded with new documents and queries. These inputs represent the results and demands of a changing world. Even if it were possible to obtain on one day a system that had the necessary representation and reasoning abilities to handle the documents and queries of that day, it would be necessary for the system to adapt to changes of the next day. Learning is needed here and the sources of data to drive and test that learning are bountiful. Not only are the queries and documents arriving abundant but the users can be asked to give feedback to the system as to their satisfaction with its performance.

8.2.2   Assment of IR data
8.2.2.1   *Formulas*

An information retrieval system accesses a document space and returns a set of documents in response to a user query. This retrieved set divides the document space into two distinct parts, namely, the retrieved and the not-retrieved. Of all the documents only some are relevant to the user's query. The determination of a set of relevant documents (which may be no easy matter in practice) also divides the document space into two distinct parts, namely, the relevant and the not-relevant. Two major measures of perfor-

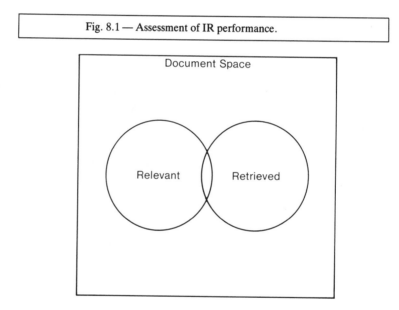

Fig. 8.1 — Assessment of IR performance.

mance of an IR system are Recall and Precision. If the document collection is separated into retrieved and not-retrieved sets and if procedures are available for separating relevant items from nonrelevant ones, Recall and Precision are defined as (Salton & McGill, 1983).

$$\text{Recall} = \frac{\text{Number of Items Retrieved and Relevant}}{\text{Total Relevant}}$$

$$\text{Precision} = \frac{\text{Number of Items Retrieved and Relevant}}{\text{Total Retrieved}}$$

Everything else being equal, a good system is one which exhibits both a high recall and a high precision.

Say there are two documents D_1 and D_2 which are retrieved in response to many queries. More specifically, say that D_1 is returned to 150 queries and that it is considered relevant to 90 of them. Say D_2 is returned to 200 queries and is relevant to 100.

Feedback

Document Descriptions	Matching Queries	Number Relevant	Number Irrelevant
D_1	150	90	60
D_2	200	100	100

According to recall, D_2 is preferable to D_1, since with D_2 more inquirers received what they wanted (100 versus 90). But the 60% precision of D_1 is better than the 50% precision of D_2.

A desirable measure of effectiveness of an IR system would

(1) assign a single number to each IR system, and
(2) this number would allow complete ordering of different performances (Swets, 1969). That is the metric would be a scale with a unit, a true zero, and a maximum value.

No such measure is, however, as popular as the covarying pair of measures known as recall and precision. Recall measures the ability of a system to retrieve relevant documents, while precision conversely measures the ability to reject nonrelevant materials.

A single-valued measure that is little used in the field of IR but attractive for some of the reasons that Swets outlines depends on rank orderings of documents to a query (Rada *et al.*, 1985). A computer system can assign values or scores to documents which scores attest to the conceptual closeness between a document and a query. Likewise, people can be asked to make the same assessments. From these scores can be derived rankings, and the rankings may be compared by such standard statistical tests as the Spearman correlation coefficient (Siegel, 1956). The assumption here as for recall is that humans are the gold-standard of performance, and the better the correlation between a computer's ranking and that of a person, the better the computer is doing.

8.2.2.2   Psychological aspects
We might point out that measures like recall are applied to what people think about documents. They are based on a person's assessment of relevant and non-relevant documents. Since these assments are subjective and often

poorly understood, the conclusions based on our measures must be guarded. To quote Taube (1965):

> Although there seems to be little agreement on what relevance means, and some doubt that it is quantifiable, there is, nevertheless, a growing agreement that a fixed and formal relationship exists between the relevance and the recall performance of any system. Thus, we will find in the literature both a frankly subjective notion of relevance as reported by individual users, and equations, curves, and mathematical formulations which presumably provide numerical measures of recall and relevance . . . The use of a single term in the same document to cover two or more distinct meanings, especially when such a usage is designed to secure the acceptance of a doctrine by attributing to it mathematical validity which it does not have, represents a more serious situation than merely careless ambiguity.

Library patrons may have many different notions of what constitutes a relevant document. One person may want the most recently published document. Another may want a document that is frequently cited by other people (Garfield, 1979). The multidimensional character of a person's assessment could be a function of many variables.

The criticisms of Taube (Taube, 1965) and others as to the subjectivity of relevance decisions can be partially countered by the results of psychological tests of large numbers of people. Psychology can be a science in the same way that physics is, except that while a physicist may talk about the statistical properties of a population of atoms, a psychologist talks about a population of people. A comparison of the ability of humans to consistently judge the relevance of documents to their general interests from bases of citations, abstracts, keywords, and total text was made under controlled experiments (Resnick & Savage, 1964). The results showed that

(1) humans are able to make such judgements consistently, and
(2) the consistency of the judgement is independent of the particular base from which it is made.

While the internal decision making apparatus is clearly complex, it does seem to produce consistent decisions about document relevance under certain circumstances. The above referenced study used a fairly homogeneous group of subjects. The consistency of relevance decisions would not necessarily hold true across all time, people, and sources of information.

One way that researchers in AI partially circumvent the challenges of measures like recall and precision is to build systems that are somehow provably like people in the way the system makes decisions about what documents are relevant. To obtain evidence that people evaluate documents with a certain set of cognitive strategies, AI researchers may use protocol analysis. Unlike traditional psychological experimentation based upon statistical analysis of the results of a task performed by many human subjects, protocol analysis focuses on in-depth examination for individual subjects performing a complex, multi-stage task (Ericson & Simon, 1984). A subject is asked to vocalize every step in the problem solving process. The experimenter correlates utterances with actions taken in the solution process and occasionally asks the subject to explain decisions not directly substantiated by prior actions or vocalizations. In one project (Carbonell, Scott & Evans, 1984) to build an intelligent information retrieval system, the researchers are using protocol analysis to obtain both a basic model of knowledge in biomedicine and models of indexers and querists for biomedical articles.

8.3 EXERCISES

Exercise 1
Propose a criterion (or criteria) by which a 'system' can be judged to be as robustly creative as you can imagine. Precisely specify how success or failure by the criteria would be measured. Then describe properties which such a system must necessarily have. Are these propeties sufficient? Delineate those parts of your system which are changeable from those parts which are not. This problem deals with abstract worlds rather than real ones. (Time 2 hours.)

Exercise 2
People need progressively more access to large-scale textual data bases. In what ways is this a good and/or bad domain for research in AI? (Time 30 minutes.) Describe an AI experiment in an IR domain which highlights what you consider good and/or bad about the appropriateness of the joining of AI and IR. (Time 90 minutes. Note again these minute requirements include reading, thinking, doodling, analyzing, and communicating.)

8.4 REFERENCES

Bethke, Albert (1980) Genetic Algorithms as Function Optimizers, PhD Thesis, Dept. Computer and Communication Sciences, University of Michigan, Ann Arbor, MI.
Buchanan, B., & Shortliffe, E. (1984), in *Rule-Based Expert Systems*; *The MYCIN Experiments of the Stanford Heuristic Programming Project*, Addison-Wesley, Reading, MA.
Carbonell, Jaime (1983) Learning by Analogy, in *Machine Learning*, T. Mitchell, (ed.) pp. 137–161, Tioga Publishing, Palo Alto, CA.
Carbonell, J. Scott, D. & Evans, D. (1984) *Toward the Automation of Content-Access Method for Large-Scale Textual Databases*, Dept. Computer Science, Carnegie Mellon University, Pittsburg, (1984), PA. Research proposal funded by National Library of Medicine.

Chikayama, Takashi (1983) ESP (Extended Self-contained PROLOG) as a Preliminary Kernel Language of Fifth Generation Computers, *New Generation Computing*, 1, 1, pp. 11–24.

Conrad, Michael (1979) Bootstrapping on the Adaptive Landscape, *BioSystems*, **11,** pp. 167–182.

Conrad, Michael (1982) *Adaptability: The Significance of Variability from Molecule to Ecosystem*, Plenum, New York.

Darden, Lindley, (1982) Reasoning by Analogy in Theory Construction. *Proc. Philosophy Science Assoc*, pp. 147–165.

Davis, Randall, (1982) TEIRESIAS: Applications of Meta-Level Knowledge, in *Knowledge-Based Systems in Artificial Intelligence*, D. Lenat, (ed.), pp. 229–491, McGraw-Hill, New York.

Ericcson, K. A. & Simon, H. A. (1984) *Protocol Analysis, Verbal Reports as Data*, MIT Press, Cambridge, MA.

Ernst, G. & Newell, A. (1969)*GPS: A Case Study in Generality and Problem Solving*, Academic Press, New York.

Fogel, L. J., Owens, A. J. & Walsh, M. J. (1966) *Artificial Intelligence through Simulated Evolution*, John Wiley & Sons, New York.

Garfield, E. (1979) *Citation Indexing: Its Theory and Applications in Science, Technology, and Humanities*, John Wiley and Sons, New York.

Holland, John, (1975) *Adaptation in Natural and Artificial Systems*, University of Michigan Press, Ann Arbor, Michigan.

Lenat, Douglas, (1982) An Artificial Intelligence Approach to Discovery in Mathematics as Heuristic Search, in *Knowledge-Based Systems in Artificial Intelligence*, D. Lenat, (ed.) pp. 229–491, McGraw-Hill, New York.

Minsky, Marvin, and Papert, Seymour, (1969) *Perceptrons*, MIT Press, Massachusetts.

Pearl, Judea (1983) On the Discovery and Generation of Certain Heuristics, *AI Magazine*, **4,** pp. 23–34.

Rada, Roy (1981) Evolution and Gradualness, *BioSystems* **14,** pp. 211–218.

Rada, Roy (1983) A Direction for AIM, *SIGBIO Newsletter*, **6,** pp. 6–8, Assoc. Comp. Mach.

Rada, Roy., Humphrey, Sussane, & Coccia, Craig (1985) A Knowledgebase for Retrieval Evaluation, *Proc. ACM '85* pp. 360–367.

Resnick, A. & Savage, T. R. (1964) The Consistency of Human Judgements of Relevance, *American Documentation*, **15,** 2, pp. 93–95.

Ritchie, G. D. & Hanna, F. K. (1984) AM: A Case Study in AI Methodology, *Artificial Intelligence*, **23,** pp. 249–268.

Rosenbloom, P., Laird, J., McDermott, J., Newell, A. & Orciuch, E. (1984) R1-Soar: An Experiment in Knowledge-Intensive Programming in a Problem-Solving Architecture, *Proc. IEEE Workshop on Principles of Knowledge-Based Systems*, pp. 65–72, IEEE Computer Soc. Press, Silver Spring, MD.

Salton, Gerald & McGill, Michael (1983) *Introduction to Modern Information Retrieval*, McGraw-Hill, New York.

Samuel, Arthur (1969) Some Studies in Machine Learning Using the Game of Checkers, *IBM Jr Res Devel*, **3,** 210–229.

Samuel, Arthur (1967) Some Studies in Machine Learning Using the Game of Checkers, Part II, Recent Progress, *IBM Jr Res Devel*, **11,** pp. 601–617.

Shortliffe, Edward (1976) *Computer-Based Medical Consultations*: *MYCIN*, Elsevier, New York.

Siegel, Sidney (1956) *Nonparametric Statistics*, McGraw-Hill, New York.

Simon, Herbert (1983) Why Should Machines Learn, in *Machine Lerning*, T. Mitchell, (ed.) pp. 25–38, Tioga Publishing, Palo Alto, CA.

Swets, John (1969) Effectiveness of Information Retrieval Methods, *American Documentation*, **20,** 1, pp. 72–89.

Taube, Mortimer (1965) A Note on the Pseudo-Mathematics of Relevance, *American Documentation*, **16,** 2, pp. 69–72.

Turing, A. M. (1963) Computing Machinery and Intelligence, in *Computers and Thought*, J. Feldman, (ed.) pp. 11–35, McGraw-Hill, New York.

Zeigler, Bernard P. (1984) *Multifacetted Modelling and Discrete Event Simulation*, Academic Press, London, England.

9

Knowledge-sparse learning

By knowledge-sparse learning we mean that kind of learning that depends on the occurrence of events in an easily detectable way. If a user of an IR system announces which documents from asset are relevant to a query and which are not and this information is used to adjust weights on document descriptors so as to improve recall of the system, then the system is engaged in knowledge-spare learning. Likewise, if a system looks at text and based on the frequency of co-occurrence of words in text decides to link co-occurring words in a classification structure, knowledge-sparse learning has taken place.

Both of the above examples of knowledge-sparse learning can be discussed from many perspectives and categorized in a variety of ways. Is the source of new data a user's response or is it text stored on the computer? What is being learned: is the thesaurus being modified, are the descriptions of particular documents changing, or is the query being refined? We will look in the next two chapters at what has been done along some of these dimensions.

Knowledge-sparse learning depends mainly on a unidimensional, reward-punishment type of feedback. This is in contrast to knowledge-rich learning which might, for instance, depend on finding similarities between complex knowledge bases and augmenting them so as to take advantage of the long history that has been distilled in the structures. We grant that all learning may be seen as having its roots somewhere along the line in adaptation to simple yes–no feedback, but it seems characteristic of intelligent systems that they take advantage of existing knowledge and employ feedback in very subtle ways.

9.1 LEARNINGS BASED ON USER YES–NO INPUT

Most operational IR systems offer an interactive search environment in which users communicate directly with the search system and responses are furnished instantaneously. It is not unreasonable in this context to solicit from the user her satisfaction with the output. The system obtains in this way feedback which can direct changes to the query or document descriptors so as to get better output for the current user and/or for future users.

9.1.1 Adjusting weights on document or query vectors

Any learning scheme relies on some kind of representation and reasoning. If the frequency of words is to be a key in learning, then a representation and reasoning that is based on word frequencies is appropriate. Assume that all the words of a given language are stored in a vector V. Any query or document might be represented by a vector of the length of V but where each word is replaced by a number between 0 and 1. Each number or weight testifies to the extent to which the corresponding word from V characterizes the query or document at issue. The learning approach in an IR system in which a vector of weights describes documents and queries often concentrates on manipulating the weights. Numbers or weights have an ordering — .1 is less than .2, .2 is less than .3, etc. If the interaction among weights is not too great, then a small change in one weight should not radically alter the performance of the IR system.

In the weight refinement problem the document space is initially described as a set of vectors

$$(w_{1,1}, \ldots, w_{1,m})$$
$$(w_{2,1}, \ldots, w_{2,m})$$
$$\ldots$$
$$(w_{n,1}, \ldots, w_{n,m})$$

where $w_{i,j}$ is the weight on the jth word of the ith document. There are m words in the language and n documents. A query likewise is represented by $(w_1, \ldots, w_m)$. One can talk about

(1) adapting a query so that it retrieves as many relevant documents as it should, or
(2) adapting the document descriptions to optimize retrieval for a given set of queries.

The problem of finding the correct weights can be viewed as a search through a search space (Rada, 1983). A search space may be formalized as a quadruple (S, I, O, G) (Banerji, 1982), where

S is a set of states,
I is a set of initial states,
O is a set of operators for moving from state to state, and
G is a set of goal states.

For the query adjustment experiments, I is a query $w_1, \ldots, w_m$ provided by a user of the IR system. The set S of states = {s|s refers to the same m-word vocabulary as I but differs in the weight assignments}. An operator in O may add or subtract from weights in s. The goal state is the weighted query that returns exactly those documents desired by the user.

A control strategy for the learning algorithm must choose which weight change operators to apply. For a given query a certain set of document are retrieved by the IR system. The retrieved documents are divided by the querist into relevant and not relevant sets. The learning algorithm moves the weights on the query so that they are more like the weights on the relevant documents. Say we have two documents

$$doc_1 = (0, 1)$$
$$doc_2 = (1, 0),$$

a query

$$query = (1, 0),$$

and the use wants only the second document doc_2. The first weight on $query$ should be raised and/or the second weight should be lowered.

It may not, however, be possible, for an arbitrary set of documents, to find a set of query weights, such that all the documents judged relevant by the person are retrieved by the computer in response to the query. This would be the case when the set of documents is not linearly separable. The query is somewhat like a perceptron, and the results of perceptron theory should apply. Perceptron theory demonstrates that perceptrons can only distinguish patterns that are linearly separable (Minsky & Papert, 1969). Assume that documents are returned to a query, if cosine(document, query) is over some threshold (Salton & McGill, 1983). Assume that the document space is defined as

$$doc_1 = (.11)$$
$$doc_2 = (.99)$$
$$doc_3 = (.01)$$

The user wants only doc_1 and doc_3. There is no query that will allow that retrieval.

Salton (Salton & McGill, 1983) talks about adaptive queries whose criterion of success recognizes that a perfect retrieval may not be possible within the confines of the weighted-vector representation scheme. He says that the best query is one that maximizes a function defined as the difference between the average query-document similarity for all relevant items and the average query-document similarity for the non-relevant items.

The attractiveness of working with numbers, as in weighted IR systems, is that the numbers have a natural metric similarity (they have a total ordering). A state which includes numbers may be slightly changed by slightly changing a number, and the resultant effect on the distance to the goal may well be small. In other words, the search space is smooth. On the other hand, the ease with which we can represent initial states, goal states, and operators that both take advantage of this smoothness and correspond to important real-world problems is less clear.

9.1.2   With the genetic algorithm

The genetic algorithm is increasingly popular in machine learning research. Gordon (Gordon, 1983) has investigated the role of the genetic algorithm as a modifer of document descriptions in response to user feedback. Good document descriptions are generated by using the querists's assessments of the documents that are returned to a given query. The document descriptions as amended by the genetic algorithm 1) have a higher probability of mathcing a query to which the document is relevant, and 2) have a lower probability of matching a query to which the document is not relevant. Adaptive document description fosters communication between a document retrieval system and the inquirers using it.

9.1.2.1   The genetic algorithm

Movitived by natural history. John Holland (Halland, 1975; 1983) has proposed a method of knowledge refinement that is based on the genetic algorithm. The genetic algorithm is an iterative 3-phase process. Strings (which could be interpreted as rules or as chormosomes) are the basic data structure of the genetic algorithm. In phase 1 each rule is assigned a value based on its performance on a learning set. In phase 2 the rules are copied in proportion to their value. In phase 3 predicates of one rule are exchanged with predicates of another rule (see the table):

RECOMBINATION		
	OLD RULES	NEW RULES
rule	☐☐☐☐☐☐☐☐	☐☐☐☐◯◯◯◯
rule	◯◯◯◯◯◯◯◯	◯◯◯◯☐☐☐☐

Albert Bethke (Bethke, 1980) has characterized the problems on which Holland's genetic algorithm works well. Bethke concludes that the space of possibilties should be smooth — that the value of one item of knowledge should not be radically different from the value of an item of knowledge that is structurally similar. The difficulty is to find a representation such that the genetic algorithm operates on strings in a smooth search space. (See also Chapter 4.)

9.1.2.2   Adjusting document descriptions

Suppose there is a document which a significant number of inquirers would judge relevant to their information need if it were presented to them. Despite this agreement among the inquirers about the relevance of this document, inquirer indeterminacy suggests each of them will ask for it differently. Suppose also that the document had several existing candidate descriptions. Which descriptions would best serve the inquirers?

These recall and precision values can be considered fitness measures for the genetic algorithm. When a query is matched against a document, the query is matched against each description of the document. Recall and precision values are collected. Next, the document descriptions are reproduced in numbers proportional to their relative fitness. Next the cross-over process randomly pairs reproduced descriptions and interchanges their components. This process repeats.

The genetic algorithm can be used to search rapidly through a large search space. The algorithm separates the more useful descriptions from the less useful and forms new descriptions which are better for retrieval.

The experiments of Gordon (Gordon, 1983) demonsrate good performance of the genetic algorithm in the context of information retrieval. The success of that work depends, however, on a description of documents that allows sets of adjacent terms in a string to be the important, meaningful terms. The manipulation by cross-over pays no attention to any special meaning about the terms or the relations that they may have one to another. Gordon did investigate other strategies of improving descriptions and concluded that with cleverness one could on an ad hoc basis find good strategies for changing document descriptions. He argued, however, that the genetic algorithm is general purpose and performs excellently. His experiments were all done on a relatively small set of documents and queries that might not accurately represent real-world situations.

9.2 LEARNING BASED ON DOCUMENT WORD FREQUENCY

We have talked about characterizing documents or queries according to word frequencies. Now the topic switches to the use of word frequencies to make decisions about relationships in the textual database. We will examine both document organizing and thesaurus building aspects of learning from word frequencies.

9.2.1 Document space adjustment

IR work often involves massive textual databases. With such databases, it is useful to superimpose an organization of the documents to facilitate storage and retrieval. One such organization is a clustering of documents according to similarity of terms. Given that terms are like concepts, such a clustering allows a searcher to more effectively and efficiently find documents by restricting the seach to those clusters known to contain the type of material that the searcher wants.

Similarity measures such as the cosine one defined earlier can be used in document clustering. First, the similarity between all pairs of documents in the document space is calculated. Then a graph is defined by making each document a node and by directly connecting any two documents whose similarity exceeds some threshold. Various connected subgraphs of the graph are then classified as clusters (Salton & McGill, 1983). In clustering one wants to set bounds on the minimum and maximum number of documents that might be in any given cluster, as well as the number and degree of overlap of clusters. By defining the centers of clusters it is then possible to assess the similarity among clusters and to add another level of organization to the classification of sets of documents. In fact this process can continue until the document space classification looks like a deep and bushy tree.

Simon (Simon, 1983) says that a machine learns, if it changes itself such that its future behavior is better because of the change. An IR system that built and continually updated document clusters in order to improve searchers results could be considered to be engaged in learning. The system is learning how to group its documents by studying the content of those documents and looking for certain similarities.

9.2.2   Thesaurus adjustment

A thesaurus is a controlled vocabulary of semantically related terms offering comprehensive coverage of a domain of knowledge (Devadason & Balasu-bramanian, 1981). There is enormous interest among many groups in the building of better thesauri. We discuss the grouping of documents based on the similarity of the words in them. Similarly we can select index terms automatically and group them into classes (Mili & Rada, 1985). Having done this we have gone a long way toward creating a thesaurus automati-cally. This kind of thesaurus building assumes that the more frequently two words tend to co-occur in a collection of documents, the more likely they are to be related in some way and substitutable for each other in searching operations.

To derive these relations among terms via their frequency, we first construct a term-term matrix which shows for each term pair how frequently the terms co-occur. Various procedurs can be applied by computer to the term-term matrix in order to isolate classes of related terms (Lancaster, 1972). For the 'string class' we take a specific term, find another connected with it, find a third connected to the second, and so on. For the 'clique class' all terms must be directly connected with each other (Sparck & Jones, 1971).

Soergel (Soergel, 1974a) claims that fully automatic thesaurus building may be attractive as an idea but is not feasible. He argues that the identification of terms and relationships by automatic methods should be considered as a king of pre-processing that results in a list of important terms and potential relationships between them. These relationships (which the computer has, in a sense, learned) can then be combed by people to establish which relationships are cognitively meaningful.

Association by frequency of co-occurrence between two terms, x and y, suggests any of the following relationships (Soergel, 1974b):

(a) y is the definition of x
(b) x and y are synonymous
(c) x is broader than y
(d) x is narrower than y

(e) x is a part-of y

(f) x and y are members of a compound term, like 'flip flop'.

For instance, we suspect that x is narrower than y, if almost all documents dealing with y also deal with x and the number of units containing y is much larger than the number containing x.

9.3 EXERCISE

Knowledge-sparse learning works well when the operator for change can help solve the problem with little knowledge of the semantics of the problem. Adjusting of weights is simpler than crossover of strings which is, in turn, simpler than adjusting hierarchies. Explore the use of the genetic algorithm to improve a hierarchy of terms. (Time 1.5 hours.)

9.4 REFERENCES

Banerji, R. B. (1982) Theory of Problem Solving: A Branch of Artificial Intelligence, *Proc IEEE*, **70**, 12, pp. 1428–1448.

Devadason, F. J. & Balasubramanian, V. (1981) Computer Generation of Thesaurus from Structured Subject-Propositions, *Information Processing and Management*, **17**, pp. 1–11.

Gordon, Michael, Adaptive Subject Description in Document Retrieval. PhD Thesis, Dept Computer and Communication Sciences, University of Michigan, Ann Arbor, MI.

Holland, John (1975) *Adaptation in Natural and Artificial Systems*, University of Michigan Press, Ann Arbor, Michigan.

Holland, John (1983) Escaping Brittleness, *Proc Intern'l Machine Learning Workshop*, pp. 92–96.

Lancaster, F. W. (1972) *Vocabulary Control for Information Retrieval*, Information Resources Press, Washington, DC.

Mili, Hafedh. & Rada, Roy (1985) A Statistically Build Knowledge Base. *Proc. Expert Systems in Government*, IEEE Computer Society Press, pp. 457–463.

Rada, Roy. (1983) Characterizing Search Spaces, *Proc Intern'l Joint Conf Art Intell*, pp. 780–782.

Simon, Herbert. (1983) Why Should Machines Learn, in *Machine Learning*, T. Mitchell, (ed.) pp. 25–38, Tioga Publishing, Palo Alto, CA.

Sparck Jones, Karen. (1971) *Automatic Keyword Classification for Information Retrieval*, Butterworth, London.

Soergel, Dagobert, (1974a) Automatic and Semi-Automatic Methods as an Aid in the Construction of Indexing Languages and Thesauri, *Intern Classificat*, **1**, 1, pp. 34–39.

Soergel, Dagobert. (1974b) *Indexing Languages and Thesauri: Construction and Maintenance*, John Wiley & Sons, New Youk.

10

Knowledge-rich learning

In the previous section we examined knowledge-sparse learning by looking first at those contexts in which users provided the important feedback and secondly at those contexts where the feedback was determined by the patterns in documents. This chapter is organized in the same broad fashion in that we begin with learning from users and end with learning from text. Additionally, in the middle of this chapter we study the merging of thesauri.

Clearly, a user can make substantial, sophisticated adjustments to an IR system by interacting with it through a smart interface. There are several inducements, however, to leaning heavily on the opportunities offered by the vast amount of already organized information on the computer. If one reads directly from text and disambiguates the important meanings from the myriad of possibilities, one has a natural language processing system beyond the current state of the art. Accordingly, we have looked for an area where the information is already on the machine but easier to understand than text — and that has led us to emphasize the merging of classification structures or thesauri.

10.1 BASED ON USERS

10.1.1 Learning the syntax

In interacting with users of a document retrieval system the computer system would ideally understand the natural language of the user. Rather than trying to build a robust natural language processing capability one could build a computer program that detects small variants from what it was prepared to handle and then augments itself so that next time it understands. At the lowest level one might look for interactive mechanisms for spelling correction and abbreviation replacement. At a higher level, the system can start with a set of understood utterances that map directly into concepts understood by the sytem in its document representation and retrieval activities. If statements come into the system from a user which the system doesn't recognize, it could look for the nearest match in its set of statements and check with the user whether that match is correct. Once the correct match has been found various strategies can be employed to change the sytem so that next time it immediately recognizes the statement. This is a kind of syntax learning (Reeker, 1971).

An example of this transformation and learning is borrowed from Reeker, deals with an insect database, and starts with the utterance 'wings are clear' (Reeker, 1984). Assume that the closest assertion to 'wings are clear' in the computer system is 'the insect has clear wings' and that the user agrees that 'the insect has clear wings' captures the correct meaning of the utterance 'wings are clear'. The syntactic analyses produce (where CV means complemented verb):

Fig. 10.1 — Parsing of synonymous queries.

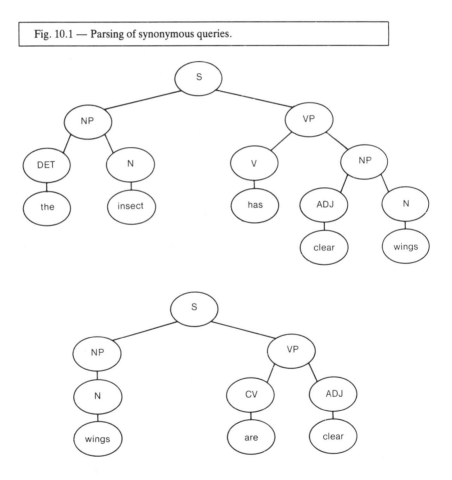

At its simplest the transformation would say 'wings are clear' should be transformed into 'the insect has clear wings', but Reeker wants something more general than that. One might want to say that the structure

S[NP[N]VP[CV ADJ]] goes into the structure S[NP[ADJ N]], where the subject 'insect' and verb 'has' are dropped. In this particular example, 'wings are clear' transforms to 'clear wings'. The program might now speculate, based on the context, as to whether the NP 'clear wings' is the object of 'insect has'. Having made these grammatical conclusions based on the example, one could now try these on other examples, such as 'wings are opaque' or 'legs are long'. One has learned something about all utterances of the form S[NP[N]VP[CV ADJ]] and S[NP[ADJ N]] and not just their superficial manifestations. One could transform further into S[NP VP[[V]NP[ADJ N]]], where categories not further expanded can match any identically labelled subtree in a valid assertion.

Other learning rules might, depending on the context, take a sentence like 'it has a heavy exoskeleton', and conclude that that sentence means 'the insect has a heavy exoskeleton'. The extent to which generalization should take place is a subject for experimentation. Most linguistic generalization programs overgeneralize, as contrasted to children, who appear to generalize conservatively. Researchers who have built models of language acquisition have included constraints based upon semantics (Reeker, 1976).

10.1.2   Learning the semantics

Researchers at SRI International (Haas & Hendrix, 1980) have been developing a system that has a basic knowledge of English and is capable of learning the concepts and vocabulary of new subject domains. Their system is called NanoKLAUS which is short for small Knowledge-Learning and Using System. NanoKLAUS comes preprogrammed with a seed vocabulary, a set of seed concepts, and a set of syntactic and semantic rules covering a small subset of English. These allow the system to engage in conversations such as:

User: A length is a measure.
System: Your'e saying that anything that is a LENGTH is also a MEASURE. Ok, now I have assimilated LENGTH.

One might try to define as seed concepts a large, comprehensive set of primitives, into which all concepts can be placed, but such a reductionist approach is difficult. Most of the seed concepts in NanoKLAUS are classes of THINGS and RELATIONS. NanoKLAUS uses principles of knowledge organization to integrate new knowledge, which simply state that there are

(1) things,
(2) subclasses of things,
(3) relations among things, and
(4) subclasses of relations.

Knowledge in NanoKLAUS is encoded into a special, first-order logic, and when new facts are learned by the system they are stored in well-formed formulas of that logic (Hendrix, 1979).

Most of the linguistic processing performed by NanoKLAUS is done with a standard pragmatic grammar (Hendrix *et al.*, 1978), but there are specific syntactic structures that define new concepts. For instance, there is a construct which basically says

<sentence> → <new-word> <is-a> <known-word>.

When a sentence satisfies this pattern, an acquisition procedure is invoked. This procedure may generate new entries for <new-word> in the system's lexicon and new well-formed formulas in the knowledge-base.

A system similar in its objective to NanoKLAUS is the Medical Interactive Knowledge Acquisition System (MEDIKAS). The goal for the MEDIKAS researcher is to analyze and explore the process of the acquisition of knowledge in order to construct a computer program that operates like an intelligent listener and automatically augments its knowledge (Baskin & Levy, 1978). MEDIKAS consists of four tasks: a dictionary manager, a semantic network manager, a rule interpreter, and a user-interface task. The dictionary manager maintains the equivalence between English words and phrases and corresponding pointers into the knowledge base. The semantic network manager operates on a semantic net, where medical concepts are presented by nodes, and relationships between concepts are represented by links between nodes. The rule interpreter automatically generates questions for the acquisition of knowledge from the user. The information in MEDIKAS is partially centred around the notions of set and set membership. If the user says 'A is an element of B', MEDIKAS also deduces that 'B has an element A'.

10.3.3 Rules for searching

One strategy for intelligent information retrieval is to have users create knowledge-bases which describe their special interests. One approach to this has been advanced by Tong and others in RUBRIC (RUle-Based Retrieval of Information by Computer) (Tong *et al.*, 1984). RUBRIC differs from traditional approaches to IR in several ways:

(1) Searching is performed over the whole document.
(2) Matching of query to document is not an all or nothing affair; documents get a match value between 0 and 1.
(3) Queries are expressed in a language of rules that allows the user to develop hierarchical knowledge structures.
(4) Users are provided with tools to help modify queries.

RUBRIC is an example of a production system (Nilsson, 1980) that performs evidential reasoning. The text of the documents provides the evidence on which the rules operate in order to determine how close a document is to a query. The knowledge on which this judgement rests is embodied in a set of rules which the user provides.

The rules define a hierarchy of topics. By naming a topic, the user invokes a goal-oriented search of the tree beneath the topic. The lowest-level topics are defined in terms of patterns in the text itself. Thus the system ultimately rests on a string search of text. But the results of the string searching are combined in a more sophisticated way than is allowed in other string-searching based systems.

Each rule may have a user-provided weight. This weight defines how strongly the user believes that the rule will contribute to correct retrieval. RUBRIC supports several calculi for interpreting rule weights. Weights are treated as certainty values and not as probabilities. Each calculus defines how to combine the uncertainties across AND, OR, and IMPLICATION. The default method is to use the functions minimum, maximum, and product to propagate the weights across AND, OR, and IMPLICATION, respectively (Tong *et al.*, 1983).

A tiny example of the operation of these rules takes a query for documents about machine learning. We design a set of rules:

(a) if *machine* and *learning* then 1.0 *machine learning*.
(b) if *computer* or *machine* then 0.8 *machine*.
(c) if *learning* or *adaptation* or *acquisition* then 0.5 *learning*.

A document with the three terms *computer, knowledge,* and *acquisition* would activate first rules b and c and then rule a. According to the default uncertainty criteria, the document would be rated as about *machine learning* at the 0.5 level. A document which said 'computer trains itself' would, according to these rules, fail to fall into the class of *machine learning* documents, although the reader realizes that a document about 'computer trains itself' is about 'machine learning'.

A number of experiments have been done with RUBRIC, and indicate that the approach allows the user to be flexible in the specification of the query. This flexibility results in both greater recall and precision when compared to traditional Boolean retrieval systems. A traditional Boolean query tends to either over-constrain or under-constrain the search procedure, giving poor recall or poor precision.

The published work on RUBRIC has emphasized the power of the numbers which are attached to rules and allow fuzzy reasoning. Rich (Rich, 1983) suggests that probabilistic reasoning be not the first course of action but the last resort and offers two guidelines for the use of probabilistic or statistical techniques:

(1) Avoid statistical representations when a better analysis of the problem would make them unnecessary or less important. This means that we should represent characters as sets of high-level features rather than as seemingly highly random collections of dots of ink.
(2) If statistical reasoning is necessary to handle either real-world randomness or genuine lack of complete information, then perform the statistical manipulations in small increments that correspond to logical steps in reasoning rather than in one large operation that fails to reflect the

structure of the problem. This argues for a probabilistic, rule-based system rather than the straightforward application of statistical techniques to a mass of data.

10.2 MERGING CLASSIFICATION STRUCTURES

10.2.1 History

Making a thesaurus is typically a labor-intensive job. It is also a job which does not stop when the first edition rolls off the press. Instead the thesaurus needs to be continually updated. Finally, a new thesaurus often repeats substantial amounts of material already present in existing thesauri (Dextre & Clarke, 1981). For these reasons people want to partially automate the process of merging thesauri.

Although the integration of ordering systems or thesauri has been spurred by the prospects of automation, the idea of integration has been of interest to classifiers for a long time. Approximately 22 years ago, C. E. Muller tried his hand at establishing a special concordance between the Universal Decimal Classification and some special classification systems without the assistance of a computer. He met with the same frustration as other researchers who embarked on that project. Too many parameters are involved which could hardly be made explicit without computer assistance (Dahlberg, 1983).

One approach to allowing users to take advantage of multiple thesauri at once is to map the terms of each thesaurus to the terms of the other. This translation could be performed for every pair of languages under consideration but only needs to be done until a connected graph is created, where nodes are terms and edges connect nodes of two different thesauri. In one example, the 'Dictionary of Equivalents' was used to link the vocabularies of the Armed Services Technical Information Agency and the Atomic Energy Commission (Svenonius, 1983). Today in Europe efforts towards language compatibility have concentrated on the construction of multi-linqual thesauri. In North America the Canadian National Library is trying to link the Canadian List of English Subject Headings with the Library of Congress Subject Headings.

In the United States Robert Niehoff of Battelle Laboratories has striven to identify, compile, and integrate existing energy vocabularies from several IR systems. Niehoff has succeeded in creating an automated, online, switching conversion guide that recognizes exact, singular–plural and synonym equivalences. Battelle Laboratories has been supported by grants for many years to engage in the development of vocabulary switching systems (Niehoff & Mack, 1985). Much of the work in developing this Vocabulary Switching System is done by hand. In other words, while the Switching System automatically switches, the construction of the Switching System was far from automated.

Another strategy is to take simple existing thesauri structures and make small maniplations that bring the thesauri together in a way that recognizes the overlap between the two but also benefits by keeping the parts which are novel to each system. The United Nations has funded a number of large projects in the construction of unified languages for the classification of documents in a number of fields including in particular the social sciences. This funded work has shown how many facets on a concept would facilitate robust comparisons between terms in different classification structures. Dextre (Dextre & Clarke, 1981) has devised a representation and reasoning scheme such that development of several microthesauri from one large thesaurus is straightforward.

10.2.2 The need for conceptual analysis

Many of the key workers in the field of merging classification structures have focused their attention on, what they call, concept analysis. This relates to what people in artificial intelligence study under the heading of knowledge representation. 'An integrated system combining the elements from different thesauri and classification systems demands clear definitions of classes by hierarchical features and preferably by indication of characteristics of division. In fact, it can only be accomplished if the necessary concept analysis of each of the elements involved in the integration has been undertaken first (Dahlberg, 1980). In 1977, UNESCO undertook the ambitious project of collecting, identifying, clarifying, representing, and delivering data on concepts in the social sciences on an international level. During the course of the project, they discovered the need to define clearer criteria for identifying the concepts and for preparing operative definitions (Dahlberg, 1981).

Concepts may be viewed as triads comprised of a referent, the characteristics of a referent, and the external, communicable form of the referent and its characteristics. A referent can take on the form of any material or immaterial object, property, dimension, fact, activity, topic or other distinguishable entity. Characteristics refer to the necessary predications or qualities which separate one referent from the next. Terms are the verbal or external form of a concept. Together, the terms, the referent, and the characteristics work to capture the tangible and intangible aspects of an element of human thought.

A concept field covers the entire realm of a concept, including its broader, narrower, and associated concepts, as well as its generic, partitive, positional, and functional relationships. A 'concept record' captures all the knowledge about a particular referent within prespecified fields (Soergel, 1974b). The prespecified fields are further broken into necessary and possible fields as follows (Dahlberg, 1983).

(A) Necessary fields

    1 name of concept
    2 notation
    3 definition

    4 next broader concept
    5 highest concept in hierarchy
    6 subject fields of concept
    7 synonyms
    8 source of concept
    9 corresponding concepts in other ordering systems

(B) Possible fields

    10 name in other languages
    20 hierarchical level
    30 additional definitions
    40 form category

        41 object, entity, abstractum
        42 quantity, quality
        43 process, activity
        44 space, time
        45 combination of above

Having identified these various fields, one can determine the degree of conceptual compatibility between ordering systems through measures such as conceptual coincidence, conceptual correspondence, and conceptual correlation. Conceptual coincidence occurs when two concepts match in all characteristics. Conceptual correspondence occurs when two concepts match in many but not all of their characteristics. Algorithms for determining coincidence, correspondence, and correlation have been devised. A first pass at an algorithm for determining coincidence based on the above representation follows (Dahaberg, 1983).

> Sort out all those concept records which have the same terms in slot 1 and check by comparing their definitions in slot 3 whether they in fact stand for the same concept. If they do, they should be checked according to their entries in slots 4, 5, and 6, and interesting deviations should be indicated under 9.

Many believe that an integrated thesaurus must necessarily be as detailed as the most detailed version of any one of the thesauri undergoing integration. Although simple conflations of the thesauri will introduce many redundancies into the ordering system, the application of harmonisation processes should be able to weed out the chaff and yield an efficient new ordering system free from overlaps (Sage *et al.*, 1981).

10.3 BASED ON DOCUMENTS

10.3.1 Indexer added

In the development of a reference retrieval system, one dilemma is whether to build a thesaurus first and then use it for indexing the documents or to index the documents by free terms and then construct the thesaurus after accumulating a good number of terms. As is often true in life, the middle ground is particularly attractive and that means in this case building a thesaurus and indexing documents hand-in-hand.

For people (and computers might simulate this process) to sumultaneously build a thesaurus and index documents requires both selecting a set of documents and creating a thesaurus around which to begin. Then the indexer scans the document and chooses in a free-form fashion a set of terms to characterize the document. In case a term is not available in the thesaurus, one of the following 3 approaches may be taken (Sudarshan, 1979).

(1) If a synonymous term is available in the thesaurus, then the thesaurus experts should be asked to include this synonym in the thesaurus. For example, if the term 'lathe' is available in the thesaurus but the indexer has chosen the synonym 'turning machine', then 'turning machine' should be added as a synonym to 'lathe'.

(2) If the indexable concept can be broken into parts which are in the thesaurus, then this breakdown should be made and the thesaurus might be augmented to indicate the relation which exists between the component terms. For instance, if 'hydrostatic thrust bearings' is initially chosen to describe the document but the index only has 'hydrostatic bearings' and 'thrust bearings', then the document is indexed under both terms and the thesaurus might be augmented to indicate that these two types of bearings are related.

(3) If steps (1) and (2) above do not produce index terms from the thesaurus, then a check is made for terms in the thesaurus which are broader than the one the indexer chose. If the initial thesaurus is well-designed, then any new term must, at least, be able to fit under some pre-existing broader term. So the indexer next asks the thesaurus group whether the indexer's term should be added to the thesaurus as a 'narrower term' or whether the existing 'broader term' itself should be used.

This hybrid method of free-text and controlled vocabulary for thesaurus construction depends on two key groups: the thesaurus group and the index group (Sudarshan, 1979). The thesaurus group consists of experts in the domain of the literature to be processed. These experts have a clear grasp of the terminology and semantic subtleties of the subject field. The thesaurus group is responsible for collecting index terms, constructing the thesaurus, and making the thesaurus as up-to-date as possible for the index group. The index group indexes the documents according to the latest version of the thesaurus and returns the document index terms which are not already in the thesaurus to the thesaurus group. The indexing group is further bound by the principle that the most recent literature in a technical area is the most important. Thus, top priority is given to the indexing of current literature, and older materials are indexed in backward chronological order as resources permit.

Partially coded document descriptions can be the basis for building a thesaurus. Some researchers have prepared formats for input statements that represent documents (Austin, 1972). One computer program that builds onto a thesaurus, reads the constrained natural language of the document, deduces what are *broader than, narrower than,* and other *related* terms to which the document description alludes, and adds those relationships to the growing thesaurus (Devadason & Balasubramanian, 1981). This effort requires humans to code documents in a stylized way that they probably find confining.

10.3.2 Dynamic memory
10.3.2.1 Memory structures
Compare the way an expert stores knowledge about books to the way a library handles the same information. The library creates a classification structure which is hard to change and into which all new material must fit (Schank, 1982). An expert, on the other hand, can make observations about what she knows and can alter the memory structures that catalog what she knows.

Our dynamic memories organize themselves so as to be able to adjust encodings to reflect growth and new understanding. We generally remember what is relevant. There is a kind of selection process at work that picks certain memories for special treatment and retention. One problem that sheds light on remembering and learning is reminding. There are several broad classes of reminding (Schank, 1982):

(1) Physical objects can remind you of other physical objects.
(2) Physical objects can remind you of events.
(3) Events can remind you of physical objects.
(4) Events can remind you of events in the same domain.
(5) Events can remind you of events in different domains.

Much of reminding is probably organized around goals. As a person reaches toward a goal, subgoals are created (Simon & Newell, 1972). If the goal is not reached, the subgoals were not correctly related to the goal. This conclusion jars memory so that changes are made into the understanding of the connections among subgoals and goals.

When processing predictions fail, a notation is made with respect to that failure. When a similar failure occurs, the memory that was stored in terms of that failure is retrieved. This conception of memory is called failure-driven memory (Schank, 1982). This is a type of reward and punishment view of memory and learning applied to cognition rather than stimulus–response behaviour.

In order to account for dynamic memory — the ability to generalize and learn from past experience — information about how memory structures are linked in frequently occurring combinations is held in Memory Organization Packets (MOPs). A MOP is both a structure and a processor. According to Schank (Schank, 1982):

A MOP consists of a set of scenes directed towards the achievement of a goal. A MOP always has one major scene whose goal is the essence or purpose of the events organized by the MOP.

A MOP pocesses new inputs by taking the aspects of those inputs that relate to that MOP and interpreting those aspects in terms of the memory in the MOP. Many different MOPs may be active at one time in response to one event. This view of memory is an embellishment of object-oriented programming (Filman & Friedman, 1984). The key to reminding and learning is the ability to create new structures that emphasize the abstract significance of a combination of MOPs. Structures that represent this domain-independent information may be called Thematic Organization Points (TOPs). In addition to MOPs and TOPs, there are scripts and scenes. Scripts are themselves fairly complex organizations of conceptual dependency diagrams (Rich, 1983). Scenes are abstractions on sets of scripts. MOPs are abstractions on scenes. TOPs are at a higher-level than MOPs.

10.3.2.2   *Generalization*

People have different MOPs. How do these structures get built and modified? Assume that each person starts with a personal script or set of MOPs that describe how that person expects to lead her life on a minute to minute basis. To succeed in life a person needs to mesh her expectations with those of society so that the expectations have a good chance of being realized. This requires an understanding of what society expects. To generalize to MOPs about what other people will do, the person needs to recognize when a current scene is similar to a previous scene and to focus on those aspects of the scenes that are similar.

People learn well, in part, because they have a limited set of universal and generalized scenes which they are able to map to new scenes. The indexing of memory is critical to all other functions of memory and to learning. How are TOPs connected to each other and to MOPs? How are scenes connected to each other and to MOPs? How, more generally, does one begin a traversal in memory and know where to step in going from structure to structure. The role of failure and explanation in learning is also intimately linked to indexing. One approach is to describe different types of failure and explanation and then to test the extent to which their descriptions are cognitively realistic by doing computer experiments. To quote Schank:

> Real tests of the ideas presented here will have to await the construction of an evolving dynamic memory on a computer. Then we will be able to see what it does in response to inputs, and alter our hypotheses accordingly.

Kolodner (Kolodner, 1984) has developed a computer system called CYRUS which tests some of the ideas that Schank has advanced about dynamic memory. She argues that memory is organized and searched in accordance with the properties of a reconstructive memory. This means that information is retrieved by reconstructing what must have happened rather than directly remembering what did happen.

Memory is automatically changed through time in CYRUS. As documents are indexed, they precipitate the modification of MOPs. The differences between the appropriate indexing for the new document and the previous indexing are assessed. Either the new document can be handled by amending existing MOPs or new MOPs are created. The memory organization that is built is a hierarchical organization of categories and their subcategories. As new events are indexed, new subcategories are created. To avoid the astronomical growth of the memory, generalizations are performed.

Lebowitz (Lebowitz, 1983) has also been investigating techniques of implementing dynamic memories. He argues that changes to a knowledge base should be based on large amounts of textual information and generalization strategies. Generalization Based Memory (GBM) has the following properties:

(1) It is inherently incremental. As instances are added to the memory, the best available generalizations are made.
(2) It handles large amounts of information. The use of a hierarchy of concepts that organizes specific instances facilitates storage and retrieval of information.
(3) Generalizations are pragmatic. No concept is removed by a single counter-example.

When GBM finds several instances that disconfirm a generalization, it tries to throw away the bad parts and keep the good parts of the generalization. To remove the overly specific parts of a generalization, GBM keeps track of the value of the generalization's components. A confidence level is maintained that indicates for each component how many times it was confirmed and how many times contradicted.

To facilitate analysis of new text and to allow appropriate generalizations, the indexing rules create many kinds of links. Building backpointers in top-down descriptions facilitates recognition (Hunter, 1985). Noting features where a case differs from a prototype is useful in both top-down and horizontal retrieval. Noting these differences depends on expectation failures and proper recognition and handling of these errors. This corresponds to credit assignment in the traditional paradigm of machine learning. One important mundane indexing rule builds indirect indices. These are links not from memory to memory, but from a memory to a set of indices. Indirect indices make it possible for a traversal scheme to refer to the class of indices it wants instead of the names of particular indices. Many of these indexing notions have been long used in the library science field but not in the context of automatic memory agumentation.

10.3.3 Cognitive graphs

Schank's work on dynamic memory emphasizes several intuitively appealing principles, while work with cognitive graphs addresses the same problems in a different, more mathematical way. The method of cognitive graphing is based on the theory of directed graphs and is motivated by the belief that knowledge of the mathematics of abstract structures is of value in cognitive simulation. Bonhamm and others (Bonham *et al.*, 1985) are studying the automatic development of a knowledge base by reading documents and translating them through a sequence of cognitive graphs.

In a cognitive graph the meaning that an edge attributes to the pair of vertices it connects, defines the role these vertices play. A vertex may have more than one meaning, when it participates in relations of different types. Vertices can play the role of symbol, concept, object, property, and value. Each role can also be viewed at a more aggregated level. For example, symbols can be aggregated in expressions. In cognitive graphs for scientific reasoning the principle type of edge is that expressing causality. Reasoning on these graphs occurs by spreading activation, set intersections, and the determination of mimimal path lengths (Shapiro & Bonham, 1982).

The first choice to be made in the construction of a cognitive graph concerns the mode in which the data is gathered. The source to be discussed here is documents. Texts are still the most widely distributed carriers of knowledge. Quoting Bonham *et al.* (1985):

> If the so-called knowledge-based systems, of which the cognitive graph is an example, are to be economically profitable to the public at large, they will need a procedure for the incorporation of the textual knowledge now represented in scientific and technical journals, handbooks, and libraries.

As the documents to be analyzed are obtained, each is translated (currently manually) into its own cognitive graph. Then the graph reasoning algorithms are applied to the task of integrating the graph of a particular document with the global knowledge base (also represented as a cognitive graph).

10.4 EXERCISES

Exercise 1
Take the table of contents of books in IR and AI, describe algorithms for merging these hierarchical classification structures, do a sample of the merging, and discuss the results. (Time 2 hours.)

Exercise 2
A system that could learn by reading text would have a large amount of fodder for the knowledge refinement mill. Read an article about such

systems and in 200 words relate the content of that article to our textbook. (Time 3 hours — this includes 1 hour to find article in library, 1 hour to read it, and 1 hour to critique it.)

10.5 REFERENCES

Austin, Derek (1972) The PRECIS System for Computer-generated Indexes and its use in the British National Bibliography, in *Subject Retrieval in the Seventies*, Wilson, T. (ed.), pp. 99–115, Greenwood Publishing Co., Westport, CT.

Baskin, A. B. & Levy, A. H. (1978) MEDIKAS—An Interactive Knowledge Acquisition System. *Proc. Second Annual Symp. Computer Applic. Medical Care,* pp. 344–350, IEEE Computer Soc. Press.

Bonham, G. M., Nozicka, G. J. & Stokman, F. N. (1985) Cognitive Graphing and the Representation of Biomedical Knowledge, *Proc. Expert Systems in Government Conference,* IEEE Computer Society Press.

Dahlberg, Ingetraut (1980) The Broad System of Ordering as a Basis for an Integrated Social Sciences Thesaurus, *Intern. Classif., 7,* 2, pp. 66–72.

Dahlberg, Ingetraut (1981) Conceptual Definitions for INTERCONCEPT, *Intern. Classif., 8,* 1, pp. 16–22.

Dahlberg, Ingetraut (1983) Conceptual Compatibility of Ordering Systems, *Intern. Classif., 10,* 1, pp. 5–8.

Devadason, F. J. & Balasubramanian, V. (1981) Computer Generation of Thesaurus from Structured Subject-Propositions, *Information Processing and Management, 17,* pp. 1–11.

Dextre, S. G. & Clarke, T. M. (1981) A System for Machine-Aided Thesaurus Construction, *Aslib Proc., 33,* 3, pp. 102–112.

Filman, Robert & Friedman, Daniel (1984) *Coordinated Computing: Tools and Techniques for Distributed Software,* McGraw-Hill, New York.

Haas, Norman & Hendrix, Gary (1980) An Approach to Acquiring and Applying Knowledge, *Proc. First Ann. Nat'l Conf. Artificial Intelligence,* pp. 235–239, American Assoc. Artificial Intelligence.

Hendrix, Gary (1979) Encoding Knowledge in Partitioned Networks, in *Associative Networks: the Representation and Use of Knowledge in Computers,* Findler, N. V. (ed.), Academic Press, New York.

Hendrix, G. G., Sacerdoti, E. D., Sagalowics, D. & Slocum, J. (1978) Developing a Natural Language Interface to Complex Data, *ACM Transactions on Database Systems, 3,* 2.

Hunter, Larry (1985) Steps Towards Building a Dynamic Memory, *Proc. Third Intern'l Machine Learning Workshop.*

Kolodner, Janet (1984) *Retrieval and Organizational Strategies in Conceptual Memory,* Lawrence Erlbaum, Hillsdale, NJ.

Lebowitz, Michael (1983) Concept Learning in a Rich Input Domain, *Proc. Internat'l Machine Learning Workshop,* pp. 177–182.

Niehoff, Robert & Mack, Greg (1985) The Vocabulary Switching System, *Int. Classif., 12,* 1, pp. 2–6.

Nilsson, Nils (1980) *Principles of Artificial Intelligence*, Tioga, Palo Alto, CA.

Reeker, L. H. (1971) A problem Solving Theory of Syntax Acquisition, *Journal of Structural Learning,* **2**, 4, pp. 1–10.

Reeker, L. H. (1976) The Computational Study of Language Acquisition, in *Advances in Computers,* **15**, Rubinoff, (ed.), pp. 181–237, Academic Press, New York.

Reeker, L. H. (1984) Adaptive Individualized Language Interfaces for Expert Systems, *Internal Proposal*, U.S. Navy Center for Artificial Intelligence.

Rich, Elaine (1983) *Artificial Intelligence*, McGraw-Hill, New York.

Sager, J. C., Somers, H. L. & McNaught, J. (1981) Thesaurus Integration in the Social Sciences, Part 1: Comparison of Thesauri, *Intern. Classif.,* **8**, 3, pp. 133–137.

Schank, Roger (1982) *Dynamic Memory: a theory of reminding and learning in computers and people*, Cambridge University Press, Cambridge, England.

Shapiro, M. J. & Bonham, G. M. (1982) A Cognitive Process Approach to Collective Decision-Making, in *Cognitive Dynamics and International Politics*, Jonsson, C. (ed.), Francis Pinter, London.

Simon, H. & Newell, A. (1972) *Human Problem Solving*, Prentice-Hall, Englewood Cliffs, NJ.

Soergel, Dagobert (1974b) *Indexing Languages and Thesauri: Construction and Maintenance*, John Wiley & Sons, New York.

Sudarshan, B.(1979) Development of Reference Retrieval System with Simultaneous Building of Thesaurus, *Lib. Sc.,* **16**, 3, pp. 77–83.

Svenonius, Elaine (1983) Compatibility of Retrieval Languages: Introduction to a Forum, *Intern. Classif.,* **10**, 1, pp. 2–4.

Tong, Richard, Shapiro, D., Dean, J. & McCune, B. (1983) A Comparison of Uncertainty Calculi in an Expert System for Information Retrieval. *Proc. Intern'l Joint Conf. Art. Intell.*, pp. 194–197.

Tong, R., Askman, V. & Cunningham, L. (1984) RUBRIC: an Artificial Intelligence Approach to Information Retrieval, *Proc. 1st Intern'l Workshop on Exert Database Systems*.

PART 2B
A CASE STUDY

In the next chapters we focus on a set of experiments that have been done in our laboratories on machine learning for information retrieval. The emphasis here is on the development of a rigorous methodology that allows repeatable experiments. We also focus on the building of classification structures because we believe that field is most fertile.

In an earlier chapter AI projects were seen as composed of representation, reasoning, and learning components. In this case study section the goal is to build languages for intelligent information retrieval. Thus the overall topic of AI is replaced by the narrower topic of 'building languages'. These languages would be used to classify documents and queries. Since the major langauges currently in use in IR take the form of thesauri, our methodology for representing knowledge is that of thesauri, and int he AI triad of represenation, reasoning, and learning, we have replaced representation with 'thesauri'. The reasoning that we do with these thesauri is tied to the IR tasks of matching of parsing. Finally, our learning strategy is to merge thesauri.

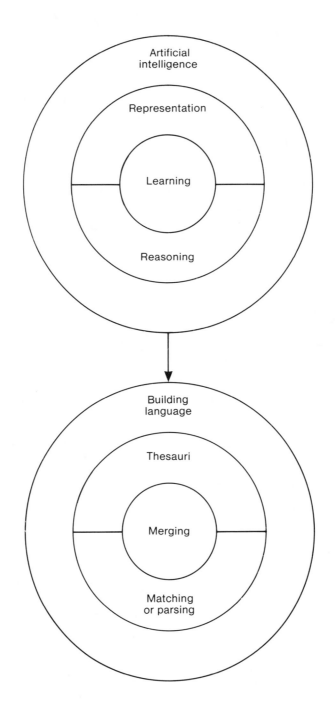

11

The MEDLARS system

We will now begin an extensive case study of work in trying to build better classification structures through machine learning. Our experiments are done within the contexts of the Medical Literature Analysis and Retrieval System (MEDLARS). The primary bibliographic system at the National Library of Medicine, MEDLARS is based on a file of terms pointing to documents (Salton & McGill, 1983). Retrieval from this system is usually performed by a librarian in interaction with a user (McCarn, 1980). The information retrieval strategies that a librarian uses are complex (Fidel, 1984). One of the approaches to alleviating the burden on the librarian is to allow the user to perform direct string-searching on the documents in the system (Bernstein & Williamson, 1984). There are, however, serious limitations to the string-search strategy for it requires the user to guess how writers have phrased the important concepts. The MEDLARS system uses a classification structure for representing queries and documents and is one of the world's most sophisticated systems of its kind.

11.1 THE GENERAL STRUCTURE

11.1.1 History

The National Library of Medicine (NLM) has long been concened with the development, maintenance and improvements of bibliographic and text retrieval systems (MEDLARS Management Section, 1982). NLM is responsible for MEDLARS. The database for this system is constructed and updated by NLM. The database is a bibliographic listing of a large segment of the articles in the biomedical periodical literature. Each bibliographic reference to an article is associated with a series of indexing terms describing the content of the article. A trained indexer scans an article and assigns indexing terms from MeSH (Medical Subject Headings) based on a NLM predetermined set of rules.

NLM first began to experiment with online bibliographic search services in the fall of 1967. The time from the original request by a health professional, through the formulation of the request by a trained analyst and processing by the computer, to the final review and mailing of the bibliography to the requester, was usually three to six weeks. In 1971 the system was upgraded so that users could acces the system via TYMNET or TELENET. The new interactive retrieval system was called MEDLARS onLINE (MEDLINE).

Soon the MEDLINE network grew to include all major medical libraries in the United States as well as many smaller hospital and medical school libraries. In addition, institutions in many other countries also access MEDLINE. Articles from over 2000 medical journals are routinely indexed in MEDLINE. Over the years many new search features were added to MEDLINE and the textual databases available for searching were also increased in number and size. In 1975 a new version of MEDLARS, called MEDLARS II, was installed that represented a sophisticated, third generation bibliographic processing system (MEDLARS Management Section, 1982).

The general structure of MEDLARS is that of a keyword system. A classification structure, from which the keywords come, provides a controlled volcabulary that helps bring the vocabulary of the indexer and searcher into coincidence. Fig. 11.1 shows a flowchart of the MEDLARS system, which emphasizes that documents and queries are encoded into MeSH terms.

11.1.2   MeSH

The effectiveness of a retrieval system is largely dependent upon the document classes in it. These classes are determined by the labels that we assign to them which in turn are determined by the classification structure or controlled vocabulary. A controlled vocabulary exists primarily to link semantically related terms; and to provide sufficient hierarchical structure to allow the conduct of generic searches (Lancaster, 1972).

For MEDLARS the classification structure is called the Medical Subject Headings. We are using MEDLARS in our learning experiments, in part, because:

(1) The Medical Subject Headings (MeSH) is one of the first and largest *classification structures*. MeSH has about 14,000 terms in an 8 level tree where nodes are biomedical terms and edges represent 'is-a' relationships.
(2) Millions of *documents* hand-encoded into MeSH are stored on the computer.
(3) Thousands of *queries* hand-encoded into MeSH arrive each day from users around the world.

MeSH consists of a set of heading arranged in a hierarchical tree structure. An article or query can be represented as dwelling at several headings (those corresponding to the indexing terms for the article or

Fig. 11.1 — Flow chart of MEDLARS system.

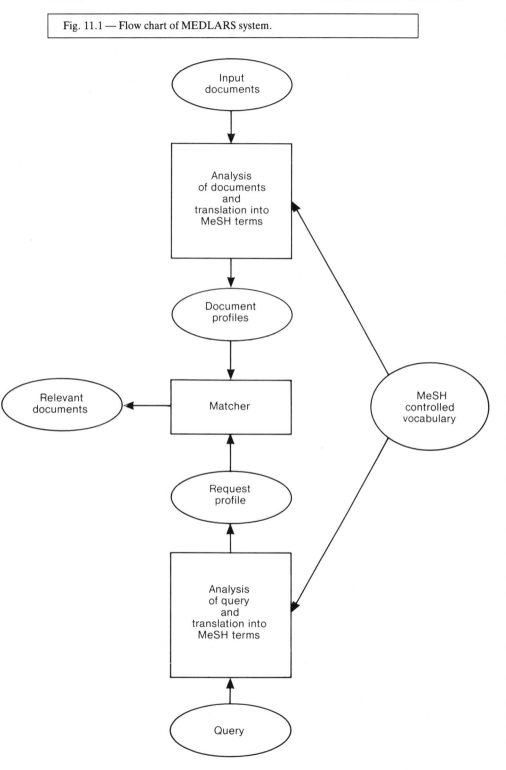

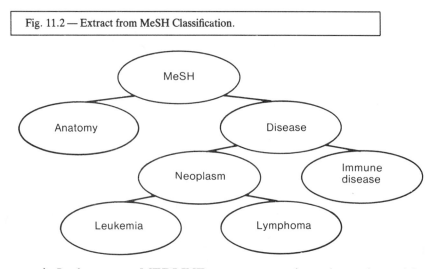

Fig. 11.2 — Extract from MeSH Classification.

query). In the present MEDLINE system, a search can be performed for articles containing a set of indexing terms satisfying the boolean combination of indexing terms in the query. Searching for an author or journal title, or doing a string matching are also practical (Humphrey, 1984). The experiments to be reported in this book are primarily concerned with searching by MeSH headings.

11.2   RELATIONSHIPS IN MeSH

11.2.1   Through queries

Even though the MeSH terms are organized in a tree structure, the retrieval system does not take as much advantage of this fact as it could. There is a special search function called EXPLODE which takes as its argument a heading from MeSH and generates a query that includes 'ored' together that heading and all its direct and indirect descendants. The system cannot, however, do finer operations automatically on the tree structure. For example, a user can not ask for all the articles indexed under arthritis and the direct descendants of arthritis. It is the responsibility of the librarian, who is generating the indexing terms for a query, to know that an article is indexed to the most specific terms possible. If a query is being made using a term that is above this most specific term in the MeSH tree structure, articles indexed with the more specific term will not be returned. When an experienced librarian is directing the search this representation scheme does not present a problem. However, if an inexperienced librarian uses the system (or, worse, a novice user generates a query on a copy of MEDLARS offered by a private information retrieval service), this problem can significantly affect the quality of a search.

MEDLARS maintains a record of all the queries that arrive in a given day. We took a random sample of queries of a certain form from this record. Only two types of queries were considered:

(1) one MeSH heading 'ored' with another MeSH heading
(2) one MeSH heading 'anded' with another MeSH heading.

The relationship that existed between MeSH terms used by queriers was studied. The hypothesis was that in 'anded' queries the distance between the MeSH terms would be large, where distance is the number of 'is-a' relationships connecting the two terms of the query. Conversely, terms from an 'ored' query would be close to each other in MeSH.

For 'ored' queries the two terms were always connected by a path that did not need to go through the root of MeSH (Smith, 1985). In fact, some of the 'ored' terms were synonyms and thus separated by no edges. One of the most frequently occurring separations was simply that between child and its parent. None of the 'ored' queries had terms that were separated by the root node of MeSH. All terms in 'ored' queries are within the same subtree of MeSH, (see Table 11.1). The 3 pairs of terms that were 4 or more edges

Table 11.1 — Distances between 'ORED' terms

	Connections	Number occurrences
Must go thru	root	0
Not thru	root	
	0 edges apart	3
	1 edge apart	3
	2 edges apart	1
	3 edges apart	0
	4 or more	3

apart in 'ored' queries were about chemicals; for example, one query was 'Glutamine D12.125.119.574 OR Acids D1.29'. Chemicals are part of a very deep subtree of MeSH.

For 'anded' queries the distribution shown in Table 11.2 obtained.

Table 11.2 — Distances between 'ANDED' terms

	Connections	Number occurrences
Must go thru	root	16
Not thru	root	
	0 edges apart	0
	1 edge apart	0
	2 edges apart	1
	3 edges apart	2
	4 edges apart	2
	5 or more	7

The majority of 'anded' queries that we examined were not in the same subtree of MeSH. One term might be in the disease subtree, while another term would be in the procedure subtree. The connection between 'anded' terms may have been very intimate in the searcher's mind but not along 'is-a' connections. Instead, 'anded' terms are more often connected by relationships such as 'treatment for' or 'cause of'.

If we assume that people believe that terms of 'ored' queries are similar along the lines of 'is-a' relationships, then these experiments suggest that MeSH is a good indicator of the relationships that people have in their mind. Likewise, assuming that terms in 'anded' queries are best connected by other than 'is-a' relationships, we again see our evidence as supporting the conclusion that MeSH has cognitively accurate, if limited information.

11.2.2 Through documents

One of the problems with MeSH is its inability to explicitly represent relationships between terms. To partially compensate for this shortcoming, subheading are used. According to the *Annotated MeSH* 'subheadings are used to subdivide MeSH headings in indexing and online searching (Medical Subject Headings Section, 1984). There are about 70 such subheadings. Definitions of two of them from the *Annotated MeSh* follow.

> Drug therapy:
> Used with disease headings for the treatment of the disease by the administration of drugs, chemicals, and antibiotics. For diet therapy and radiotherapy, use specific subheadings. Excludes immunotherapy and treatment with biologicals for which 'therapy' is used.
> Therapeutic use:
> Used with drugs, biological preparations, and physical agents for their use in the prophylaxis and treatment of disease; includes veterinary use.

The National Library of Medicine basically treats the subheadings as a refinement of a heading. Explicit connections between hadings are not made. Yet, as is obvious from the above definitions of the 'Drug Therapy' and 'Therapeutic Use', subheadings may imply relationships. A document is typically indexed in MEDLINE with about ten headings. If one of those headings is a disease whose drug therapy is discussed, then the odds are high that the drug used in therapy will also be indexed and qualified with the subheading of 'Therapeutic Use'. Thus one can deduce that the disease is treated by the drug. A careful study of the millions of indexed documents might reveal a wealth of knowledge about relationships in medicine.

In our surveys of the indexing of documents in MEDLARS it has seemed that the implicit relationships of the subheadings could often be safely made explicit. For instance, a search on 'arthritis, rheumatoid/drug therapy', naturally enough, produced articles where drugs used in the treatment of rheumatoid arthritis were mentioned. The following two sets of indexing terms represent two articles from a MEDLINE search on 'arthritis, rheuma-toid/drug therapy' and show that gold compounds and adrenal cortex hormones are used in the therapy of rheumatoid arthritis.

MeSH terms from Article 1:
  Arthritis, Rheumatoid/DIAGNOSIS/DRUG THERAPY
  Azathioprine/THERAPEUTIC USE
  Clinical Trials
  Comparative Study
  Gold Thioglucose/THERAPEUTIC USE
  Gold Thiomalate/THERAPEUTIC USE
  Human
  Joint/PATHOLOGY
  Penicillamine/THERAPEUTIC USE
  Statistics
  Support, U.S. Gov't, P.H.S.
MeSH terms from Article 2:
  Adrenal Cortex Hormones/THERAPEUTIC USE
  Adult
  Aged
  Arthritis, Rheumatoid/COMPLICATIONS/DRUG THERAPY
  English Abstract
  Female
  Human
  Middle Age
  Osteoporosis/CHEMICALLY INDUCED/ETIOLOGY

There is a wealth of information that could be semi-automatically gleaned from the existing body of index terms by paying attention to the grouping of those terms by document in MEDLARS.

The above should not suggest that subheadings invariably, readily suggest connections among MeSH terms. Relationships may be inferred between terms in an encoding that are actually non-existent in the article. This is demonstrated by the article with the title 'Rheumatoid Arthritis and Granulomatous Hepatitis: a New Association'. One MeSH encoding of this title is

  Arthritis, Rheumatoid/COMPLICATIONS
  Granuloma/COMPLICATIONS
  Hepatitis/COMPLICATIONS
  Liver/PATHOLOGY.

Just looking at the encoding one might infer that the article discusses granuloma in joints, since rheumatoid arthritis and joints are closely associated. But this document is about granulomas in the liver not the joints. Algorithms for making explicit links from the implicit subheadings would need to take advantage of a variety of information in order to be robust.

11.3 AMENDING MeSH

As literature evolves through time the classification structue needs to also evolve to reflect these changes in the literature. At NLM changes to MeSH are continually being studied and at yearly intervals new versions of MeSH are publsiehd. The procedure for this updating is not rigorously defined but is a combination of responding torequests from library patrons and of NLM initiated studies.

With the enormous proliferation of information retrieval systems the importance of coordination among different classification structures is apparent. We discuss here briefly two examples of manual efforts with MeSH to achieve this coordination. For the purposes of coordination, thesauri are sometimes placed along the spectrum from microthesaurus to macrothesaurus. A microthesaurus covers a smaller domain of literature but in greater detail than a macrothesaurus.

The Cancer Information Thesaurus (CIT) has been developed as a microthesaurus from MeSH (MeSH serving as the macrothesaurus) (Kirtland, 1981). Most of MeSH's hierarchical tress and more than one half of its vocabulary are retained. Terminology specific to cancer and not included in MeSH has been added to CIT.

Despite itssimilarity to MeSH, CIT differs in some ways. For instance, in CIT all descriptors relate to cancer; in MeSH their scope covers the whole health field. In making a map between MeSH and CIT, a faceted classification structure was designed that facilitated comparison of tems from each classification scheme. Nevertheless, the mapping process is at times difficult and somewhat arbitrary.

An exaple of taking two thesauri and making them more harmonious has occurred with MeSH and the *Diagnostic and Statistical Manual of Mental Diseases* (DSM) (Committee on Nomenclature & Statistics, 1952). In 1968 the American Psychiatric Association published a revised DSM. MeSH was then updated to reflect the many changes in the psychiatric terminology. When another revision of DSM was published in 1980. N. again revised MeSH (Calhoun, 1980). In selecting some new terms of MeSH, NLM took into account compatibility with DSM and also with the *International Classification of Diseases* (United States National Center for Health Statistics, 1980), but there has never been a clear algorithm for how this merging of classification structures is done at NLM. Instead, painstaking assessments are made and learned decisions are made.

11.4 EXERCISE

If you have to access to MEDLARS, generate several queries of 'anded' and 'ored' MeSH terms on MEDLARS. Use the 'neighbor' function MEDLARS to help you learn about MeSH terms. Find the distance in MeSH between terms in your query by using the 'tree' function in MEDLARS. Turn in report. (Time is 3 hours because of the difficulty of using a new computer system.)

11.5 REFERENCES

Bernstein, Lionel & Williamson, Robert (1984) Testing of a Natural Language Retrieval System for a Full Text Knowledge Base, *Jr American Soc Inform Sc*, **35**, 4, pp. 235–247.

Calhoun, Edith (1980) Mental Disorders in MeSH, *NLM Technical Bulletin*, **136**.

Committee on Nomenclature and Statistics, (1952) *Diagnostic and Statistical Manual of Mental Diseases*, American Psychiatric Association, Washington, DC.

Fidel, Raya (1984) Online Searching Styles: Case-Study-Based Model of Searching Behavior, *Jr American Soc Inform Sc*, **35**, 4, pp. 211–221.

Humphrey, Susanne (1984) Biomedical Computing Awareness via MEDLINE, *SIGBIO Newsletter*, **6**, 4, pp. 21–32, ACM.

Kirtland, Monika (1984) Macro and Microthesauri: Changes Occurring in MeSH–Derived Thesauri and a Solution to Some Related Search Handicaps, *Jr Amer Soc Inform Sc*, pp. 249–252, July.

Lancaster, F. W. (1980) *Vocabulary Control for Information Retrieval*, Information Resources Press, Washington, DC.

McCarn, D. B. (1980) MEDLINE: an Introduction to On-Line Searching, *Jr American Soc Inform Sc*, **31**, 3, pp. 181–192.

MEDLARS Management Section (1982) *Online Services Reference Manual*, National Library of Medicine, Bethesda, MD.

Medical Subject Headings Section (1984) *Medical Subject Headings, Annotated Alphabetical List*, 1985, National Library of Medicine, Bethesda, MD, Publication S84–223156.

Salton, Gerard & McGill, Michael (1983) *Introduction to Modern Information Retrieval*, McGraw-Hill, New York.

Smith, Cindy (1985) MEDLINE Queries and Distances in MeSH, *Internal Report*, National Library of Medicine.

United States National Center for Health Statistics (1980) *The International Classification of Diseases*, *9th Revision, Clinical Modification*, Health Care Financing Administration, Washington, DC. DHHS Publication PHS 80–1260.

12

Matcher

12.1 INTRODUCTION

We have developed algorithms that reference a hierarchical network and calculate the conceptual closeness between a document and a query. The network is MeSH. Documents and queries are each encoded as sets of MeSH terms. The practical goal of our work that is reported here is to:

(1) provide evidence that an algorithm can access MeSH and rank documents so as to simulate the rankings of people, and
(2) suggest ways to semi-automatically improve retrieval through MeSH.

In general, the focus of the research is on the systematic study of ways that a computer can use its knowledge so as to serve its users better.

The measure of success for our information retrieval system is how well it recalls the literature in response to a query and decide how relevant the article is to the query. The people who present the queries are familiar with the literature in the subject domains and also assess the relevance of each title retrieved. As we vary the methods of retrieving documents, we assess retrieval power by comparing the computer's ranking to that of the person's.

In traditional, keyword retrieval systems, the documents returned by the computer are compared to those people consider relevant. Both the people and the computer make binary (relevant or non-relevant) decisions. Recall and precision are calculated from this data. In word-frequency retrieval systems, such as SMART, the computer ranks n articles from 1 to n (Salton & McGill, 1983). A cutoff point is determined above which documents are considered relevant and below which documents are considered non-relevant; from this data recall and precision are calculated. In the experiments reported in this paper both the people and the algorithms rank n articles on a scale from 1 to n. Retrieval performance is considered good to the extent that the algorithms' rankings correlate with the people's rankings.

An important step in the representation of memory was Quillian's development of the 'semantic network' (Quillian, 1968). The basic notion is that knowledge is embodied in the nodes and edges of a graph. The relevance algorithm that is presented in this chapter takes advantage of earlier work in 'spreading activation' (Collins & Loftus, 1975). The terms from a document and from a query initiate broadcasts which go through a semantic net. The distances between the document and query correspond to the conceptual distance between the two. This chapter shows how the 'is-a' relationships are powerful in determining document–query closeness.

12.2 METHODOLOGY

12.2.1 The algorithms

Our algorithms say how close an article is to a query. For instance, if the article is classified as 'rheumatoid arthritis' (RA) and the query is classified as 'juvenile rheumatoid arthritis' (JRA), we expect that the article and query are close. On the other hand, if the article is about RA but the query asks for 'History of Medicine', we expect that the article is not particularly relevant to the query (see Fig. 12.1 for RA and History). Information about

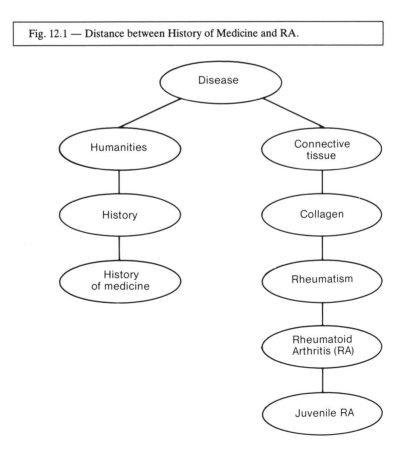

Fig. 12.1 — Distance between History of Medicine and RA.

this conceptual distance is available in MeSH. MeSH shows that JRA is an immediate descendant of RA, whereas History of Medicine is only very distantly related to RA. Our algorithms are designed to measure this distance between terms that characterize an article and a query.

The query is initially a well-formed expression of MeSH terms and logical operators *and, or,* and *not.* The expression is converted into minimal disjunctive normal form with the Quine–McCluskey algorithm (McCluskey, 1956). Each minterm (a conjunction of terms) in the disjunctive normal form is then treated as a separate query. Negated terms make a contribution to relevance or distance that is the opposite or negative of what an unnegated term would. The final value for a document–query pair is the best value over those values obtained from the minterms.

The query (a minterm with no negations) is represented in our equations as

$$Q = \{t_{Q,1}, \ldots, t_{Q,m}\}.$$

The document likewise is represented as

$$\text{Doc} = \{t_{Doc,1}, \ldots, t_{Doc,n}\}.$$

Given our representation of MeSH as a conceptual graph where edges are relationships, we define the distance between two terms as

$$d(t_i, t_j) = \text{minimal number of relationships between } t_i \text{ and } t_j.$$

We define unnormalized relevance as:

$$Relevun\ (\text{Doc,Q}) = \sum_{t_i \in Doc} \sum_{t_j \in Q} \frac{1}{1 + d(t_i, t_j)}$$

and normalize it as:

$$RELEVANCE\ (\text{Doc,Q}) = \frac{Relevun\ (\text{Doc,Q})}{\min\{m,n\} + \frac{1}{2}(m \times n - \min\{m,n\})}$$

The denominator in the normalized calculation gives the maximum possible unnormalized value (this formula was devised by Michael Dominiak) (Dominiak, 1984).

RELEVANCE represents our first attempt at an intuitively attractive assessment of document–query relevance. Our second equation DIS-TANCE for measuring the distance between a document and query satisfies several mathematical properties that the first equation RELEVANCE doesn't. DISTANCE is defined as follows:

$$DISTANCE\,(\text{Doc},\text{Q}) = \frac{1}{n\,m} \sum_{t_i \varepsilon Doc} \sum_{t_j \varepsilon Q} d(t_i, t_j)$$

$$= 0, \text{ if } Doc = Q.$$

12.2.2   Programs

Our computer programs were written in Franz Lisp on a VAX-780 running UNIX. We connect to the MEDLARS system for retrieving documents. We have stored MeSH in a frame-based language. An example of the output of the program is shown in Fig. 12.2.

12.3   DATA RETRIEVAL PROPERTIES

12.3.1   Observer reliability

Before comparing the performance of the relevance algorithm to people, we studied the performance of people. Twenty-two graduate students in computer science at George Washington University were given a query about 'computers and medicine' and 7 titles from MEDLARS about 'computers and medicine'. Each student was asked to rank the titles to the query at two different times separated by 24 hours. The average Spearman ρ correlation coefficient (Edwards, 1964) between two different rankings by the same person was 0.63. This suggests high intra-observer reliability; with less than 0.05 probability would such a difference occur by chance. A Kendall's concordance (Siegel, 1956) performed on the 22 first-time rankings of the students gave a value of 0.19. At the 0.05 confidence level we can reject the null hypothesis that the student ranks were independent; i.e., inter-observer reliability is high.

For the population of 6 titles and 10 queries about 'rheumatoid arthritis and knee prosthesis' rankings by two people were compared. To analyze the data we grouped articles with queries in a way that allowed the 60 article-query pairs to be treated as one population for a ranking. Then Spearman's correlation coefficient was used to compare two different rankings. The correction for tied ranks and t-test transformation were both employed. The null hypothesis that the 2 rankings are independent can be safely rejected. In other words, there was significant agreement among the 2 rankers.

Fig. 12.2 — Example output from matcher program.

(now doing article)article83231880(the article is:)

(AbstractingandIndexing EvaluationStudies MEDLARSMEDLINEInformationSystem SubjectHeadings UnitedStates)

(the query is:)
(AbstractingandIndexing)

(the list of paths from article to query is)

(setq answer
    ((AbstractingandIndexing)
    (EvaluationStudies MiscellaneousTechnicsNonMesh
                AnalyticalDiagnosticandTherapeuticNonMesh
                MeSHkb
                InformationScienceCommunicationNonMesh
                InformationScienceNonMesh
                Documentation
                AbstractingandIndexing)
    (MEDLARSMEDLINEInformationSystem OnlineSystems
                Computers
                InformationScienceNonMesh
                Documentation
                AbstractingandIndexing)
    (SubjectHeadings Documentation AbstractingandIndexing)
    (UnitedStates NorthAmerica
          America
          GeographicalsNonMesh
          GeographicalsZNonMesh
          MeSHkb
          InformationScienceCommunicationNonMesh
          InformationScienceNonMesh
          Documentation
          AbstractingandIndexing)))

(RELEVANCE is) 0.575

(DISTANCE is) 4.6

12.3.2   Basic agreement

For the 10 queries and 6 articles about 'rheumatoid arthritis and knee prosthesis' the average of the two people's rankings was compared to the computer's rankings. For both RELEVANCE and DISTANCE the agreement between the computer and the people was significant at the 0.05 level.

    To show that this ranking by the computer depended on more than the exact matches among terms of the query and document, the experiments were repeated but now with path lengths constrained. If only exact matches between terms in the query and document descriptions are used, then there is negative correlation between the people's and computer's rankings. If all paths between terms of length greater than 5 are excluded from consideration, the correlation between the people and the computer remains negative. To obtain a significant positive correlation, it seems necessary to keep track of long sequences of 'is-a' paths.

Two people also ranked 52 documents to the search 'Lipids and EBP'. Each document was represented by all the MeSH terms stored in MED-LINE for that document. The 52 documents were retrieved from MED-LINE by a search that included the children of lipids. The correlation between the rankings of the 2 people was significant at the 0.05 level. One person's ranking produced a t-test value of 3.07 when compared to the ranking of RELEVANCE. The other person's ranking gave a t-test of 1.77 when compared to RELEVANCE. Anything greater than 1.7 would occur by chance for these data-set sizes with a probability less than 0.05.

12.3.3 Recall and broadened searches

In order to further explore the ability of RELEVANCE or DISTANCE to improve both recall and precision, we embarked on a set of tests that are more reproducible than the earlier ones. In our new experiments we took queries directly as they came into MEDLARS from arbitrary users. Since we wanted to look at the ability of DISTANCE to find the best documents from a broadened search, we needed to use queries that could be broadened. In particular, we looked for queries that had two terms which were 'ANDED' together and for which, at least, one of the terms had children in MeSH. Arbitrarily selecting a day from early February 1985, we found the following four queries in the MEDLARS traffic files:

(1) Liver Diseases and Peritoneoscopy
(2) Biocompatible Materials and Dental Implantation
(3) Suicide and Substance Dependence
(4) Shock and Endorphins.

The children of a term X or a term Y in each query (X and Y) were found. All the documents were retrieved for the broadened query ((X or (children X)) and Y) or (X and (Y or (children Y))). Two members of our staff scored each retrieved document's MeSH terms against the original query X and Y. After documents were scored on the scale of 1 to 10 each set of documents was ranked. Also, the documents scored by the computer's DISTANCE algorithm were ranked.

Consider the universe of documents under consideration for any query to be all those retrieved by the broadened search. The set could be separated into those returned by search with both parents and those by search with a parent and the children of the other parent. Call the number of documents returned by the search with the parents alone NumParents.

The scores from $Person_1$, $Person_2$, and DISTANCE were analyzed. First, the t-test was run between $Person_1$ and $Person_2$, between $Person_1$ and DISTANCE, and between $Person_2$ and DISTANCE. Second, within the top NumParents of documents, the number of articles which came from the children and which came from the parents were compared.

To the query 'Liver Diseases and Peritoneoscopy' 41 documents were returned. The query '(children of Liver Diseases) and Peritoneoscopy' also returned 41 documents, but they were all different from the first 41. Between $Person_1$ and DISTANCE the t-test result was 6.78 which is significant at the 0.05 level. Between $Person_2$ and DISTANCE, it was 7.48 which is also significant. Between $Person_1$ and $Person_2$, the result was 6.21 which is still very significant. This means that the rankings between persons and computer, and between person and person were all correlated such that the probability of these ranks occurring by chance is less than 0.05.

In the query of 'Biocompatible Materials and Dental Implantation', there were 12 documents retrieved from the parents and 37 documents from the children ('Biocompatible Materials and children of Dental Implantation'); therefore there were 49 documents in total. The t-test results between $Person_1$ and $Person_2$, between $Person_1$ and DISTANCE, and between $Person_2$ and DISTANCE showed significant correlation. Once again, the t-test results showed a high corrrelation between persons and the computer and between person and person.

In the query of 'Suicide and Substance Dependence' and of 'Shock and Endorphins' all the correlations, namely, between $Person_1$ and $Person_2$, between $Person_1$ and DISTANCE, and between $Person_2$ and DISTANCE were significant.

For the universe of documents retrieved by the broadened search, both $Person_1$, $Person_2$, and DISTANCE assigned scores. From these scores were derived rankings which we have already determined were significantly correlated. In the top NumParents documents of the four queries, more than half came from the children. With more than half of top NumParents documents from the children, the question now becomes whether

(1) the people agree as to which documents from the children belong in the top NumParents, and
(2) the computer could via DISTANCE produce the top NumParents.

$Recall_1$ and $Recall_2$ were used to this end and are defined as follows:

Between $Judge_x$ and $Judge_y$:

$Recall_1$
   Within $Judge_x$'s top NumParents documents, the number of documents which came from the parents.
$Recall_2$

The number of common documents in $Judge_y$'s top NumParents documents and the top NumParents documents of $Judge_x$.

$Recall_1$ gives the recall measure which $Judge_x$ would have, if only the documents from the original search (without broadening) were retrieved. If

(1) the computer can determine the most relevant documents from a broadened search, and
(2) $Judge_x$ is a person and $Judge_y$ is DISTANCE,

then $Recall_2$ should be larger than $Recall_1$.

Since we consider people the gold standard and want our computer programs to achieve this standard, we first tested the ability of $Judge_{DISTANCE}$ to raise $Recall_2$ over $Recall_1$ when compared to $Judge_{Person\,1}$ or $Judge_{Person\,2}$. Over the 4 queries and against $Judge_{Person\,1}$, DISTANCE did significantly raise $Recall_2$. However, against $Judge_{Person\,2}$ DISTANCE produced an insignificantly larger $Recall_2$ than $Recall_1$. Accordingly, we next tested whether $Person_1$'s ($Person_2$'s) top NumParents documents would satisfy $Person_2$ ($Person_1$) more than just the return from the parent query. The statistical test shows that $Recall_2$ did improve significantly from $Person_1$ to $Person_2$ and from $Person_2$ to $Person_1$. Although with the broadened search, one could get better article retrieval, $Person_1$ and $Person_2$ help each other more than DISTANCE helps. This suggests that the computer could rank more effectively.

12.3.4   Further investigation
12.3.4.1   Another query
Why didn't DISTANCE help recall for $Person_2$? What parts of MeSH and/or DISTANCE could be changed so as to further improve recall? To investigate this phenomenon a query was submitted of 'studies of interactions between lipids and encephalitogenic basic proteins'. The translation of this query into MeSH produced 'lipids and encephalitogenic basic proteins', which we call Search I.

Query and search terms

Query: studies of interactions between lipids and encephalitogenic basic proteins.

Searches:
Search I : Lipids and Encephalitogenic Basic Proteins.
Search II: (children of lipids) and EBP.

Search I over MEDLARS retrieved 9 documents for the period 1/84–6/85. These documents are referred to as the parent documents, in keeping with the language of tree structures. The documents were ranked in order of relevance to the query by two computer algorithms and the research biochemist who initiated the search. The researcher and the algorithms used

the documents' MeSH headings obtained in the retrieval to interpret the
document contents. The closeness of the Document Terms and the Query
Terms was evaluated by Relevance and by Distance, and the documents
were ranked in order of closeness to the query. The researcher also ranked
the closeness of each document to Search I, by using the document MeSH
headings as the document descriptor. The results are presented in
Table 12.1 which compares computer rankings and researcher rankings of

Table 12.1

Article Number	Researcher Rank	Researcher Score	Relevance Rank	Distance Rank
1	9	C	6	5
2	8	C	9	9
3	3	A	1	1
4	6	B	8	8
5	1	A	3	3
6	2	A	5	4
7	4	B	7	6
8	7	C	2	7
9	5	B	4	2

documents retrieved for Search I and Query I.

One measure of the value of the rankings by the algorithms is the recall
they provide. The researcher may make a binary decision about articles
retrieved as being sufficiently relevant or not, where some decision about a
relevance threshhold is required. Thus,

$$Recall = \frac{|W \cap R|}{|W|}$$

where W is the number of articles at or above the relevance threshhold set by
the researcher; R is the number of articles retrieved by the algorithm; $W \cap R$
is the intersection of W and R; and $|W|$ is the cardinality of the set W.

If we require that documents be scored A to be relevant, then the
number of relevant articles available from the combined Searches I and II is
6. All documents returned by Search I constitute the retrieved set R. The
number of documents retrieved and relevant is 3. Therefore the recall for
Search I is

RECALL = 3/6.

and the precision, the number of documents retrieved and relevant divided
by the number of documents retrieved, is

PREC = 3/9.

12.3.4.2   Broadening the search

The search was broadened by including the children of the search terms, that is, the immediate descendants of the search terms in the subtree. The search term 'EBP' is a leaf in the MeSH tree and has no descendants. The search term 'Lipids' has 17 immediate descendants, which were linked by 'or's to form one term labelled 'children' for Search II. Search II terms consisted of 'children of Lipids' and EBP. 19 documents were returned by MEDLARS for Search II. These were scored and ranked by the research biochemist and by the algorithms, Relevance and Distance. The results are presented in Table 12.2.

Table 12.2 — Scores and ranks of documents returned by Search II

Article Number	Researcher Rank	Researcher Score	Relevance Rank	Distance Rank
10	5	B	10.5	6.5
11	2	A	14.5	18
12	13.5	D	4	5
13	8	C	8	9
14	12	D	1.5	4
15	19	E	14.5	11
16	2	A	7	2
17	11	D	14.5	14.5
18	5	B	14.5	13
19	10	C	17	17
20	13.5	D	1.5	1
21	2	A	10.5	12
22	9	C	9	10
23	15	D	18	19
24	17	D	5.5	8
25	5	B	3	6.5
26	17	D	5.5	3
27	7	B	14.5	16
28	17	D	14.5	14.5

The recall and precision for the collection of 9 top-ranked articles for Search II (children of lipids and EBP) are

$$RECALL = 1/6$$

$$PREC = 1/8$$

for both the Relevance and Distance algorithms. As would be expected, both recall and precision are less when children of lipids are substituted for lipids. It is more interesting to examine recall and precision for the broadened search (Search I and Search II combined) for two algorithms. With Relevance as the judge of the top 9 of the 28 documents:

RECALL = 3/6

PREC = 3/9

With Distance as the judge:

RECALL = 2/6

PREC = 2/9

Thus we see that Relevance leads to no better retrieval than the parent search alone would, and Distance actually worsens recall and precision in returning what it sees as the best of the broadened search.

12..3.4.3 Improved recall by eliminating anomalous edges

A significant number of MeSH terms occupy multiple nodes in the MeSH tree. For example, artificial insemination occupies a node both in the Miscellaneous Technics subtree, where its parent node is Reproduction Technics, and in the Genetics subtree, where its parent node is Breeding. In both cases the edge linking the node to its immediate predecessor is of the 'is-a' type. In cases where a choice of tree nodes is available for one or both terms in a query-document term pair, the pair of nodes which yields the shortest pathlength is selected by Relevance and Distance.

A problem, however, occurs in the MeSH terms assigned to a number of documents returned by Search II. The MeSH term 'Proteolipids' occurs both as a child of 'Lipids' and as a child of 'Proteins'. Yet, the relationship between 'Proteolipid' and its two possible parents is quite different (Fig. 12.3). Because proteolipids and encephalitogenic basic proteins are

Fig. 12.3 — Anomalous link between proteolipids and parents.

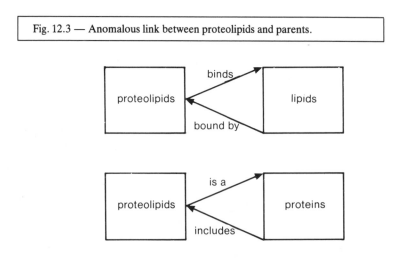

both important components of myelin membrane, the MeSH term proteoli-pids occurs commonly in the documents returned with the search term 'EBP'. Additionally, proteolipids is used as a search term in the broadened search as a child of lipids. One would expect that misranking of documents having the document term 'proteolipids' is likely to occur for this query because the shorter path of proteolipids to lipids will be selected by the algorithms, yet the evaluation of closeness of the document term proteoli-pids to the query terms by the researcher emphasizes that proteolipids is-a protein. The remedy to this situation may be to alter the evaluation of Relevance and Distance by allowing only the proteolipid node in the protein subtree to be used for the document term 'proteolipid'.

The effect of the document term 'proteolipids' was investigated by noting all documents assigned the MeSH term 'proteolipids' and excluding those articles from the retrieval. The top 9 articles when ranked by Relevance and Distance now contain, respectively, 3 and 4 documents scored A. Thus recall and precision are given by

$$RECALL = 3/6 \text{ for } Relevance \text{ and}$$
$$= 4/6 \text{ for } Distance$$

and

$$PREC = 3/9 \text{ for } Relevance \text{ and}$$
$$= 4/9 \text{ for } Distance.$$

Some improvement in recall and precision are observed for Distance when the appropriate 'proteolipids' node is used.

12.3.4.4   Retrieval using added query terms

Not all terms of the query 'studies of interactions between lipids and encephalitogenic basic proteins' are MeSH terms and therefore the use of the Search Terms (Lipids and EBP) as Query Terms may not be the most powerful set of query terms that could be used to produce the best recall for the English language query. The effectiveness of adding query terms to aid Relevance and Distance to retrieve documents close to the English query was investigated. The English query word 'interactions' is not equivalent to any MeSH term, but is closely related by a variety of types of relationships to a number of MeSH terms. A number of these terms were identfed by the researcher, and ones we tested are listed here.

Query Terms

Set 1: $Q_1 = \{q_{A,1}, q_{A,2}\} = \{\text{Lipids, EBP}\}$

Set 2: $Q_2 = \{q_{B,1}, q_{B,2}, q_{B,3}\}$
$\qquad = \{\text{Lipids, EBP, Analytical Diagnostic \& Therapeutic Techniques}\}$

Set 3: $Q_3 = \{\text{Lipids, EBP, Chemistry Analytical}\}$

Set 4: $Q_4 = \{\text{Lipids, EBP, Biological Sciences \& Occupations}\}$

Set 5: $Q_5 = \{\text{Lipids, EBP, Miscellaneous Technics}\}$

Set 6: $Q_6 = \{$Lipids, EBP, Physical Sciences$\}$
Set 7: $Q_7 = \{$Lipids, EBP, Biological Sciences & Occupations, Miscellaneous Techniques, Physical Sciences$\}$

The DISTANCE algorithm was applied to the documents retrieved for Searches I and II with each of the 7 queries just listed. Whereas recall is 2/6 for Q_1 and precision is 2/9 for Q_1, the average recall for queries 2 through 7 is 2.67/6 and the average precision is 2.67/9. We thus see a definite improvement secondary to the augmentation of the queries with terms consonant with what the queriest had in mind.

12.4   MATHEMATICAL AND COMPUTATIONAL PROPERTIES

12.4.1   A metric

DISTANCE (D) satisfies the properties of a metric. If X, Y, and Z are sets of MeSH terms, this means

(1) $D(X,X) = 0$, (zero property)
(2) $D(X,Y) = D(Y,X)$, (symmetry property) and
(3) $D(X,Y) + D(Y,Z) \geqslant D(X,Z)$ (triangle inequality property).

The proof of properties 1 and 2 follows almost immediately from the definition. The proof of 3 is more involved but basically rests on the fact that $d(x,y) + d(y,z) \geqslant d(x,z)$, where x, y, and z are single nodes in the graph. About 10 algebraic manipulations (each fairly simple in and of itself) is needed to demonstrate the triangle inequality.

The nice mathematical properties of DISTANCE as a metric continue into other types of mathematical properties. Under what conditions are two slightly different documents closer or further to a given query? If we add a certain node to document X, will that bring the augmented X closer to a certain query? If $Z = \{X$ union (some term t not in X)$\}$, then we can determine whether $D(Z,Y)$ is greater than, equal to, or less than $D(X,Y)$ by determining whether $D(t,Y)$ is greater than, equal to, or less than $D(X,Y)$, respectively. In other words, if the average distance between t and Y is greater than $D(X,Y)$, then $D(Z,Y)$ will be larger than $D(X,Y)$. If the (sum of the distances between t and all the terms in Y) divided (by the number of terms in Y) is equal to $D(X,Y)$, then $D(X,Y) = D(Z,Y)$. All these arguments, of course, hold equally well, when the term document is replaced by the term query. They only depend on X, Y, and Z being a set of nodes.

This issue of when one document is or is not closer to another document is part of the more general question of how can we expeditiously find those documents which are close to a query. If we

(1) replace a query X by one Y, such that the nodes of Y are neighbors of the nodes of X (call Y a broadened version of X),
(2) retrieve from a keyword system all those documents that include the terms of Y, and

(3) assess the relevance of the retrieval from Y along with the retrieval from X,

will we find substantial improvements in recall and precision. This question can not be answered in a purely mathematical way because the document set is only exhaustively understood. But we can do experiments to partially characterize the kind of documents we receive in response to queries X and Y. We generated three queries, X, Y, and Z, such that Y is a broadened version of X and Z is a broadened version of Y. All pathlengths for all paired query, article terms were tabulated. The function of pathlength frequency vs pathlength is described for the three searches in Table 12.3, where PL means

Table 12.3 — Frequency of pathlengths

PL	0	1	2	3	4	5	6	7	8	9	10	11	12	13	14	15	16
S1	7	0	0	0	0	0	3	15	2	3	8	2	0	0	0	0	0
S2	11	5	7	2	5	6	8	32	10	12	20	3	0	0	0	0	0
S3	7	1	6	0	3	9	9	24	14	12	14	5	0	0	0	0	0

PathLength and Si means Search i. For search I (lipids and EBP), peaks appear for pathlengths equal to 0, 7, and 10. For searches II (children of lipids and EBP) and III ((children of children of lipids) and EBP), the pathlength distribution also shows maxima at 0, 7, and 10. However, pathlengths in the range of 1 through 5 appear in searches II and III. This suggests that there are documents in the document space under consideration such that retrieval based on a broadened search might find documents closer to the original query than some of the documents returned to the original query itself.

12.4.2 Efficiency

People typically believe that the efficiency of a parallel computer ranges from 0 to 1. When the implicit computation that occurs in the message space is considered, however, a parallel computer is seen to have efficiency exceeding 1 on certain classes of problems. To appreciate this parallel power one must adopt an unconventional view of how processors communicate. The message space stores messages that are moving in time, and a single processor (or serial) machine must explicitly store these messages and calculate when they would reach various destinations. This and other factors permit an n-processor machine to compute in 1 time step more than a 1-processor machine can in n time steps.

Given a class of machines, a class of algorithms, and a class of problems how good are machine + algorithm on problem? The challenge of computer science is to characterize the constraints that allow a given machine–algorithm–problem triad to be useful. The accepted wisdom is that one processor should receive a message from only one other processor in one time step. Yet, examples abound in which nature defies this 'wisdom'. In a group of n physical particles, each is affected by the gravitational field of the other $n - 1$ particles at every instant. In principle, a network on n neurons may behave such that each neuron responds in each time step to the sum of messages from the other $n - 1$ neurons.

Traditionally, when all n processors of an n-processor machine are active, an optimal efficiency of 1 has been obtained. On the other hand, the definition of efficiency does not preclude that efficiency exceeds 1. The time for a 1-processor machine to solve a class C of problems is $T_1(C)$, and for a n-processor, is $T_n(C)$. The speedup $S_n(C)$ of an n-processor machine on C is defined as:

$$S_n(C) = \frac{T_1(C)}{T_n(C)}.$$

The efficiency $E_n(C)$ of a n-processor on C is defined as:

$$E_n(C) = \frac{S_n(C)}{n}.$$

We argue that efficiency can exceed 1. The message space can be viewed as a dynamic storage that performs implicit computations. Because of these computations n-processors can do in 1 time step more than 1 processor can do in n time steps. Of course, only certain classes of problems lend themselves to solution by a parallel algorithm that achieves great efficiency. Such problems are becoming more apparent as the technology for solving them becomes more available.

Some work in analog and stochastic computing (Neville & Mars, 1979) allows one processor to simultaneously integrate 2 or more incoming messages. Fahlman (Fahlman *et al.*, 1983) has described 3 kinds of communication networks in parallel machines: message-passers, mark-passers, and value-passers. Both the stochastic and value-passing networks have features in common with the network that we propose. Gottlieb and Schwartz (Gottlieb & Schwartz, 1982) stress that E_n is usually much less than 1. Wilkes (Wilkes, 1977), however, has shown that there exists a class C of problems and a machine such that $E_n(C)$ may be arbitrarily large. The efficiency described in this chapter depends on different features of a parallel computer than those discussed in other published work.

The decreasing cost of processors is stimulating the search for efficient uses of parallel computers. Work on very-large, textual databases is turning to parallel machines to deal with the need for reasonable response times (Ozkaharan, 1983). Researchers in artificial intelligence are developing parallel architectures such as those in the brain (Hinton & Anderson, 1981). 'Much of the progress in the fields constituting cognitive science has been based upon the use of explicit information processing models, almost exclusively patterned after conventional serial conputers. An extension of these ideas to massively parallel, connectionist models appears to offer a number of advantages' (Feldman & Ballard, 1982).

12.4.2.1   Architecture

The parallel machine NATURE (Rada, 1981) has cells each of which resembles a random-access, stored-program computer (Aho *et al.*, 1974). A single cell contains a central processor (CPU), memory, and an input–output processor (IOP) (Fig. 12.4). The CPU performs the traditional fetch and

Fig. 12.4 — Sketch of one cell.

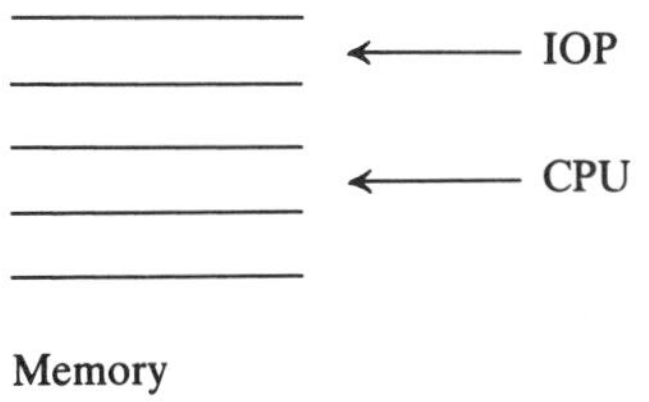

$$\begin{array}{c} \underline{\qquad\qquad} \\ \underline{\qquad\qquad} \end{array} \longleftarrow \text{IOP}$$

$$\begin{array}{c} \underline{\qquad\qquad} \\ \underline{\qquad\qquad} \end{array} \longleftarrow \text{CPU}$$

Memory

IOP and CPU might be viewed as having read–write heads on the memory.

execute cycle. The IOP at each time step broadcasts and receives a message. Our memory model says that for the IOP or CPU to reach a word of memory at address j in its own cell takes j time steps.

When there is more than one cell of NATURE those cells are distributed along a straight wire or other medium such that each two adjacent cells are the same distance D apart (Fig. 12.5). The communication protocols among

Fig. 12.5 — Line architecture of NATURE.

$$-x_{i-2}-x_{i-1}-x_i-x_{i+1}-x_{i+2}-$$

The cells x_i are located along a line and evenly spaced.

cells are synchronized. The time for a message to travel from $cell_x$ to $cell_y$ is directly proportial to the distance between $cell_x$ and $cell_y$.

12.4.2.2   Proof of benefit

The computation of DISTANCE could benefit from the availability of parallel architectures. To simplify analysis we will constrain the problem in the following ways:

(1) The graph of terms in the 'knowledge base' is a line with each pair of adjacent terms separated by the same distance.
(2) The number of terms in the query and document is of the same order as the number of terms in the 'knowledge base' (kb). The kb has n terms.
(3) For both the single and multi-cell cases the algorithms to implement DISTANCE are in the machine but no particular kb, document, or query is. Each term of the kb, document, and query is represented by log n alphabetic characters. The input for DISTANCE is 3 lists: one contains the terms of the kb in an order which corresponds to the conceptual distance between each pair of terms. Document and query are each presented in an arbitrary order. Each word in the memory of a cell of NATURE has $O(\log n)$ bits.

12.4.2.2.1   Single processor

For the serial approach to DISTANCE the kb has to be placed into memory at a cost of, at least, $1 + 2 + \ldots + n = O(n^2)$ time steps. Each term's location in memory corresponds to its position in the kb. In the best serial algorithm for DISTANCE Document and Query are sorted according to their *location* in the kb. The algorithm DISTANCE is separated into a 'right' and 'left' part (Fig. 12.6). Once the distance between one Query term $t_{Q,i}$

Fig. 12.6 — Fast serial algorithm.

Main routine
(0) Preprocessing — including sorting of kb.
(1) Determine the distance between $t_{Query,1}$ and all terms in the Document that are to the right of $t_{Query,1}$ in the kb. Store the sum of these distances in $s_{Query,1}$, and store the number of Document terms to the right of $t_{Query,1}$ in $Dright_{Query,1}$.
(2) For $j = 2$ to n/c_Q create a sum for all the distances between $t_{Query,j}$ and the Document terms to the right of $t_{Query,j}$ in the kb.
(3) Repeat 1 and 2 with right everywhere replaced by left.

Subroutine
To do the inner part of step 2 for 'right' (done similarly for 'left'):
(i) Locate the Document terms between $t_{Query,j-1}$ and $t_{Query,j}$ in the kb. Say there are k such terms. Subtract the distances between $t_{Query,j-1}$ and these Document terms from $s_{Query,j-1}$ and store in $s_{Query,j}$.
(ii) Multiply the distance between $t_{Query,j-1}$ and $t_{Query,j}$ by $Dright_{Query,j} - k$. Subtract this product from $s_{Query,j}$.

The basics of an $O(n^2 \log n)$ algorithm for DISTANCE
on a serial machine.

and all the Document terms to its right in the kb has been determined, that result can be used in the calculation of the distance between $t_{Q,i+1}$ and the

Document terms to its right. (A similar argument holds for the 'left' part). The number d_i of Document terms whose *location* lies between the *locations* of $t_{Q,i-1}$ and $t_{Q,i}$ satisfies the equation:

$$\sum_{i=2}^{O(n)} d_i = O(n).$$

After the preprocessing, the cost of this version of a serial DISTANCE is $O(n^2)$. However, the preprocessing has a cost of $O(n^2 \log n)$.

Without sorting, an algorithm cannot solve DISTANCE in $O(n^2 \log n)$ time. Examination of operation on the non-sorted input shows the high cost of finding needed information. The lower-bound on sorting time is well-established. Thus $T_1(\text{DISTANCE})$ equals $O(n^2 \log n)$.

12.4.2.2.2   *Multiple processor*

Given n terms in the kb, our multiprocessor approach to DISTANCE will use n processors or cells. Each cell corresponds to a term in the kb. The cell with which a term is associated testifies to the geometrical position of that term in the kb. Each cell is separated from its neighbor by a distance that is equal to the time that it takes ($\log n$) bits to pass from the one cell to the other.

The terms of kb are fed into $NATURE_n$ from the leftmost processor (LP). LP broadcasts a message that identifies a term. Each term takes one time step for LP to emit and it reaches the cell for which it is destined within $O(n)$ time steps. The terms of Document and Query are also fed into $NATURE_n$ from LP. The cell corresponding to a Document or Query term that is being transmitted will take note of that term and subsequently be an actor (Filman & Friedman, 1984) (as in object-oriented programming) for that term. This priming of $NATURE_n$ involves the sending of messages for each of the $O(n)$ terms. Although each message may take $O(n)$ time to reach its destination, LP does not have to wait till a message has reached the other end of $NATURE_n$ before it begins another broadcast. The time to prime $NATURE_n$ is just $O(n)$.

After the system is primed, each cell in $NATURE_n$ with a Query term broadcasts a value to its right — this is synchronized so that the broadcasts all start at the same time. This value is the same for each broadcasting cell and could be simply a sigle pulse. Each cell in $NATURE_n$ with a Document term is tuned to receive this pulse. $NATURE_n$ is designed so that a signal travels the distance between two adjacent cells in one time step. Since all cells begin the broadcast phase at the same time, each receiving cell x knows how far a pulse has travelled before it reaches x. As a pulse is received, x determines the time since the pulse originated its travel, and x then adds the corresponding distance to its tally of distances.

Within n time steps each Document cell has received the sum of all Query term contributions to the left of the Document cell. Next the program process except that they now broadcast to the left. This right and left directional broadcasting prevents undesirable interference. After enough time has passed for each Document cell to receive whatever signals are destined for it, the summation of values in each Document cell has finished. The time consumed thus far is only $O(n)$.

The Document cells need to get their final values to the LP cell in order that DISTANCE can be computed. The Document cells essentially reverse the process by which they were sent information from LP. Each Document cell sends a message that conveys the value of the summed signals that Document cell had received. The message fits in $O(\log n)$ bits, and each document cell originates its message at the same time. Within $O(n)$ time LP has received each value and created the sum. The computation of DISTANCE on $NATURE_n$ takes $O(n)$ time.

12.4.2.3   *Discussion of efficiency*

The advance of intelligent information retrieval systems is dependent on advances in hardware. A host of reasons ranging from

(1) the parallel nature of the brain, to
(2) the computational constraints imposed by the speed of light on a single-processor architecture.

dictate the emergence of distributed or parallel computing as one of the cornerstones of future computing. Unfortunately, we as people have an almost insurmountable legacy of serial thinking and have great difficulty to conceive of parallel algorithms for most problems that we currently consider interesting. A key advantage to DISTANCE is that it lends itself to implementation on a truly parallel machine. Not only does DISTANCE do well by conventional standards on a new, parallel architecture, but it is able to solve its problem with greater efficiency on a parallel machine than most people have believed is possible.

$NATURE_n$ is a computer architecture with n simultaneously interacting processors and a dynamic message space. This departure from traditional architectures allows efficiency to exceed n^2 on certain problems. There are definitions such that efficiency can never exceed 1, but this author argues that implicit processing in the message space can provide efficiencies far greater than 1. We have seen that

$$S_n(\text{DISTANCE}) \ = \ \frac{O(n^2 \log n)}{O(n)} \ = \ O(n \log n)$$

and

$$E_n(\text{DISTANCE}) \ = \ \frac{O(n \log n)}{n} \ = \ O(\log n).$$

$NATURE_n$ takes substantial advantage of the geometric characteristics of DISTANCE and obtains an efficiency of $O(\log n)$.

12.5   EPILOGUE

We argue that the MeSH knowledge-base can be advantageously utilized by the computer so as to produce better retrieval. We have developed relatively simple computer algorithms (RELEVANCE and DISTANCE) to quantitatively assess the conceptual distance between documents and queries. We initially applied these algorithms to MeSH with the expectation that their ranking of documents would compare poorly to those of people. However, the algorithms perform surprisingly well. The extent to which the performance of RELEVANCE (or DISTANCE) + MeSH simulates the performance of people depends on the meaningfulness of the 'isa' relations in MeSH.

Our principle interest in RELEVANCE and DISTANCE is to evaluate the cognitive realism of a knowledge base like MeSH, as we explore new ways to build bigger and better knowledge bases. Along the way we have discovered how powerful for certain purposes, such as comparing the content of a document to that of a query, MeSH can be. Our algorithms are readily applied to the results of a MEDLARS query and can help a user know which documents are worth obtaining in their entirety. We have also investigated automatically broadening a search to include the children of the query terms. The resultant documents often prove to be more relevant to the original query than many of those documents returned to the original query.

12.6   EXERCISES

Exercise 1

Do a query of MEDLARS, rank documents, apply DISTANCE (by hand or via computer), and compare the rank implied by DISTANCE with your own rank. (Time 2 hours.)

Exercise 2

Devise a DISTANCE algorithm that treats *isa* links directionally. Say that x *isa* y means that x is a narrower term than y. Then y is a broader term than x, i.e., y $(isa)^{-1} x$. In your family tree the number of relationships separating you and your greatgreatgrandparent is the same as the number separating you and your cousin. Yet, psychologically it might be true that your sense of distance to your greatgreatgrandparent is different from that to your cousin. The distance to your greatgreatgrandparent goes over 4 *isa* links or is isa^4, while the distance to your cousin is $isa^2 (isa^{-1})^2$. The significance of *isa* and isa^{-1} depends on the hierarchy of terms with which you are dealing. Investigate mathematical and/or data-retrieval properties of your modified DISTANCE. Is it still a metric? Does it lead to better or worse recall than the original DISTANCE? (Time is 3 hours.)

Two students answered this question in particularly provocative ways. Joseph Maline said: 'Intuitively, it seems that as long as you preserve one of the relationships *isa* or *isa* $^{-1}$ and do not mix the relationships, the distance relationship is linear. The problem is to capture this relationship mathematically not just intuitively. For a first pass at this, I propose the following formula for pathlength

$$[(1 + |isa|)|isa|] + [(1 + |isa|)|isa^{-1}|]$$

Hafedh Mili said: 'Given an $\alpha \neq 0$ a direct isa link is assigned the weight 1-α. A reverse isa link (or isa^{-1}) is assigned the weight $1 + \alpha$. Paths with more isa links would be preferred to paths with more isa^{-1} links (assuming the two paths have the same length). The shortest path between two terms (t_i and t_j) in the knowledge base can be written as

$$dnew(t_i, t_j) = p(1 - \alpha) + q(1 + \alpha),$$

where p is the number of isa edges and q is the number of isa^{-1} edges. In general,

$$dnew(t_i, t_j) \neq dnew(t_j, t_i).$$

Thus here we have an asymmetric measure (which, of curse, cannot be a metric). Define DISTANCEnewdoc as

$$\text{DISTANCE}newdoc\ (\text{Doc,Q}) = \frac{1}{nm} \sum_{t_i \in Doc} \sum_{t_j \in Q} dnew(t_i, t_j)$$

For 2 documents D_1 and D_2 that were equally ranked by DISTANCE, how will they be ranked by DISTANCEnewdoc? For $\alpha > 0$, if on the average the terms of D_1 are higher in the hierarchy than those of D_2, it is very likely that D_1 will be ranked better than D_2. In other words, the document that has the broader scope would be preferred. If we reverse the order of Document and Query in the measure to give

$$\text{DISTANCE}newq\ (\text{Q,Doc}) = \frac{1}{nm} \sum_{t_j \in Q} \sum_{t_i \in Doc} dnew(t_j, t_i)$$

then with the same 2 documents as in the preceding case, D_2 will be better ranked by DISTANCEnewq. If α is negative the behavior of these computations will be reversed. Each user could set her own choice of α depending on whether she preferred broader or narrow documents.

12.7 REFERENCES

Aho, A., Hopcroft, J. & Ullman, J. (1974) *The Design and Analysis of Computer Algorithms*, Addison-Wesley, Reading, MA.
Collins, A. M. & Loftus, E. F. (1975) A Spreading Activation Theory of

Semantic Processing, *Psychological Review,* **82**, pp. 407–428.

Dominiak, Michael (1984) Weight Refinement for Information Retrieval, unpublished, Department of Computer Science, George Washington University.

Edwards, Allen (1964) *Statistical Methods for the Behavioral Sciences,* Holt, Rinehart and Winston, New York.

Fahlman, S., Hinton, G. & Sejnowski, T. (1983) Massively Parallel Architectures for AI: NETL, THISTLE, and Boltzmann Machines, *Proc. Amer. Assoc. Artif. Intelligence,* pp. 109–113.

Feldman, J. & Ballard, D. (1982) Connectionist Models and their Properties, *Cognitive Science,* **6**, pp. 205–254.

Filman, Robert & Friedman, Daniel (1984) *Coordinated Computing: Tools and Techniques for Distributed Software,* McGraw-Hill, New York.

Gottlieb, A. & Schwartz, J. (1982) Networks and Algorithms for Very-Large Scale Parallel Computation, *Computer* **15**, 1, pp. 27–36.

Hinton, G. & Anderson, J. (1981) *Parallel Models of Associative Memory,* Erlbaum, Hillsdale, New Jersey.

McCluskey, E. J. (1956) Minimization of Boolean Functions, *Bell System Tech. J.,* **35**, 6, pp. 1417–1444.

Neville, R. & Mars, P. (1979) Hardware Design for a Hierarchical Structure Stochastic Learning Automaton, *Jr. Cybernetics and Inform. Sc.,* **2**, 1, pp. 30–35.

Ozkaharan, E. A. (1983) Desirable Functionalities of Database Architectures, *Proc. of IFIP World Congress.*

Quillian, M. R. (1968) Semantic Memory, in *Semantic Information Processing,* Minsky, M. (ed.) MIT Press, Cambridge, MA.

Rada, Roy (1981) Evolution and Gradualness, *BioSystems,* **14**, pp. 211–218.

Salton, Gerard & McGill, Michael (1983) *Introduction to Modern Information Retrieval,* McGraw-Hill, New York.

Siegel, Sidney (1956) *Nonparametric Statistics,* McGraw-Hill, New York.

Wilkes, M. V. (1977) Beyond Today's Computers, *Information Processing,* **77,** North Holland, Amsterdam, pp. 1–5.

13

Adding an Edge

In this chapter we explore three strategies for automatically augmenting a knowledge base (kb). In the first effort the frequency of word co-occurrences in documents is used as a guide to the construction of a hierarchy of terms. In the second method two existing kbs are automatically compared and relationship from one that are mising in the other lead to the construction of a new kb. In the third method we try to discover new knowledge by reasoning analogically between two fields of scientific knowledge.

13.1 STATISTICALLY BUILDING A CLASSIFICATION STRUCTURE

13.1.1 Introduction

Knowledge representation is a central issue in Information Retrieval (IR) systems. Knowledge bases (kbs) may be referenced by algorithms that measure the distance between a document and a query. Tests have been performed on a manually built knowledge base (kb) and a kb automatically constructed using frequencies of words. We hypothesized that the statistically constructed kb would participate in poorer document retrieval than the manually constructed kb. Surprisingly, retrieval based on the kb built automatically from word-frequency data was no poorer than the retrieval based on a hand-crafted kb.

For IR systems, the knowledge base is often a preconstructed structure, containing controlled vocabulary. These knowledge bases are built by human subject experts. The first experiment deals with this kind of knowledge base: given a set of terms (basically index terms), we tried to relate these terms by placing them in a graph. In the graph nodes represent index terms and edges reflect the hierarchical relations among the terms. For the second experiment, the knowledge base was built in a systematic way, involving no semantic analysis, only available data about frequencies of words in the document set. Some heuristic rules were used to relate words to each other.

13.1.2   Method

In our first experiments we built knowledge bases manually. The document set consists of the titles of the following fifteen articles. We used a rather elementary strategy to choose the index terms: removal of prepositions and some stem generation (removal of suffixes and grouping of similar word forms). To drive the construction of the kb we first chose a set of documents. Our kbs were intended to reflect the information in these documents. In response to a query for all documents about computers and information services from the June 1985 file of MEDLINE 15 documents were returned (see Fig. 13.1).

Fig. 13.1 — 15 titles used in first experiment

1 TI — The pharmacy computer system at the New England Medical Center.
2 TI — Role of medical cybernetics in the improvements of diagnosis, prognosis and choice of treatment method in pulmonological patients.
3 TI — Computer applications in radiation therapy treatment planning.
4 TI — System for widespread application of microcomputers to vascular surgery.
5 TI — Development of a computerized vascular registry for large-scale use.
6 TI — Microcomputer-based programs for the practicing vascular surgeon.
7 TI — Basic information for microcomputer data base management.
8 TI — Modular algorithm for tardive dyskinesia diagnosis (MALTD): a demonstration of a methodological concept for diagnostic decision making.
9 TI — The use of MUMPS in a departmental computerized clinical data system.
10 TI — A computerized diagnostic system for comparing alternative classification schemes of depression.
11 TI — A computerized record and verify system for radiation treatments.
12 TI — A computer-assisted monitoring system for arrhythmia detection in a medical intensive care unit.
13 TI — On the optimum selection of diagnostic tests in computer-aided differential diagnosis.
14 TI — A computerized database–management system for curriculum analysis.
15 TI — Use of a viewdata system to collect data from a multicentre clinical trial in anaesthesia.

To manually build the kb we first chose key terms from the titles. The 45 key terms thus obtained were next organized into a heirarchical classification structure (or kb). If term x was positioned as a parent of term y in the hierarchy, that meant that y was an instance of x. Building the knowledge base was difficult, mainly due to the small number (45) of nodes in the knowledge base. These nodes wee sparsely distributed over the large field of 'computers and medicine'. Nodes which would have been placed at different hierarchical levels in the tree had there been more terms were placed at the same level since there were no other terms to separate them from their parent in the tree.

In our second experiment we automatically generated a knowledge base from the frequency of word co-occurrences. The same fifteen documents of the first experiment were used in the second experiment. However, while in experiment one only titles were used, in experiment two the entire compu- terized record of a document as stored on the MEDLARS (National Library of Medicine, 1984) system was studied. On MEDLARS a document is stored as a record of several fields including title, abstract, author name, date of publication, and country of publication.

An algorithm was used to extract terms from the document space for the second experiment. This algorithm is similar to one in Salton (Salton & McGill, 1983):

(1) Identify all the unique words in the document set.
(2) Remove all common function words included in a stop list.
(3) Remove all suffixes and combine identical word forms (stems).
(4) Group low frequency words in thesaurus classes.
(5) Give a range of frequencies for words to be considered for indexing. All the words that are within the range are index terms.
(6) Take high frequency words — whose frequencies of occurrences exceed the high threshold — and compute for each pair the number of times both terms occur in the same document, that is the frequency of co- occurrence of both terms. If the frequency is below the low threshold, the pair is not considered. Otherwise, the pair is 'retainable' for indexing. Compute, for the retainable pairs, the 'cohesion'. The co- hesion of a pair of terms (t_i, t_j) is the quantity:

$$\text{COHESION } (t_i, t_j) = \frac{\text{frequency of co-occurence of } t_i \,\&\, t_j}{\sqrt{(\text{frequency of } t_i \times \text{frequncy of } t_j)}}$$

Retain as index terms those pairs whose cohesion is above a certain threshold.

The algorithm for statistically constructing the kb relies on the following assumptions:

(1) High frequency words have broad meaning, while low frequency words have narrower meanings. With this assumption we will position the different words at the different levels (depths) of the tree.
(2) Give a word W_k of medium frequency and a word W_j of high frequency. If W_k has a density function over the document set of the same shape as the one of W_j, then the two words have similar meanings but W_j is more specific than W_k. W_k is then a descendant of W_j.

We group key terms into several classes by giving ranges of frequencies. Let $F_1 > F_2 > \ldots > F_k$ be the different thresholds. Terms of group 1 will be a level 1 in the knowledge base (children of the root which is level 0). Similarly, terms of group i will be children of the terms of level i-1, and so on to level k where the terms are leaves (see Table 13.1).

The exact method for determining parent–child relationship follows.

Table 13.1 — Frequency of terms by group

Group	Range	Terms
1	$F_1 +$	$Term_1^1, \ldots, Term_{n_1}^1$
2	$F_2 - F_1 - 1$	$Term_1^2, \ldots, Term_{n2}^2$
...	...—...	....
...	...—...	....
k	$F_k - F_{k-1} - 1$	$Term_1^k, \ldots, Term_{n_k}^k$

(1) For a term $Term_{k_0}^i$ of level i, compute the number of co-occurrences of this term with all the terms $Term_i^{i-1}$ of level i-1.

(2) If $Term_{k_0}^i$ appears most with $Term_0^{i-1}$, then it is a child of $Term_0^{i-1}$. Two special cases may occur:

(2.1) More than one term of level i-1 satisfies the condition:

$$occcur\ (Terms_{k_0}^i, Term_{l_0}^{i-1}) \geq occur\ (Term_{k_0}^i, Term_i^{i-1})$$

In this case, we allow $Term_{k_0}^i$ to have as many parents as there are l_0 satisfying the above condition.

(2.2) All the terms of level i have been assigned parents and a term $Term_{m_0}^{i-1}$ of level i-1 is left without a child. In order to keep all the leaves at level k we 'propagate' this node by a 'dummy node' $Term_{n_i+1}^i$. $Term_{n_i+1}^i$ has the same 'meaning' as $Term_{m_0}^{i-1}$. If $Term_{n_i+1}^i$ is assigned a child from level $i+1$, we have saved a 'meaningful' relation in the knowledge base. Otherwise, continue the process of propagating dummy nodes.

13.1.3 Results

To evaluate both the manually and statistically build kbs we applied our DISTANCE function to a query and the 15 aforementioned documents. We did this both with the manual and with the statistically build kbs. The ranking produced by DISTANCE was then compared to the ranking that people had considered appropriate. If DISTANCE on kb_1 better simulated people's decision than DISTANCE on kb_2, we would conclude that kb_1 was better than kb_2.

The manual knowledge base was tested for the query 'I want all documents about computerized data base systems in health care'. The query was encoded as 'COMPUT DATA-BASE SYSTEM'. Comparison of the people's and DISTANCE's ranking gave a correlation coefficient of 0.41.

For the word frequency experiment the initial number of words was 920. The frequencies ranged from 1 to 45. We chose a low threshold of 8 and a high threshold of 28. After suffix stripping and the grouping of low-frequency words into thesaurus classes, the frequencies ranged from 1 to 65. To obtain phrases, we grouped words whose frequencies were above 28. The thresholds were chosen such that a reasonable number of nodes would be obtained at each level of the kb. A graphical representation of the statistically built kb is given in Fig. 13.2.

The query 'I want all documents about computerized database systems inhealth care' was encoded as 'COMPUT DATA-SYSTEM MEDIC'. The correlation between the computer and manual ranking again produced a correlation coefficient of 0.41.

To further test the utility of the statistically built kb, two more specific queries were studied. QUERY2 is 'Use of Computers in Vascular Surgery', encoded as 'COMPUT VASCULAR SURG'. Hand ranking versus machine ranking lead to a correlation coefficient of 0.67. QUERY2 is 'Use of Computers for Diagnosis and Treatment', encoded as 'COMPUT DIAGNOS TREAT'. Hand ranking versus machine ranking led to a correlation coefficient of 0.69.

13.1.4   Discussion

We have addressed the role of word co-occurrences as a guide to knowledge-base building. The test of the knowledge has been its ability to help indicate the conceptual distance between documents and queries. Regarding the query 'computerized database systems in health care', the manual and frequency based methods yield the same Spearman correlation coefficient (0.41). The probability that two uncorrelated rankings give a correlation coefficient of 0.41 is slightly greater than 5%. That the correlation was not closer may be due to the nature of the query. The query used for this test is close to the query that retrieved the initial set of data. QUERY2 and QUERY3 were intended to be more precise, thus to differentiate better the articles from the query. As expected, the algorithm seems to perform better on these two queries. Being aware of the bias of the experimental conditions — small data set and a number of empirical decisions — the present results are obviously insufficient to definitively assess the effectiveness or non-effectiveness of the frequency-based knowledge construction algorithm.

Does the statistically derived knowledge base indicate terms and relationships that people generally accept as important? Examination of the statistically produced kb reveals a number of meaningful 'is-a' links (Brachman, 1983). For instance, record 'is-a' data-system 'is-a' system. On the other hand, the link between microcomputer and vascular is not the same kind as that between record and data system. The current word co-occurrence

Fig. 13.2 — First 6 levels of knowledge-base developed from frequencies of co-occurrence.

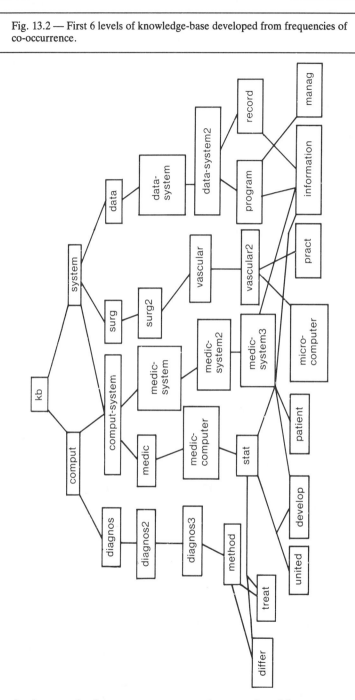

method says whether or not two words are related but not exactly how. These results suggest that natural language processing techniques might be used with the frequency method to help isolate the types of relationships which should be emphasized in the kb. Also, we are contemplating experiments in which parts of various manually designed kbs (such as MeSH and the ACM classification scheme) are merged and used in document retrieval. Guidance for these merging operations might be most profitably derived from a kb that was produced with frequency information about the particular document space at hand.

Does the statistically-derived knowledge-base rank documents to a query in the same way that a person would rank the documents? Would the method work on larger document spaces and more queries? We were surprised that the frequency-derived heirarchy of terms allowed our ranking algorithm to simulate people's ranking. Yet, it should work even better with larger samples because the statistical methods depend on substantial data sets. Many researchers have used word frequencies to classify documents and queries as weighted vectors. Then distances between vectors are calculated and indicate relevance. Clustering of documents and terms has been investigated on the way to building hierarchies of documents and terms, but no one has, to our knowledge, tried the combination of hierarchy construction and distance evaluations that are described here.

13.2   BETWEEN TWO KNOWLEDGE BASE

Attempts to automatically refine knowledge-based systems must rely on delicate relationships between structure and function. Changes to the structure or representation of the system are intended to produce beneficial improvements in the function or reasoning of the system. To capture the regularity in the problem space the generate and test mechanisms of the problem solver must capture substantial information about the problem. In the library problem one knowledge base kb_1 was augmented with structure from another knowledge base kb_2. These augmentations to kb_1 have necessitated a redesign of the knowledge representation and reasoning scheme so that the structure–function relationships of the amended kb_1 could incorporate those of kb_2. The information retrieval work illustrates how the reliance on structural information to the exclusion of functional information can lead to errors. In particular, when a knowledge base of 'is-a' relations has 'agent–object' relations added to it, then the means of processing relations must also be amended.

13.2.1   Sources of new edges

Another 'knowledge base' *Current Medical Information and Terminology* (Finkel *et al.*, 1981) (CMIT) has been used because it expresses some relationships that MeSH doesn't. CMIT is organized as a series of records with the following format:

CMIT Major Heading (Disease Name)
CMIT Minor Heading (Label of a devision of disease descriptors)
    Information (Listing of disease descriptors)

The range of CMIT Major Headings is the set of all major diseases as selected by the American Medical Association. The CMIT Minor Headings include etiology, symptoms, pathological findings, and prognosis.

We have worked in the domain of rheumatoid arthritis for our first experiments because a number of computerized data bases and knowledge bases cover rheumatoid arthritis (Kingsland *et al.*, 1983). Rather than asking experts what constitute important relationships in rheumatoid arthritis, we thought that we could extract that information automatically from already codified and computer-stored information. For instance, we refer to the structure of the massive, rheumatology database (not the data itself) developed by the American Rheumatism Association and called ARAMIS (Hess, 1976). A part of the ARAMIS structure that was used in our experiments is shown in Fig. 13.3:

Fig. 13.3 — ARAMIS database structure.

```
JRA
  Surgical therapy
    Synovectomy (specify joint)
    Reconstructive surgery without prosthesis (specify joint)
    Reconstructive surgery with prosthesis (specify joint)
    Other surgery
```

Because CMIT is partially text (greatly abbreviated, but still text), we MeSH-encode the information in CMIT before doing knowledge-acquisition experiments. For instance, the CMIT phrase 'relationship to immune phenomena' is MeSH classified as 'immunology'. A search is performed on CMIT's major headings for the MeSH terms produced from the MeSH encoding of an article or query. When a match occurs between a MeSH term of an article or query and a CMIT major heading, a search for MeSH terms under the CMIT information section that match MeSH terms generated by the encoding of the query or article is begun. If a match is found, a relationship is added to MeSH. Given

(1) an article title of 'Granulomatous Inflammation in Rheumatoid Joints' that encodes to 'Granuloma; Rheumatoid Arthritis/pathology', and
(2) a CMIT entry of

> Rheumatoid Arthritis
>   Pathological Findings
>   Granuloma.

an edge is added to MeSH between Rheumatoid Arthritis/pathology and Granuloma.

Fig. 13.4 — The effect of augmenting MeSH on RELEVANCE.

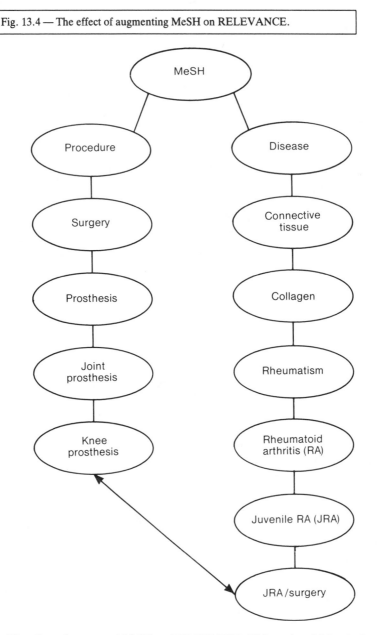

The effect of augmented MeSH on RELEVANCE. Without the additional edge,
RELEVANCE$(Q_5, A_2) = (1 + 1/12)/(1 + 1/2)$.

13.2.2   Results with Augmented MeSH

With an earlier set of articles, our algorithm for reasoning by analogy from
CMIT and MeSH inserted the following 3 edges into MeSH: RA/pathology
← → granuloma, RA/diagonosis ← → edema, and RA/pathology ← →
synovial-membrane. The information in ARAMIS allowed the following

edges to be added to MeSH: RA/surgery $\leftarrow \rightarrow$ knee-prosthesis, RA/surgery $\leftarrow \rightarrow$ hip-prosthesis, JRA/surgery $\leftarrow \rightarrow$ knee-prostesis, and JRA/surgery $\leftarrow \rightarrow$ hip-prosthesis.

To our surprise these additional edges did not improve retrieval. We compared the rankings produced by RELEVANCE on augmented-MeSH to the lumped rankings of the two people (see Tables 13.2 and 13.3). We

Table 13.2 — Lumped rankings by P_1 and P_2

Queries 1–10 versus Articles 1–5

	Q_1	Q_2	Q_3	Q_4	Q_5	Q_6	Q_7	Q_8	Q_9	Q_{10}
A_1	1	1	2	1	3.5	4	3.75	3.5	3.75	2
A_2	2.5	2	3	2	4.5	5	4.25	4	4.25	1
A_3	4	3	1.5	3.75	1.5	2.75	2	2.75	3.5	
A_4	5	5	5	5	4	1	1	3	1	5
A_5	2.5	4	3.5	3.25	1.5	3	3.25	1.5	3.25	3.5

Table 13.3 — Rankings by RELEVANCE on augmented MeSH

Queries 1–10 versus Articles 1–5

	Q_1	Q_2	Q_3	Q_4	Q_5	Q_6	Q_7	Q_8	Q_9	Q_{10}
A_1	1.5	1.5	1.5	1.5	1.5	2.5	2	2.5	1	2
A_2	1.5	1.5	1.5	1.5	1.5	2.5	2	2.5	2	1
A_3	4	4	3	4	4	5	5	5	4	4
A_4	5	5	5	5	5	1	2	1	5	5
A_5	3	3	4	3	3	4	4	4	3	3

could not show at the 0.05 level of confidence that the two rankings were correlated. If we examine the worst case, namely Q_5 where the Spearman correlation coefficient went from .88 when MeSH + RELEVANCE was compared to people to $-.13$ when augmented-MeSH + RELEVANCE was compared to people, we see why the extra edges hurt (see Table 13.4).

Table 13.4 — Spearman ρ

Queries 1–10 versus Articles 1–5

	Q_1	Q_2	Q_3	Q_4	Q_5	Q_6	Q_7	Q_8	Q_9	Q_{10}	ave
P_1 vs P_2	.90	1.0	.70	.98	.60	1.0	.75	.50	.75	.90	.81
MeSH vs Lumped	.75	.58	.75	.97	.88	.83	.81	.56	$-.11$	.96	.70
Aug vs Lumped	.68	.88	.75	.97	$-.13$	.08	.36	.14	$-.42$	.96	.43

'ave' means average of ρ for Q_1 through Q_{10}
'Aug' means augmented MeSH

The extra edge connecting knee-prosthesis and JRA/surg causes relev(Q_5, A_2) to rise above relev(Q_5, A_3) because of the increased closeness between knee-prosthesis and JRA/surg. This ranking is, however, not consistent with how people rank. In these tests the edges added to MeSH did not help retrieval.

13.2.3 Neo-RELEVANCE on augmented-MeSH

Our representation of MeSH creates special nodes for the qualifiers that MeSH calls subheadings. These special nodes always contain both a term and a qualifier separated by a slash (term/qualifer). When edges were added to MeSH by referring to CMIT or ARAMIS, those new edges had to connect a term1/qualifier1 node (which was already connected to the term1 node) to a term2 node. The augmenter algorithm created ternary relationships like JRA–JRA/surg–knee–prosthesis.

RELEVANCE treated these special term1–term1/qualifier1–term2 relationships no differently than it would handle the more general 'is-a' relationships such as JRA–RA. The 'is-a' relationships are transitive: the fact that JRA 'is-a' RA 'is-a' arthritis also means that JRA 'is-a' arthritis. A path that goes through a term/qualifier node is not following 'is-a' relationships and can *not* generally be assumed to satisfy transitivity.

Accordingly, we revised RELEVANCE to take advantage of some of the different kinds of relationships that exist in augmented MeSH. This new RELEVANCE or neo-RELEVANCE can only follow a term1/qualifier1 link to term2 when the query which is being processed contains qualifier1. For example, a query = {RA/surg} can follow the path from RA/surg to kee-prosthesis in augmented MeSH, but a query = {knee-prosthesis} can not go from knee-prosthesis to RA/surg.

The application of neo-RELEVANCE to augmented-MeSH produced good rankings (see Table 13.5). The Kendall's concordance between these

Table 13.5 — Rankings by neo-RELEVANCE on augmented MeSH

	Queries 1–10 versus Articles 1–5									
	Q_1	Q_2	Q_3	Q_4	Q_5	Q_6	Q_7	Q_8	Q_9	Q_{10}
A_1	1.5	1.5	1.5	1.5	3.5	3.5	3.5	4	1	2
A_2	1.5	1.5	1.5	1.5	3.5	5	5	4	2	1
A_3	4	4	3	4	2	3.5	3.5	4	4	4
A_4	5	5	5	5	5	1	1	1	5	5
A_5	3	3	4	3	1	2	2	2	3	3

new rankings and the lumped-people was 0.83, which shows significant correlation at better than the 0.05 confidence level (see Table 13.6).

We are not, however, able to show substantial improvement over RELEVANCE on MeSH-alone, in part, because RELEVANCE on MeSH-alone gave rankings which alrady well-simulated people.

Table 13.6 — Kendall's concordance and significance at 0.05 level. Summary of data analysis

	Kendall's Concordance	Significant
P_1 vs P_2	0.89	yes
MeSH vs Lumped	0.81	yes
Aug MeSH vs Lumped	0.66	no
Neo vs Lumped	0.83	yes

For an explanation of the entries please see text and other tables.

Study of the one query on which all the computer rankings did poorly does reveal the need for additional edges to be added to MeSH. RELEVANCE performs well on all the queries except Q_9. Q_9 asks for articles about 'treatment of infectious complications of total knee arthroplasty'. Our indexer encodes this query into MeSH as 'knee-prosthesis and (surgical-wound-infection/drug-therapy or surgical-wound-infection/prevent&control or surgical-wound-infection/surgery)', P_1 and P_2 think that A_4 most closely matches Q_9. RELEVANCE says A_3 is closer to Q_9 than A_4. The explanation for the discrepancy in the computer rankings on Q_9 and the human ranking rests on a missing edge in augmented-MeSH. A_4 is classified as 'knee-prosthesis/adverse-effects and surgical-wound-infection', but there is no edge between these two nodes which are, however, clearly related nodes. A_3 is classified as 'follow-up-studies and knee-prosthesis'. The minimal distance in MeSH between 'knee-prosthesis/adverse-effects' and 'surgical-wound-infection' is 8 edges. Seven edges separate 'knee-prosthesis' and 'follow-up-studies'. If an edge were placed between 'knee-prosthesis/adverse-effects' and 'surgical-wound-infection', then Q_9 would be, appropriately, closer to A_4 than to A_3.

13.2.4 Discussion
Our initial experiments in edge augmentation did not support the hypothesis that the extra edges would improve retrieval. We were dealing at the wrong level of granularity when we added simple edges to MeSH. In terms of gradualness, the small change in structure which a single edge constitutes does not correspond to a small change in the meaning of the knowledge base. Manipulation of the larger structural unit of labelled edges gives more gradualness to the search space.

13.3 HOW SCIENTISTS ADD EDGES

13.3.1 Hypothesis generation
The history of the gene shows us the important role of hypothesis generation based on identity and part–whole relations. Studies of the genetic literature provide valuable pointers to the representation and reasoning mechanisms that scientists use. Computers now offer the opportunity to further make explicit and explore in greater detail strategies for the addition of relationships to a kb. We have taken representations of the gene and chromosome as given in Darden and Maull (Darden & Maull, 1977). Although this rep-

resentation leaves many assumptions implicit, it serves as a useful starting point. We placed the gene and chromosome concepts into a frame system and manipulated them with a computer program that embodied our first approximation of the identity-driven hypothesis-generator or edge-adder. The program was able to correctly change one property of the chromosome based on recognizing the matching property in the gene. However, the same program also incorrectly concludes that the chromosome and gene are equal in 'number'.

The property of number is connected to the part–whole relation which needs to be incorporated into the discovery process. Our second program specifies conditions under which the part–whole relation should be postulated and actions to be taken. This program can determine that genes that are part of the same chromosome are linked to each other in inheritance. We are elaborating the reasoning algorithm and the representation of the concepts on which it works so that we better understand the conditions under which a given reasoning and representation pair work well together.

13.3.2 Particular concepts and rules

We initially elaborated the following chromosome and gene concepts, which were meant to represent what scientists knew about these concepts in the early 20th century. The concepts are represented as LISP association structures (Winston & Horn, 1984).

Chromosome concept

```
(setq chromosome '((problem heredity)
    (prop1 pure)
    (prop2 pairs – maternal + paternal)
    (prop3 maternal + paternal – pairs – not – mixed)
    (prop4 half – in – gametes)
    (prop5 number: few)))
```

Gene concept

```
(setq gene '((problem heredity)
    (prop1 pure)
    (prop2 pairs – maternal + paternal)
    (prop3 maternal + paternal – pairs – mixed)
    (prop4 half – in – gametes)
    (prop5 number: many)
    (prop6 independent – assortment)))
```

Simultaneously, we developed a rule for part–whole. For part–whole hypothesizing between two concepts x and y that are defined like the gene and chromosome above we can readily use a rule with preconditions and actions.

Rule for part–whole

Preconditions:
(1) Concept y has $number_y$ and concept x has $number_x$, where $number_x < number_y$.
(2) x and y have the majority of their properties in common.
Actions:
Conclude x is a part of y.

When we applied the part–whole rule to the gene and chromosome concepts, the rule correctly concluded that genes are part of chromosomes. Yet, we readily recognize that there are many concepts on which this part–whole rule incorrectly operates. Accordingly, we launched a refinement of both the concepts and the rule.

Beginning of second version of chromosome concept
(setq chromosome
 '((problem: heredity)
 (field: cytology)
 (location: nucleus of cell)
 (individuality: retained
   time: cell cycles
   space: cell nucleus)
 (relation to other chromosomes: pairs)
      .

      .

      .

Beginning of second version of gene concept
(setq gene
 '((problem: heredity)
 (field: genetics)
 (location: in gametes and elsewhere)
 (individuality: retained
   time: through generations
   space: somewhere in organism)
 (relation to other genes: pairs)
      .

      .

      .

Our first rule for part–whole worked because of its harmony with our first representation. Our second rule operates on more primitive properties, namely, time and space, than we have been able to adequately incorporate into our representation of the chromosome and gene.

Second version of part–whole rule
Preconditions:
(1) y is in place1 and x is in place1.
(2) y is at $t1$ and x is at $t1$
(3) y has $number_y$ and x has $number_x$, where $number_y < number_x$.
Actions:
Conclude some xs are part of one y.

The conceptual units of our first chromosome and gene are not primitive enough, but those of our second rule are too primitive. We are modifying the representation of the chromosome and gene and of the part–whole rule, so that they fit together and are robust.

If we can detect that two frames or concepts participate in a relationship like part–whole, we can then add that information or edge to our knowledge base. In this work on hypothesis generation for the development of the theory of the gene we are focusing on two kinds of relationships, namely, identity and part–whole. These relationships are far from comprehensive, but they are important. A precise understanding of how to use them so as to augment a knowledge base would be a step towards a more complete theory of knowledge acquisition.

13.4 EXERCISE

Find a situation where the ability of DISTANCE to simulate human ranking of documents is suboptimal. Then investigate changes to the classification structure on which DISTANCE operates and changes to DISTANCE itself such that the performance of DISTANCE is closer to optimal. For instance, you could find a query on MEDLARS that returned documents such that the documents you judged most relevant hardly agreed with those considered most relevant by DISTANCE. Then you might add new edges to MeSH and modify DISTANCE and rerun your recall tests. (Time is 3 hours.)

13.5 REFERENCES

Brachman, Ronald (1983) What IS-A Is and Isn't: An Analysis of Taxonomic Links in Semantic Networks. *Computer* **16**, 10, pp. 30–36.

Darden, Lindley & Maull, Nancy (1977) Interfield Theories, *Philosophy of Science*, **44**, pp. 43–64.

Finkel, A., Gordon, B., Baker, M. & Fanta, C. (1981) *Current Medical Information and Technology*, American Medical Association, Chicago.

Hess, Evelyn (1976) A Uniform Database for Rheumatic Diseases, *Arthritis and Rheumatism*, **19**, 3, pp. 645–648.

Kingsland, L., Lindberg, D. & Sharp, G. (1983) AI/RHEUM: A Consultation System for Rheumatology, *Jr Medical Systems*, **7**, 3, pp. 221–227.

National Library of Medicine, (1984) *Programs and Services, Fiscal Year 1983*, US Government Printing Office, Bethesda, MD.

Salton, Gerald & McGill, Michael (1983) *Introduction to Modern Information Retrieval*, McGraw-Hill, New York.

Winston, Patrick, & Horn, Berthold (1984) *LISP*, Addison-Wesley, Reading, MA.

14

Indexer and additional terms

Our 'Indexer and Additional Terms' project has two main aspects: (1) the augmentation of MeSH via a learning algorithm, and (2) the evaluation of the augmented knowledge base. Work with 'Matcher and Additional Edges' showed that adding helpful *non-isa* edges was no easy matter. Adding new terms that are connected by *isa* relationships seems more straightforward. There are many classification structures that depend on *isa* relationships which have significantly different coverage of the terminology in a domain. For instance, in biomedicine there is a 40,000+ term classification structure for patient records called the Systematized Nomenclature of Medicine (SNOMED) (Cote, 1979). Many of the terms of SNOMED could be readily added to MeSH. We have also examined the Computing Reviews Classification Structure (CRCS) (Association of Computing Machinery, 1984).

While our first objective in these indexing experiments was to test strategies for adding subtrees of SNOMED to MeSH, the need for a good reasoning or indexing algorithm became a major concern. The last sections of this chapter address the indexing problem. One section looks at morpho-semantic analysis as an aid to indexing, and the other, at grammatical parsing.

14.1 AUGMENTATION

14.1.1 SNOMED classification structure

SNOMED was developed by the College of American Pathologists as a systematic nomenclature for use in hospital records (Cote, 1979). Much as MeSH terms are used to describe documents, SNOMED terms are used to describe patients. SNOMED contains approximately 50,000 terms divided into 6 major categories: Topography, Morphology, Etiology, Function, Disease, and Procedure. Ideally, a physician can completely describe any patient by choosing one or more terms from each of the 6 categories. *Topography* terms describe what part of the patient is affected by the disease. *Morphology* terms describe what the disease looks like on both the gross and histological levels. *Etiology* terms describe the cause of the disease, if it is known. *Function* terms describe how the disease affects the patient's normal physiology. *Disease* terms describe the name given to the patient's particular constellation of signs and symptoms. *Procedure* terms describe what is being done to treat the disease.

True to the pathologists that developed it, SNOMED is an extremely detailed classification structure. For example, the Topography category contains two terms for most of the paired structures of the body, one term designating the left structure and one term designating the right structure. Where MeSH has about 10 terms dealing with blood group antigens and antibodies, SNOMED has 150 terms for the major and minor blood groups.

SNOMED terms are grouped into a rough hierarchical tree structure, but this structure is much less explicit than it is in MeSH. Given the way SNOMED was designed to be used, it was not essential to have clear hierarchical organization beyond that of the 6 major categories. Despite its loose organization, SNOMED has been used as a knowledge base for the automatic indexing of pathology reports (Dunham *et al.*, 1978).

14.1.2 Augmentation algorithm

Suppose knowledge base A (kb A) can be represented as a tree structure with nodes $\{A_1, A_2, \ldots, A_n\}$. Suppose we would like to augment knowledge base A with knowledge base B (kb B), which has nodes $\{B_1, B_2, \ldots, B_n\}$ (see Fig. 14.1). A simple augmentation would be to identify any subtrees in kb B whose root corresponds to a node in kb A. (This could be as simple as finding any nodes in kb B that are also in kb A.) The augmentation of kb A would then be accomplished by mapping the entire subtree identified from kb B into the node identified in kb A. For example, if A_5 and B_4 represented the same concept, the above augmentation scheme would result in the tree of Fig. 14.2. In the present project, kb A is MeSH and kb B is SNOMED. Having defined an aumentation algorithm, SNOMED was analyzed for subtrees that could be automatically identified and augmented into the MeSH classification structure.

One clear instance of a potentially useful parent–child relationship was found in SNOMED. Many SNOMED terms are followed by the modifier 'NOS', which means 'Not Otherwise Specified'. Usually, such a term (the parent) is immediately followed by more specific variants of the term (the term's children), as in the following excerpt from SNOMED:

    E–2710 Rickettsia, NOS
    E–2711 Rickettsia prowazekii
    E–2712 Rickettsia typhi
    E–2713 Rickettsia rickettsii
    E–2714 Rickettsia siberica

Fig. 14.1 — Two tree-structured knowledge bases.

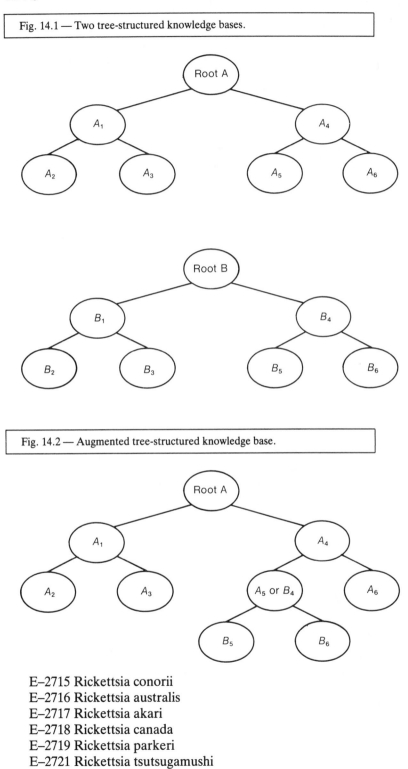

Fig. 14.2 — Augmented tree-structured knowledge base.

E–2715 Rickettsia conorii
E–2716 Rickettsia australis
E–2717 Rickettsia akari
E–2718 Rickettsia canada
E–2719 Rickettsia parkeri
E–2721 Rickettsia tsutsugamushi

Here, Rickettsi is the parent and the various species of Rickettsia are the children. The corresponding entry in MeSH for Rickettsia is less comprehensive:

B03.700.651.801.733	Rickettsia
B03.700.651.801.733.501	Rickettsia prowazekii
B03.700.651.801.733.601	Rickettsia rickettsii
B03.700.651.801.733.701	Rickettsia tsutsugamushi
B03.700.651.801.733.801	Rickettsia typhi

By the augmentation algorithm, any child of a SNOMED parent should also be a child of a MeSH parent if the same parent appears in both classification structures. From the Rickettsia example, we start with the two trees of Fig. 14.3 and Fig. 14.4.

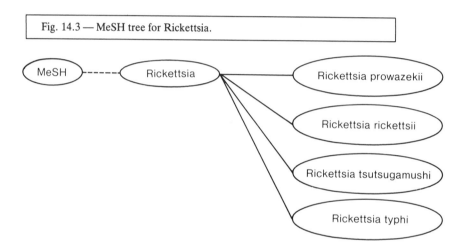

Fig. 14.3 — MeSH tree for Rickettsia.

Applying the augmentation algorithm, MeSH would be given new children from SNOMED as in Fig. 14.5. An advantage of this simple augmentation scheme is that it is readily automated. SNOMED children eligible for augmentation into MeSH are flagged by the NOS modifier of the parent terms. The augmentation scheme is to add these parent–child relationships to the MeSH tree when the parent exactly matches a MeSH term and the child does not already exist in MeSH. In the above case, 6 of the 10 children of Rickettsia, NOS were added to MeSH.

14.2 INDEXING AND AUGMENTING

14.2.1 Improved indexer

Say for the purposes of this exposition that we have as input a noun phrase and want to assign a single code number or key term to it (Rada & Evans, 1979). In the exhaustive table approach to indexing, a table contains every problem statement encountered in actual practice and its matching code number. Each time a problem statement is presented to the automatic coder

Fig. 14.4 — SNOMED tree for Rickettsia.

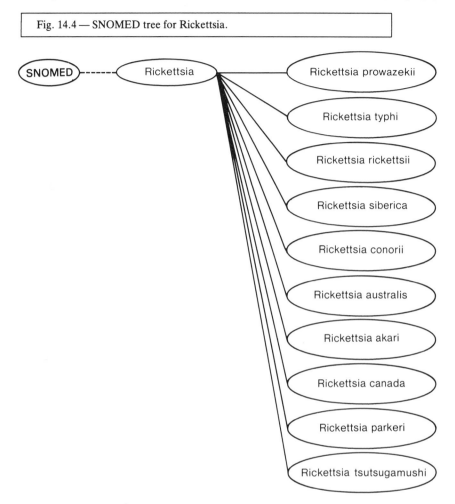

it is matched against the statements already incorporated into the table. If an identical entry is not found in the table, the automatic coder will reject the new statement, which must then be manually coded. A study of a sample of noun phrases revealed that a truly exhaustive table would be very large (Greenwood, 1972).

As coding schemes need less and less space for the storage of tables, thesauri, or dictionaries, their coding algorithms require ever increasing complexity, and significant costs can be incurred in algorithm development as well as in table preparation. Modern coding systems use morphologic, syntactic, and semantic analyses to classify medical language (Dunham *et al.*, 1978) Restricting themselves to obstetric and gynecologic noun phrases, researchers have developed a coder that requires only 24K bytes of memory for the program and a glossary of 690 entries. Developing the glossary, however, involved a lengthy consideration of some 200,000 items from hospital data and medical dictionaries (White, 1977).

A modified table look-up procedure has been developed by Howell and

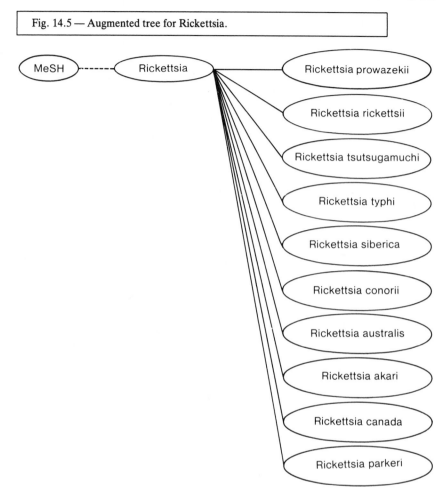

Fig. 14.5 — Augmented tree for Rickettsia.

Loy (Howell & Loy, 1968). It utilizes a table that stores each word occurring in a noun phrase along with the code numbers that have been assigned to the noun phrase of which the word is a part. Each word in the table points to all the codes(s) applicable to it. To code a problem statement, a computerized encoder separates the statement into words, references the table, notes the codes to which the words are pointing, and chooses the codes to which every word of the statement points. For example, let the code for 'chronic otitis' be 102 and for 'otitis' be 101. Since chronic points to 102 and otitis to both 101 and 102, the correct code for choronic otitis is 102 (see diagram).

chronic	102
otitis	101, 102

When every word in a statement points to the same code (word order is irrelevant), that code is the correct one for the statement.

KODIAC (Greenwood, 1972) is an adaptation of Howell and Loy's scheme. Since more than one code may have a pointer from each word in the statement being coded, in the KODIAC table a final digit is added to each code to indicate how many words should be in a statement receiving that code. Returning to our previous example, code 102 is followed by the digit 2 for the two words in chronic otitis, while code 101 for otitis is followed by the digit 1, as shown in the diagram.

chronic	102/2
otitis	101/1, 102/2

When asked to code otitis, the computerized program, after obtaining both 101/1 and 102/2, compares the number of words in the statement to the final digit in the code (called the code marker), and selects 101 to code otitis on the basis of the code marker 1.

14.2.1 Illustrative experiment

We have done a few experiments on the indexing and term augmentation project. Our hypothesis has been:

> The addition of subtrees from other classification structures to MeSH can improve the function of MeSH as a tool in indexing.

The method of the preliminary experiments is

(1) Form dictionary of words in classification structure; each word pointing to all the terms from which it came.
(2) Break the title into words and match to terms via the dictionary.
(3) MeSH merged with SNOMED and CRCS.
(4) Return to 1.

An example of how augmentation could help indexing follows. Assume we are looking at the term 'Diagnosis, Computer Assisted' and that our dictionary looks as follows:

Dictionary
Assisted L1, E0, . . .
Computer L1, . . .
Diagnosis L1, . . .

For a title of *Computer Diagnosis of Depression* the indexer would conclude that L1 occurs most often.

Now suppose that MeSH is merged with part of CRCS such that 'Expert Systems' points to 'Diagnosis, Computer Assisted'.

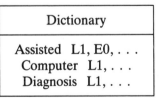

The dictionary is now augmented to include:

Dictionary
Assisted L1, E0, . . . Computer L1, . . . Diagnosis L1, . . . Expert L1, . . . Systems L1, . . .

Now the title *State of Expert System CADIAG* is correctly indexed under L1, whereas prior to the augmentation this indexing would have been missed.

14.2.3   Experimental results

Due to its modular design, the System for Augmenting and Indexing (SAI), is not limited to manipulating MeSH and SNOMED. Any hierarchical-knowledge base can be used for the augmentation, provided a pre-processing program can be written to select the subtrees for the subsequent augmentation. Given these subtrees, the SAI can complete the experiment.

In building the required dictionaries, SAI processed MeSH and SNOMED in their entirety. The unaugmented MeSH dictionary contained entries for 11,977 words; the SNOMED-augmented MeSH dictionary had 12,951 entries. (The actual number of words in each dictionary fluctuated slightly for each experiment.) From MEDLARS, 247 titles from the recent medical literature were chosen randomly. The titles were not constrained to any particular topic.

For each title, INDEXER (the indexing part of SAI) printed the MeSH terms assigned to the article by NLM indexers (set A) and the MeSH terms assigned by INDEXER (set B) according to the indexing algorithm explained previously. INDEXER also printed the number of agreements with the NLM staff indexers, i.e., how many terms are in the intersection of sets A and B. A term that is in both sets A and B is called a 'hit'. The average hit percentage (AHP) is calculated as the number of hits divided by the number of terms assigned by INDEXER (set B). Set B is used in the divisor instead of set A, since set A can contain terms not deducible from just the title. To summarize.

A = {terms assigned by NLM}

B = {terms assigned by INDEXER}

Hits = A ∩ B

AHP = |A ∩ B| ÷ |B|

where '∩' is the symbol for set intersection and '$|x|$' denotes the cardinality (number of terms) of set x.

Four experiments were performed with the INDEXER system; the results are summarized in Table 14.1. Each experiment used the same 247 randomly chosen titles. The third column of the table is the total number of MeSH terms used by NLM indexers to represent the 247 titles. The fourth column is the total number of MeSH terms INDEXER proposed, employing its indexing algorithm. The other coloumns should be self-explanatory.

Table 14.1

Experimental results.

Experiment	Knowledge base	Total NLM terms	Total INDEXER terms	Total hits	AHP
1	Unaugmented	1929	—	—	~5%
2	Unaugmented	1929	1373	284	21%
3	Unaugmented	1929	665	273	41%
	Augmented	1929	616	259	42%
4	Unaugmented	1929	524	255	49%
	Augmented	1929	493	239	48%

Experiment 1

Using the indexing algorithm as stated above, INDEXER performed rather poorly. The AHP was approximately 5%. Analysis of the results at this stage revealed several problems with the indexing algorithm:

● By decomposing each title into words, INDEXER matched words completely out of their context in the title. This was especially a problem when no MeSH terms matched more than one word in the title. Such one-word matches were frequently the 'best' match INDEXER could find. In such one-word matches, a fairly non-specific word like 'chemical' caused a match to every MeSH term that happened to have the word 'chemical'. In the initial experiment, some of the titles were assigned hundreds of MeSH terms by INDEXER.

● INDEXER was biased against short MeSH terms: single-word MeSH terms would not match if two or more words from any other MeSH term occurred in the title. For example, if given the title, 'OXIDATION OF NAD DIMERS BY HORSERADISH PEROXIDASE', INDEXER would match the MeSH term 'HORSERADISH PEROXIDASE' (a two-word match) but not 'NAD' (only a one-word match) even though 'NAD' is a correct term.

● Relatively meaningless stopwords like 'the', 'and', 'or', etc. often misled INDEXER into ridiculous assignments.

● Simple suffixes prevented some obvious matches. For example, the word 'XYLAN' occurred in the title of an article that should have been matched to the MeSH term 'XYLANS', but INDEXER failed to find the match because of the differing 'S'.

Experiment 2

To correct these problems, several simple modifications were made to INDEXER for this experiment:

- Stopwords were removed from the dictionaries, subtree lists, and titles.

- Plural suffixes were removed from the dictionaries and titles according to three simple rules: (1) drop any final '–s' if preceded by a consonant; (2) if a word ends in '–ies' then change the ending to a '–y'; and (3) drop '–es' if it ends a word.

- Before a MeSH term was assigned to a title, INDEXER required greater than 50% of the words in the MeSH term to appear in the title.

Experiment 3

If one word in a MeSH term occurred twice in a title, then the original indexing algorithm counted this as a two-word match. This counting method led INDEXER astray in many cases. For example, if the word 'RAT' occurred twice in a title, this would be counted as a two-word match to any MeSH term having the word 'RAT' even though 'RAT' was only one word in the MeSH term. In this experiment, the problem was corrected by ignoring multiple occurrences of a word in a title.

Experiment 4

For this experiment, INDEXER required *all* the words of a MeSH term to appear in the title before that MeSH term was assigned to the title.

14.2.4 Discussion of results

Simple alterations to the indexing algorithm rather dramatically improved INDEXER's performance, as shown by the results of Experiments 2–4. Similar results have been described in the literature (Niehoff & Mack, 1985). In Experiment 3, the simple modification of removing repeated words from a title doubled the AHP. At its best average performance (Experiment 4), one out of every two MeSH terms returned by INDEXER agreed with NLM's assignments.

The total number of hits remained fairly constant throughout the experiments while the number of MeSH terms generated by INDEXER decreased during the course of the experiments. As a result, the AHP was a true indicator of INDEXER's discriminative ability during the four experiments.

INDEXER generated approximately one-fourth as many MeSH terms as NLM indexers used to classify the titles. This is a reasonable result since upon inspection of the 247 titles, it was noted that less than half of NLM's MeSH term assignments could be deduced from the title alone. This is not surprising since NLM indexers base their MeSH assignments on the entire contents of each document, not just the title.

The results of Experiment 3 and 4 do not show that INDEXER benefited from the augmentation of MeSH with SNOMED. In fact, both the number of hits and the number of INDEXER-assigned terms decreased in the augmented runs.

The augmentation algorithm seems eminently reasonable, yet no benefit was observed in these experiments. At least two explanations can be offered to explain the lack of improvement. First, perhaps our yard stick for the knowledge bases, namely, how they perform with INDEXER, is not sensitive enough. This hypothesis was probably true in Experiment 1, where INDEXER's performance was quite poor. Given the great improvement over the succeeding experiments, however, it is unclear whether INDEXER still lacks adequate sensitivity.

Another possible explanation is that the augmentation did not cause any improvement of the knowledge base. A close inspection of SNOMED reveals many similarities between it and MeSH. For example, there is a strong correspondence between SNOMED's Topography category and MeSH's Anatomical Terms section. SNOMED's Etiology category closely corresponds to the Organisms and Chemicals sections in MeSH. There are many other sections of correspondence between the two knowledge bases; perhaps the augmentation failed because SNOMED offers MeSH few new conceptual pathways toward the root of the knowledge base.

14.2.5 Experiment by hand

We did a small experiment by hand to test to what extent extra terms in MeSH would help. We were only checking to what extent our method could find one particular index that was appropriate for a document. For two sets of documents the indexing accuracy dramatically increased.

An outline of the methodology for these 2 hand experiments follows:

(1) Documents were retrieved from MEDLINE under 'blood transfusion' and 'diagnosis, computer assisted'.
(2) Documents were encoded by our automatic method (with some augmentations to be described shortly) based on MeSH and evaluated for their hit-rate on 'blood transfusion' and 'diagnosis, computer assisted'.
(3) MeSH 'blood transfusion' was augmented with children of 'transfusion reaction' in SNOMED and MeSH 'diagnosis, computer assisted' was augmented with children of 'artificial intelligence' in CRCS.
(4) Documents were indexed by our algorithm via augmented MeSH.

14.2.5.1 CRCS

We took the most recent 20 titles from a search for '*diagnosis, computer assisted' and tested the extent to which MeSH alone would give us the heading Diagnosis, Computer Assisted. The steps of the experiment follow:

(1) We noted the MeSH numbers associated with several MeSH words, such as Computer, Diagnosis, and Intelligence.
(2) We found in each title the occurrence of any of the words from 1 above. Next we obtained the most frequent MeSH number from a dictionary

that has each word in MeSH followed by a list of the numbers of the terms in which that word occurred along with an indicator of the number of words in the term. The dictionary matcher removed all suffices of words so as to increase the likelihood of match. In case of a tie, we resolved it, if possible, by choosing the MeSH number whose indicator agreed with the number of words from the title used to select that MeSH number.

Using the 20 titles we were able to encode 2 into 'Diagnosis, Computer Assisted' based on MeSH alone.

Then we augmented MeSH with CRCS by adding to the dictionary the artificial intelligence component of CRCS. A small sample of the Artificial Intelligence part of CRCS follows:

i.2 artificial intelligence

i.2.0 general

i.2.1 applications and expert systems

i.2.6 learning

i.2.6.1 analogies

i.2.6.2 concept learning

i.2.6.3 induction

i.2.6.4 knowledge acquisition

Each of these CRCS terms is coded with the MeSH number for Diagnosis, Computer Assisted, and then the dictionary is appropriately augmented. Upon repeat of the indexing procedure, none of the correctly identified titles were changed in their indexing. Of the 18 titles that previously were not encoded into Diagnosis, Computer Assisted an additional 9 are now correctly encoded. Of these 9, many had the words expert systems which matched two words of a CRCS term. This shows a positive effect of an augmented MeSH in indexing.

14.2.5.2   SNOMED

We took the most recent 22 titles from a search for '*blood transfusion/ adverse effects and not AIDS'. Then we tested the extent to which MeSH alone would give us the heading Blood Transfusion. To do this:

(1) We noted that transfusion occurs in 8 mesh terms, such as Blood transfusion, autologues. Blood occurs in many MeSH terms.

(2) Next we found in each title the occurrence of any of the words from 1 above and proceeded as we had in the earlier described experiment.

Using the 22 titles we were able to encode 7 into blood transfusion based on MeSH alone.

Then we augmented MeSH with SNOMED by adding to the dictionary a part of SNOMED that included:

```
(TRANSFUSION REACTION)
(TRANSFUSION REACTION HEMOLYTIC)
(TRANSFUSION REACTION HEMOLYTIC IMMEDIATE)
(TRANSFUSION REACTION HEMOLYTIC DELAYED)
```

Each of these SNOMED terms is coded with the MeSH number for Blood Transfusion, and then the dictionary is appropriately augmented. Upon repeat of the indexing procedure, none of the correctly identified titles were changed in their indexing. Of the 15 titles that previously were not encoded into Blood Transfusion an additional 5 are now correctly encoded. Of these 5, 3 had the words delayed hemolytic transfusion reaction which matched perfectly into a SNOMED term.

14.2.5.3　Discussion
The addition of terms like 'transfusion reaction' to 'blood transfusion' helps indexing. 'Transfusion reaction' is not an instance of 'blood transfusion'. We have, in these hand experiments, added terms to MeSH that were not instances of their new parents. A 'transfusion reaction' occurs in response to a 'blood transfusion' but is not an instance of a blood transfusion. These other links led INDEXER to some excellent guesses about the content of the document. We would like to explore more fully the significance of this kind of result in the context both of machine learning and expectation-driven parsing.

14.3　MORPHOSEMANTIC ANALYSIS

14.3.1　Introduction
One important part of an IR system is a mechanism for enabling the computer to recognize what a document is about. For the case of MED-LARS we would like a computer to recognize what MeSH terms fit a document well. This is a complex undertaking, being in certain respects similar to natural language comprehension. The language which MeSH and many medical articles and abstracts use is not, however, natural English. It is, rather, a subset of natural English, so-called 'medicalese', which displays certain qualities of diction and syntax which make it easier for a computer to parse such written material than would be possible were it not so limited. Some of these qualities are the following:

— Medical titles and headings are usually terse, nominalized, simple declarative sentences using unambiguous terms.
— Pronouns, adjectival or adverbial clauses, and adverbs are used infrequently, and often can be ignored without losing the meaning of the title or sentence.
— Slang, rhetorical forms, puns, self-referential material, and ellipsis are rare.

It has been found that, due to this stereotypy, word order is of lesser significance than in natural language (Dunham *et al.,* 1978; Ulmschneider & Doszkocs, 1983). Therefore, procedures which concentrate on recognizing words and phrases held in common between two pieces of text may be sufficient to determine whether such pieces are closely related. Several other problems remain: aside from the formidable undertaking of matching two terms which are similar only if one understands their medical meaning (such as 'malabsorption syndrome' and 'celiac sprue'), medicalese employs a convention infrequently seen in natural English: the use of a single word to represent a complex action or condition, e.g.

> coagulopathy: a disease involving abnormal clotting of blood

> pancreaticoduodenostomy: a surgical procedure wherein the pancreas is drained into an opening made in the duodenum

> galactosemia: a condition involving abnormal amounts of galactose in the blood.

While a learned human can easily see that 'coagulopathy' and 'clotting' have something to do with one another, this similarity is opaque to the computer without somehow enabling it to discern:

(a) that 'coagulopathy' is formed from two root words, 'coagulo' and 'path' with a nominal ending;

(b) that 'coagulo' means 'blood clotting'.

Fortunately, as medical terms are overwhelmingly derived from a limited number of greco-latin roots (Dunham *et al.*, 1978), instructing the computer to recognize such word parts seems a feasible task.

14.3.2   Method

An algorithm, called STAR (for STemming And Replacement) was written to perform morphosemantic analysis of medical terms (Brylawski, 1985). The first task, that of decomposing a word into its component root forms (morphemes) is called 'stemming'. We used a thesaurus-oriented approach which works as follows: first, we constructed a list of medical prefixes, suffixes, and root words (note that many root words are prefixes and/or suffixes, but not vice versa). Then, for any given word, the algorithm does the following:

(1) Remove a prefix from the beginning of the word, if possible.
(2) Remove a suffix from the end of the word.
(3) If 1 succeeded, try to remove a root from the beginning of the word.
(4) If 2 succeeded, try to remove a root from the end of the word.
(5) Return the fragmented word.

The distinction between 1 and 3 (or 2 and 4) is significant because many morphemes are meaingful only if they begin or end a word, e.g. pre-, -ize, -s, whereas most other morphemes can be found anywhere, e.g. -mast-, -troph-, etc.

The second tool used is a thesaurus of synonyms. This consists of a long list of paired terms. If the computer finds as it is processing a word that the word is in its thesaurus, it stops trying to stem the word and instead translates it to the term or phrase it is paired with. For example: REN- and NEPHR- would both be replaced with KIDNEY. This accomplishes three goals:

(1) It maps all like-meaning words or morphemes onto a common word or phrase so that the computer can subsequently recognize that they are similar. This permits the computer not only to recognize different combining forms of a single root word (e.g. NEOPLASM and NEOPLASTIC), but also to recognize different roots or words that mean the same thing (e.g. HEM-, HEMAT-, SANGUIN, and BLOOD).

(2) It prevents the computer from decomposing certain words inappropriately, e.g. normally DIALYSIS would be decomposed to DIA and LYSIS; this would partially match BACTERIOLYSIS, which is wrong. Obviously, DIALYSIS is an exception to the normal decomposing rules in that it loses its primary meaning when broken down. The easiest way to prevent this is to put DIALYSIS (and its other form DIALYZ) into the thesaurus, so that the algorithm will recognize that it should not attempt to fragment the word. Another method of preventing this breakdown is to put DIALYSIS into the allowed list of suffixes; this, however, is clumsier and does nothing to match other forms of the word, e.g. DIALYZED.

(3) It enables inclusion of implied terms; for instance, normally the computer would recognize no similarity between COAGULOPATHY and HEMOPHILIA, but this can be partially overcome by having HEMOPHILIA and its combining forms translate to HEMOPHILIA BLOOD CLOTTING DISEASE, which will match COAGULOPATHY quite well when it is decomposed and translated. Terms which naturally match phrases can be assigned those phrases as a meaning, e.g. HYPERTENSION can translate to HIGH BLOOD PRESSURE easily.

In addition to these two tools, the algorithm also has a list of 'junk words' and 'junk suffixes', i.e., words or suffixes which are meaningless in themselves and which only serve to delimit or modify other words. Examples include A, THE, OR, AND, -S, -TION, -ISM, and -ATIC. If these words or morphemes are left in, the computer will find similarities between terms whose only resemblance is a grammatical ending or article (e.g., HEMATOLOGY and PATHOLOGY); thus, all such words and suffixes are removed by the algorithm as well.

The method used to test whether the STAR algorithm would work in a fashion similar to a knowledgeable human involved the following steps:

(1) A sample list of 30 titles concerning medical topics was processed by STAR.

(2) The dictionary of all MeSH terms was similarly processed.

(3) Via an indexing algorithm, each title was compared to the MeSH dictionary. A term was considered to match the title by either of two protocols:

Protocol 1

If at least three words were shared by title and term, or if more than half the words in the term were in the title, the term was considered to match.

Protocol 2
A term matched only if every word in the term was also found in the title.

(4) If the user desires, any terms which are wholly a subset of another term which matched are discarded. For example, if both BLOOD TRANS-FUSION and BLOOD TRANSFUSION REACTION matched, then the former would be discarded.

(5) The resultant terms matched by STAR were then compared to the title and to the MeSH terms assigned by human researchers at the National Library of Medicine, to see how close the computer came and whether it matched terms which had nothing to do with the title given. The performance of the algorithm was also compared to the number and accuracy of terms matched by employing the same protocols on the unSTARred text and MeSH terms.

14.3.3   Results

The results of indexing the sample list of 30 titles were as shown in Table 14.2.

Table 14.2

Indexing results

Terms and titles processed?	Protocol	Discard subsets?	True positives	False positives	False negatives
no	1	nop	27	120	205
no	2	no	20	20	69
yes	1	no	74	762	158
yes	2	no	56	163	176
yes	1	yes	31	540	201
yes	2	yes	51	61	181
using a complete synonym and root thesaurus					
yes	2	yes	75	40	157
removing terms not descernible from title					
yes	2	yes	75	40	97

True Positives =
    Terms assigned by the program and assigned by the NLM indexers.
False Positives =
    Terms produced by the program but not assigned by the NLM indexers.
False Negatives =
    Terms assigned by NLM but not by the program.

Pre-processing the titles and term index proved to greatly increase the number of matches found, at a cost of also greatly increasing the number of extraneous terms assigned by the computer. Some of these false positive terms are, however, 'near misses', i.e. are closely related topics to those assigned by NLM but not exact matches. The number of such false positives was considerably decreased by the use of protocol 2, while the number of matches suffered to a much lesser extent (769 to 163, versus 74 to 56).

The use of a post-processor to remove terms which were subsets of other terms, combined with the exact match protocol (No. 2), greatly decreased the number of false positives while leaving the matches relatively intact.

Since the processor in this experiment used only a small, incomplete thesaurus of roots and synonyms, an approximation of the results obtained using a complete thesaurus was obtained by indexing by hand. In addition, it was recognized that many of the NLM-assigned terms were assigned on the basis of reading the whole article and were in no way discernable from the title itself. The last line of the table shows approximately what would result from eliminating (for purposes of this experiment) those terms.

14.3.4   Discussion

Note that the number of matches using protocol 1 decreased sharply when the subset remover was applied. This occurred because the subset filtering algorithm is very crude: if LOW BLOOD PRESSURE appeared in the title, while LOW BLOOD PRESSURE and LOW BLOOD PRESSURE, ORTHOSTATIC appeared in the term index, the STAR would match them both (since over 50% of the words match), then discard the exact match, LOW BLOOD PRESSURE, in favor of the more specific term. Modifying the subset filter such that exact matches are not touched would avoid this.

The method of removing both prefixes and suffixes from a word, seems to work better than methods involving only suffix removal in cases where the term involved is not completely 'known' to the algorithm. For example, a suffix-only routine working on the word LYMPHOPROLIFERATIVE would come a cropper if it did not have the root word LYMPHOPRO-LIFER and ATIVE. The combined prefix-and-suffix routine, however, could do better if LYMPHO- were known to it, which is likely as this is a common prefix.

Another problem with a suffix machine is that often 'exceptions', such as DIALYSIS (see above), are prefixed, e.g. HEMODIALYSIS. A suffix-stemmer will not recognize that an exception word is buried in the above term and will go ahead and render it HEMODIA LYSIS or HEMO DIA LYSIS, both poor. STAR will of course split HEMODIALYSIS to HEMO and DIALYSIS first, then will recognize that the latter fragment is not to be stemmed further. In all, the prefix-and-suffix routine seems to be the most robust when encountering words which are foreign or exceptional.

STAR discards all nonmeaningful suffixes and words in order to avoid spurious matches; a more sophisticated processor would instead retain these extra words and morphemes but mark them in some fashion so as to use them for later or concurrent syntactic analysis. We employed titles instead of abstracts or complete documents for two reasons. First, titles are terse noun phrases relatively free of syntactic variability, containing very few unnecessary terms; this avoided having to do syntactic analysis on the text to determine which portions were most relevant to the whole. Second, the indexing procedure is computationally inefficient, and it was considerably easier to test the STAR algorithm's performance on a variety of topics by using very short pieces of text.

The subset filter was added when we realized that many of the false positives generated by the program were due to the program matching both a general term and a specific term to a title: for example, HEMOLYTIC ANEMIA matched HEMOLYTIC ANEMIA and ANEMIA both, whereas the NLM indexers would only select the specific term. The simplest way to have the computer handle this difference was to have the computer decide that if one term was included in another, then the former was more general and the latter more specific. A better approach for future test might employ some explicit test for generality, using the MeSH tree itself.

14.4   PARSER IMPROVEMENTS

14.4.1   General

Our simple INDEXER does not take advantage of our knowledge of language in any sophisticated way. The INDEXER reads in a classification structure and from that builds a table or dictionary which then guides the indexing. Given any classification structure, the INDEXER automatically bootstraps itself into operation.

A major question in our research in automatically merging knowledge bases is 'how can we evaluate a knowledge base?'. Two major alternatives offer themselves as we adjust our experiment so that the evaluation is more sensitive. One alternative is to measure how close the program's index is to the person's. The other alternative is to put more knowledge into the program's parser.

Others (Resnick & Savage, 1964) have studied how well the assessment of a title corresponds to the assessment of an entire document and concluded that there is significant agreement between the two assessments. The title says less than the document, but it carries the same general message. Can we use our earlier-developed metric among sets of nodes in a cognitive graph to say how far the computer's indexing of the title is from the human's indexing of the document? Yes, we can. Furthermore, since we can easily run an effectively endless number of indexed documents through the system, our system should be sensitive to small differences in the performance of a MeSH-driven indexer versus that of a MeSH+SNOMED- driven indexer.

The alternative of adding more information to the INDEXER is also being pursued. We have already completed a program (written by Debbie Bennett) that reads MeSH and decomposes each term into its keyword and modifier components. An adequate strategy (as suggested by Rebecca Lewis) roughly says:

(1) If the term is of the form 'word1 word2', then word2 is the keyword and word1 is the modifer. For example, in 'blood transfusion' transfusion is the keyword and blood is the modifier.

(2) If the term is of the form 'word1, word2', then word1 is the keyword and word2 is the modifier. In the term 'diagnosis, computer-assisted' diagnosis is the keyword and computer-assisted is the modifier.

Given this division of MeSH, our parser of titles is now obligated to

divide titles into components called keywords and modifiers. One example
of a grammar we are testing was written by Lewis in DYPAR-1 (Boggs *et al.*,
1984). In DYPAR-1 a vertical bar '|' means 'or' and a question mark '?'
means 'optional'.

Fig. 14.6 — General grammar for titles.

‹title› → (‹noun_plus› | (‹noun_plus› ‹prep› ‹rest›) | (‹noun_plus›
    ‹rest›))
‹rest› → (‹noun_plus› | (‹verb_plus› ‹prep› ‹rest›) | (‹noun_plus›
    ‹verb_plus› ?‹prep› ‹rest›) | (‹noun_plus› ‹prep› ‹rest›) | (‹conj›
    ‹noun_plus› ‹rest›))
‹verb_plus› → (‹verb› | (‹verb› ‹adverb›) | (‹adverb› ‹verb›))
‹noun_plus› → ((?‹art› noun) | (?‹art› ‹adj› ‹noun›) | (?‹art› ‹adj›
    ‹noun_plus›))
‹verb› → (design | diagnose | treat | administered | following | com-
    bined | used)
‹prep› → (of | to | for | in | with | through | under | over)
‹adverb› → (with | as | daily | once | twice | regularly)
‹conj› → (and | or | plus)
‹noun› → [keyword-list as developed from MeSH]
‹adj› → [modifier-list as developed from MeSH]
‹art› → (the | a)

The parser shown in Fig. 14.6 is meant to produce sublists of keywords
and modifiers. Lewis also designed a matcher program that would determine
from the keyword and modifier dictionaries an indexing of the title. We have
not tested Lewis's strategy yet.

14.4.2 Domain specific
The above grammar is very general and would apply to titles from any
discipline. An alternative approach to evaluating the 'knowledge base' is to

(1) focus on a narrowly constrained domain within the biomedical
    literature,
(2) write a grammar that is designed specifically for that domain,
(3) isolate the part of the classification structure or knowledge base that is
    concerned with that domain.
(4) index titles by first parsing them with the grammar of 2 and then
    referring to the structure of 3,
(5) compare the results of the indexing of 4 to those of people,
(6) automatically augment the structures of 3 by referring to other existing
    organizations of information like SNOMED, and
(7) as long as the results seem interesting, go to step 4.

This kind of strategy is typical of that in artificial intelligence. In contemporary learning experiments the problem of evaluation is usually sidestepped by narrowly constraining the domain the system must understand and handcoding so much human knowledge into the system that performance of the system in that domain is readily comparable to that of a person.

Susanne Humphrey has developed a grammar for a certain subset of titles in the biomedical literature about clinical trials. In the United States clinical trials are monitored by the government, and rules for their proper execution are clearly detailed (Rosenbloom *et al.*, 1985; Food & Drug Administration, 1975). This makes an attractive domain for computer work because the knowledge in the domain has been well organized by people. Humphrey's grammar was written in DYPAR-1 (Boggs *et al.*, 1984) and a small sample of it follows.

Three high-level productions of the grammar are shown in Fig. 14.7.

Fig. 14.7

‹MedTitle› → (‹ExogDrugTreatmentTitle›)

‹ExogDrugTreatmentTitle› → (?(‹Measurement› ‹ForOf›) ?(‹EffectExp›
‹AfterDuringFollOfToWhileWith›) ‹EDTTitle›?‹InNumPts›)

‹EDTTitle› → ((
 ((((‹Disease› (‹ModifiedTreatment› | ‹Treated›)) | (‹ModifiedTreat-
 mentNoun› ‹ForInOf›) | (‹ModifiedTreatingNoun› ?of)) ‹Disease›
 ‹ByUsingViaWith› ‹ExogDrug› ?‹CompWithExogDrug› ?(‹After-
 Foll› ‹Surg› ?((‹ForInOn› ?((‹TreatmentNoun› ‹ForInOf›) | (‹Treat-
 ingNoun› ?of)) | (‹To› ‹TreatNoun›) | ‹ForInOfOn›) ‹Disease›))
 ?CompWithExogDrug›)|
 (‹ExogDrug› ?‹AdminAppliedGivenUsed› (‹ForInOn› | (?‹AsForl-
 nOn› ((‹ModifiedTreatmentNoun› ‹ForInOf›) | (‹ModifiedTreat-
 ingNoun› ?of))) | (‹To› ‹TreatNoun›)) ‹Disease› ?‹CompWithExog-
 Drug› ?(‹AfterFoll› ‹Surg› ?(((‹ForInOn› ?((‹TreatmentNoun›
      ‹ForInOf›) | (‹TreatingNoun› ?of))) | (‹To› ‹Treat
 Noun›) | ‹ForInOfOn›) ‹Disease›)) ?‹CompWithExogDrug›))

Two low-level productions of the grammar are shown in Fig. 14.8.

Fig. 14.8

‹AdminAppliedGivenUsed› → (administered | applied | given | used)
‹PhysiolNoun› → (lactation | tachyphylaxis | (exercise tolerance))

Two of the titles about clinical trials from MEDLARS that were used to guide the development of the grammar are shown in Fig. 14.9.

> Fig. 14.9

Title1: Adjunctive use of magnesium sulfate with ritodrine for pre-
term labor tocolysis.

Title2: Clotrimazole treatment of oral candidiasis in patients with
neoplastic disease.

Humphrey's grammar successfully parsed 17 of 47 titles on which it was tested.

Where do things stand? We are forging ahead with a number of experiments that are establishing a method for evaluating a classification structure by using it in indexing. Our principle objective is to experiment with different methods of automatically augmenting the classification structure, but our ideas about that cannot be tested without a sensitive tool for assessing the value of what has been augmented. This is not primarily a project in natural language processing, but rather a learning experiment that happens to involve natural language.

14.5 EXERCISE

Explore the effects of partial matches between two kbs on the performance of INDEXER. Refer to the experiments of this chapter in which direct matches between MeSH and SNOMED-NOS terms, followed by merging of the children of SNOMED-NOS terms with MeSH, led to no improvement in indexing. The few, hand-experiments which allowed partial-matching led to much better indexing. Would these partial matches continue to help when done without the guidance of a human? (Time 3 hours.)

14.6 REFERENCES

Association of Computing Machinery, (1984) The Full Category System, *Computing Reviews.*

Boggs, Mark, Carbonell, Jaime, Monarch, Ira, & Kee, Marion (1984) *DYPAR-1: Tutorial and Reference Manual,* Department of Computer Science, Carnegie-Mellon University, Pittsburgh, PA.

Brylawski, Brandon (1985) Augmentation of Information Retrieval by Word Decomposition and Analysis, *Internal Report,* NationaL Library of Medicine, October.

Cote, Roger (1979) *Systematized Nomenclature of Medicine,* College of American Pathologists, Skokie, Illinois.

Dunham, G., Pacak, M., & Pratt, A. (1978) Automatic Indexing of Pathology Data, *Jr Amer Soc Inform Sc.*

Food and Drug Administration, (1975) *Notice of Claimed Investigational Exemption for a New Drug.* FD Form 1571.

Greenwood, R. (1972) KODIAC, a System for Disease Coding by a Medium-Sized Computer, *Bio-Med Comp*, **3**, pp. 123–134.

Howell, R. & Loy, R. (1968) Disease Coding by Computer: The Fruit Machine Method, *Brit J Prev Soc Med*, **22**, pp. 178–181.

Niehoff, Robert & Mack, Greg (1985) The Vocabulary Switching System, *Int Classif*, **12**, *1*, pp. 2–6.

Rada, Roy & Evans, Lynn (1979) Automated Problem Encoding System for Ambulatory Care, *Computers and Biomedical Research*, **12**, pp. 131–139.

Resnick, A. & Savage, T. R. (1964) The Consistency of Human Judgements of Relevance, *American Documentation*, **15**, *2*, pp. 93–95.

Rosenbloom, D., Brooks, P., Bellamy, N., & Buchanan, W., (1985) *Clinical Trials in the Rheumatic Diseases*, Praeger Publishers, New York.

Ulmschneider & Doszkocs, T. (1983) A Practical Stemming Algorithm for Online Search Assistance, *Online Review*, **7**, *4*.

White, W. (1977) A Method for Automatic Coding of Medical Information in Patient Records, *Method Inform Med*, **16**, pp. 1–10.

15

Conclusion

15.1 SUMMARY OF EXISTING WORK

The Information Age provides us an opportunity and a responsibility to create more intelligent machines. Two dominant themes of this age are:

(1) More automatic means of intelligently classifying and retrieving documents are needed.
(2) The construction and augmentation of knowledge bases for the information age should not be totally relegated to painstaking human effort.

These two themes merge in the work on 'machine learning for information retrieval'.

In an information retrieval system Language plays a central role. Queries and Documents are mapped into a Language, and within that Language matches between Queries and Documents are made.

Fig. 15.1 — Language in information retrieval.

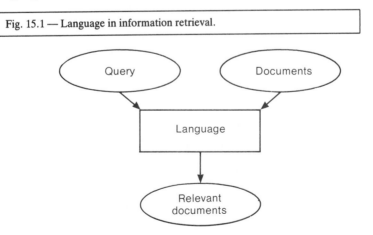

Of those Information Retrieval (IR) systems which require humans to index the documents and queries, two of the more popular types of languages are:

(a) a hierarchy of terms as in the Medical Subject Headings of the National Library of medicine (MEDLARS Management Section, 1982), and
(b) the multi-relation scheme, as in PRECIS of the British National Library (Austin, 1984).

Those IR systems which don't require humans to index documents depend on either word-frequency assessments or string-searching. Research is ongoing into natural language processing systems that would both obviate the need for human indexing but retain its robustness.

Intelligent systems have representation, reasoning, and learning components. To manifest learning a system should try to extend itself and be amenable to gradual improvements. No one understands how, in general, to build computer systems that have gradualness, although it is the *sine qua non* of living things.

A sound methodological approach to research in machine learning requires that experiments be easily performed. Given our poor understanding of the nature of human knowledge, we can not mathematically characterize the knowledge that we want intelligent machines to learn. We need to do experiments with people, and this is facilitated when we do research in domains where people normally interact with the computer. Information retrieval systems are excellent examples of important systems which are often computerized and with which people regularly interact in a knowledge-intense way. Ways of assessing the quality of this interaction through recall–precision measures or protocol analysis make it easier for scientists to devise repeatable experiments in IR.

Existing work in machine learning can be divided, on a first pass, into two categories: knowledge-sparse learning and knowledge-rich learning. Knowledge-sparse situations are those which take little advantage of the complexity in knoweledge; for instance, yes—no decisions by a person represent knowledge-sparse decisions. Knowledge-rich situations show many facets to representation and reasoning. When a person adds rules to an existing set of rules in order to refine the retrieval that those rules create, knowledge-rich augmentation of rules has occurred.

We can further divide the area of knowledge-sparse learning into

(1) the subarea where users provide yes—no decisions about the relevancy of documents, and
(2) the subarea where the frequency of co-occurrence of words in text is the source of new information for the learning algorithm.

The representation of documents and queries that facilitates knowledge-sparse learning is typically of the numeric sort. Vectors of weights can be readily modified so that the vector, whether it represents a query or a document, comes closer to what the user expects in terms of query-document similarity. Some of the more interesting work in knowledge-sparse learning tries to build richer structures than just weight adjustment typically allows. The genetic algorithm (Gordon, 1983) recombines substrings so as to compose better document descriptions. Automatic thesaurus refinement through word-frequencies leads to hierarchical structuring by taking the results of one grouping and using them in a subsequent grouping.

Some of the knowledge-rich learning experiments ask users whether certain queries are similar or not, and then based on a substantial knowledge of the structure and function in language try to build new syntactic (Reeker, 1984) or semantic rules (Hass & Hendrix, 1980). Here the learning is rich not because of the similarity-decision of the user but because of the wealth of complex information that the program brings to bear in processing the decision. Some of the most exciting work in knowledge-rich learning relies on text—of which massive quantities already exist on the computer to drive changes in a knowledge-base. Schank's (Schank, 1982) group has applied the term 'dynamic memory' to the work which starts with a sophisticated knowledge-base, language parser, and explainer and based on the novelties in a document improves the computer system so that it now appreciates those novelties. Work like Schank's but of a more mathematical sort is being done with cognitive graphs (Bonham *et al.*, 1985).

15.2 SUMMARY OF A CASE STUDY

A group at the National Library of Medicine has been investigating ways to automatically improve classification structures (Rada *et al.*, 1985). The Library is an excellent grounds for such testing because of its massive involvement in automated retrieval of documents. The Library largely depends on a classification structure called the Medical Subject Headings (MeSH) both for representing documents and queries. Millions of document descriptions are stored on the computer, and thousands of queries each day reach the library computer. MeSH has substantial structure which is reflected in the connections that exist among MeSH terms in a query and in a document.

To make the Library's computer more intelligent, we have to strengthen MeSH. In order to evaluate whether changes that we make to MeSH are indeed helpful, we need to do reasoning with it. In other words, we need to establish a structure—function relationship on MeSH and then see how alterations in the structure correspond to alterations in function. To this end, reasoning mechanisms for adjudicating the conceptual closeness of documents to queries and for indexing titles have been built over MeSH. These reasoning mechanisms provide a function on the MeSH structure.

The algorithm to match documents to queries relies on a metric called DISTANCE. DISTANCE has several attractive mathematical and computational properties. For instance, it can be computed by a parallel computer with efficiency greater than 1 (Rada, 1984). More germane to our learning experiments are the data-retrieval properties of DISTANCE when it operates on MeSH. When DISTANCE ranks documents to a query and people do the same task, the computer and the people have significantly correlated rankings. This attests to the power and soundness of the 'is-a' links on which MeSH is founded. By placing further demands on the performance of DISTANCE and MeSH, we were able to isolate a circumstance under which the two together did not adequately simulate people's behaviour in the ranking of documents:

(a) Searches or queries were automatically extended or broadened to include the children in MeSH of terms in the originally query.
(b) The best documents from the broadened query were determined by people and the computer.
(c) There was not significant improvement in recall by the computer under these very special circumstances.

This weakness led to finer studies of the relationships in MeSH and queries. By removing an edge from MeSH that was misleading and adding terms to the query that partially captured an important relationship in the querist's mind, we were able to operate DISTANCE so that it improved both recall and precision.

DISTANCE depends for its success on the cognitive realism of the edges or relationships in MeSH. It seems that MeSH could be substantially improved by adding to it edges that exist in other organized bodies of information. Current Medical Information and Terminology (CMIT) (Finkel et al., 1981) is a computerized knowledge base that has seven kinds of relationships that MeSH doesn't. We added some of these relationships to MeSH but were surprised that the behaviour of DISTANCE then deteriorated. Further study showed that the new edges which were not of the 'is-a' kind needed to be handled in special ways.

We have also done other experiments in edge augmentation. One was based on the frequency of word co-occurrences and surprisingly showed some substantial ability of the statistically built classification structure to allow good relevance calculations (Mili & Rada, 1985). From the other end, we are developing a sophisticated edge-augmenter that reasons by analogy from highly developed concepts. This analogical reasoner posits that certain kinds of relationships exist among concepts in biology and makes changes to concepts based on the specific types of similarities that it finds.

Classification structures emphasize 'is-a' relationships, and experiments in merging classification structures naturally focus on the addition of subtrees of terms from one structure to the other. DISTANCE is not particularly sensitive to this kind of change in a classification structure, but a measure of function that depends on vocabulary is. Our INDEXER takes document titles and maps them into terms of the classification structure. Properly increasing the number of terms in the structure ought to lead to better indexing. Results to date indicate that more subtleties of

(1) indexing must be taken into account in order to have a sensitive measure of the effect of changes in the classification structure, or

(2) learning must be invoked in order that terms and relations are added to MeSH which improve indexing.

15.3   REQUESTS FOR WORK

There are many directions which might be fruitfully pursued in intelligent information retrieval. Our thesis has been that learning must be considered as important as representation and reasoning. Furthermore, one of the most opportune areas for work in the combination of representation, reasoning, and learning is that of automatically merging classification structures or knowledge bases. A discussion of how to proceed with these learning experiments should address both generic and domain-specific issues.

15.3.1   Representation
15.3.1.1   General
At the generic level, a reasonable representational primitive, given the state of the art of artificial intelligence, is a frame. This structure rather arbitrarily allots four levels of detail to a frame—frame, slot, facet, and value. Nevertheless, the software and experimentation that have been done with frames in mind is enough to merit continuation of that paradigm till one can demonstrate that something simpler or more complex should be used.

How to organize a set of frames in the computer is unclear. For the typical, academic experiment with frames, the number of frames is so small that storing them at the same time in directly addressable memory (core) is feasible. Then processing of the frames occurs through traversal of the relationships that lead from frame to frame. This is efficient so long as all frames are in core. In realistically large knowledge bases for intelligent information retrieval no directly addressable memory could be large enough to hold all the knowledge at once. We are not talking about the documents which, all would agree, in a modern library require secondary storage devices but about the meta-level information that allows access to the documents. That meta-level is itself so vast that it cannot fit into core. All directly addressable memory must be reachable from a single processor in one time step. Technological abilities will not be able to overcome the limitations of time and space that upperbound the size of such memory.

So the question becomes: How do we organize the knowledge so that those parts which can be accessed quickly can efficiently connect to those parts which have to be fetched from a secondary device. In the long-run, the solution may rely on highly distributed or parallel computers, and our notions of memory storage and retrieval may then be radically different from our current notions. In the meantime, the research is largely done on single-processor machines. The general solution must pay attention to the hard-learned lessons from large-scale database work—namely, make easily accessible that which is frequently needed.

15.3.1.2 Specific

Further discussion of efficiency is hard to pursue without further elaboration
of the nature of the knowledge and how it is used, and that leads us to the
issue of what content primitives should the system have. Schank argues for
conceptual primitives that have to do with motion, ingestion, and like
(Schank, 1975). In a particular domain, such as medicine, the meaningful
primitives might well be more specific. Say we have a merging of the terms
and structure in MeSH and SNOMED with the main subtrees being those of
SNOMED's etiology, morphology, topography, function, disease, and
procedure (Cote, 1979). MeSH has about 70 subheadings which actually
specify a kind of relationship that can exist among headings. For instance,
the subheading 'drug therapy' is applied to a disease which is being treated
by a drug: the link implicitly exists between that disease and the drug which
treats it. The relationships implied by these subheadings were not conceived
with the thought that a computer might need to take advantage of the links
that they imply. Someone should try to mak these relationships clear and to
connect terms in MeSH by these approximately 70 relationships. Other
sources of medically dependent links are given in CMIT and SNOMED, and
these should also be incorporated into a new and better MeSH.

After important, non-'is-a' relationships have been added to a classification structure, the classification structure has become a knowledge base. If
this knowledge-base is used for measuring the distance between queries and
documents by finding path-lengths between terms along certain types of
relationships, then one breakdown of the information would be into separate files for each type of relationship. One file would have all the terms
connected by 'is-a' relationships. Another file would show the 'drug therapy'
links. Each of these files would itself be too large to fit into core. Accordingly, they could be futher decomposed into subfiles, where each subfile had
a meaningful grouping of terms. For the 'is-a' links a grouping of terms into
subfiles might be done by putting all the terms in the etiology subtree
together, the terms in the morphology subtree together, etc.

Once a query and a document have been obtained in their parsed form
for input to the revised DISTANCE, the terms of the parsed query and
document could be grouped so that all the computations on a subfile of the
knowledge base could be done in one pass. The reasoning of DISTANCE
would have to be significantly amended over what was described earlier so
that passing from one subfile to another was meaningful and simple. Such an
approach to memory management is fairly straightforward and bound
largely by practical, computer-science like considerations. An alternative
strategy would rely more on the many, excellent studies that have been
made of how humans manage their own memory (Rummelhart & Norman,
1983).

15.3.2 Reasoning

A matcher and parser are the fundamental reasoning components of an
intelligent information retrieval system. The matcher assumes documens
and queries are parsed but some method is needed for ascertaining the

degree of similarity between documents and a query. The kinds of reasoning that are needed for this could be useful in many contexts where similarity is at issue. The parser must build on what is known in natural language parsing and take advantage of the constrained domain in which a particular information retrieval system operates.

15.3.2.1 Matcher

The matcher described in an earlier chapter needs expanding along several fronts. Relationships other than 'is-a' need to be handled in particular ways. Inheritance of properties should make practical the storing and processing of information that would otherwise be impossible.

The 'is-a' links that we have used are directionless. In other words the 'is-a' connection between 'joint disease' and 'disease' is handled no differently whether one goes from 'joint disease' to 'disease' or from 'disease' to 'joint disease'. Clearly, humans see these links differently. 'Joint disease' is a narrower term than 'disease', and 'disease' is a broader term than 'joint disease'. In traversing MeSH our algorithm might be improved were it to be sensitive to the difference between a broader and a narrower link. We might create subgraphs of concepts that have locally meaningful 'is-a' links, but connections among these subgraphs would imply a qualitatively different type of link.

When relationships like 'drug therapy' are encoded into the knowledge base and used to represent documents and queries, then DISTANCE should pay great attention to such links. Many levels of indirection might be appropriate here. At the lowest level, a disease x treated by drug y, when both are mentioned as such in a document and query, should allow DISTANCE to conclude great similarity. If a broader term x' of x and a broader term y' of y are connected by the drug therapy link, but x and y are *not* directly so connected, DISTANCE should take this into consideration but with less force than when the connection is direct. This indirection can appropriately be called inheritance. The terms x and y have inherited the relationship 'drug therapy' because their parents shared in that relationship.

15.3.2.2 Parser

Our parser, as it stands, takes negligible advantage of our knowledge of English. We have sketched some parsing procedures that would allow more sophisticated breakdowns of MeSH and titles and thus also allow better matches between titles and MeSH terms. The FIDDITCH parser (Hindle, 1984) is an appealing tool because it has a large built-in grammar and vocabulary. It is fast because it does no backtracking and only handles syntax. A more robust approach might use DYPAR-4 for a case-frame, semantic, expectation-based parsing.

Evaluating the performance of the computer indexer by checking for exact matches between the human encoding of the documents and the computer's indexing of the titles of the documents is unrealistically harsh on the computer's indexing. Instead, we should assess the distance between what the computer and person produce. This extension to the indexer would be important to the development of a sensitive tool for measuring knowledge base soundness, which is our main, current objective behind the indexing.

15.3.3   Learning

While the focus of this book is on machine learning, the critical trimuvirate of representation, reasoning, and learning has led us to spend much of our time with representation and reasoning. One cannot fruitfully address learning without the other members of the triumvirate present. In particular, good strategies for learning must be sensitive to the ways in which representation and reasoning depend on each other.

One standard condition for learning is to have operators which make small changes in a representation that produce small changes in reasoning. Our experiments with edge augmentation have shown the importance of the structure—function relationship. The function of CMIT is very different from that of MeSH. When we added non-isa links to MeSH from CMIT we payed inadequate attention to the differences in function of the two systems. We had required some striking structural similarities before making changes, but they weren't the correct structural similarities.

When comparing two hierarchies like MeSH and SNOMED, what are the conditions under which parts of one should be merged with parts of another? How many nodes of two subgraphs should be the same before the two are considered homologues? What levels of abstraction or what depth of a tree should be given most attention? How is functional similarity measured? These are some of the many questions that could be readily posed and to varying degrees investigated in the kinds of learning experiments that we have devised.

The problem of finding structure–function similarity is recognized but not solved. There are a variety of paradigms and constraints discussed in the litarature which might guide the selection of parameters to vary in the study of structure–function measures. Carbonell (Carbonell, 1985) argues for a small set of learning strategies as being necessary and sufficient for intelligent behavior . Darden (Darden, 1983) has a partial taxonomy of discovery mechanisms in science. Lenat (Lenat, 1983) has heuristics for discovery. This other work in machine learning should be referenced and related to the work in merging of classification structures.

15.4   EPILOGUE

An intelligent information retrieval system would deploy plausible reasoning to establish a connection between a request and a candidate document (Sparck Jones, 1983). Because in practice requests are ill-specified in relation to the descriptions of documents, effort of a non-trivial kind is required to select appropriate documents. It might be claimed that the various statistical processes, proposed as means for improving search, embody learning characteristic of intelligent behaviour. However, only little effort has been put into knowledge-intensive learning for retrieval systems.

Capturing the user's knowledge of a domain is no mean task. Knowledge engineering has been successful in some areas, but it remains to be shown that effective knowledge-based computer systems can be constructed for document searching. Top-down and bottom-up approaches to building intelligent IR systems are ongoing in several laboratories. The top-down approach is partially exemplified by the work of Pollitt (Pollitt, 1983). Pollitt is forcing MeSH into production rules that operate on the text descriptions and connect the user to the text. Pollitt is seeking an adequate intelligent front-end for users by assuming that the organization of MeSH adequately embodies the knowledge of the subject at hand. The bottom-up approach has been pursued at SRI with the Hepatitis Knowledge Base (Walker, 1982); here a knowledge base is constructed from scratch. This construction is itself a major task and leaves unsolved the problem of linking this autonomous characterization of the domain to the text itself.

Rada and his colleagues are trying to build onto MeSH so as to have a knowledge base for reasoning about document retrieval (Rada, 1985). Starting with MeSH could be considered a top-down approach, but trying to automatically merge MeSH with other, existing thesauri is a kind of bottom-up approach. It seems incumbent on workers in intelligent systems to not try to rewrite all of human knowledge by starting manually at the bottom. On the other hand, existing codified forms of knowledge are typically not immediately suitable for many of the intelligent tasks that we would like computers to perform. Accordingly, we might profitably try to automatically combine bodies of information that we find already on the computer.

We hope that the second half of this book has shown two things (at least): firstly that learning methods do have a contribution to make in the quest for intelligent information retrieval; and secondly that more research needs to be done in the area of representation before fully automated knowledge acquisition can occur in practice.

The reader who has followed through the whole book has been exposed to a wide variety of learning systems from the simplest trainable pattern recognizer to the constructor of complex knowledge bases. He or she should by now have a deeper understanding of the problems and payoffs of machine learning in several fields — including a complex real-world application, namely IR. The extended case study of Part 2 was intended to bring into sharper focus the difficulties of credit assignment, the various modes of feedback, the choice of error-correction procedures, and so on, which were introduced in Part 1.

In particular, we hope to have illustrated the central role of the description language by our concentration on the themes of reasoning and representation. Computers can learn, and in future will learn much that is economically valuable, but they can never learn what cannot be expressed symbolically in a form suitable for reasoning. In Wittgensteins's words: 'the limits of my language are the limits of my world'.

15.5 EXERCISE

Prepare a mini-contract proposal in response to some part of the request for work.

15.6 REFERENCES

Austin, Derek (1984) *PRECIS: A Manual of Concept Analysis and Subject Indexing,* British Library, London.

Bonham, G. M., Nozicka, G. J. & Stokman, F. N. (1985) Cognitive Graphing and the Representation of Biomedical Knowledge, *Proc Expert Systems in Government Conference,* pp. 397–403, IEEE Computer Society Press.

Carbonell, Jaime (1985) AI Languages for Problem Solving, in *The Role of Language in Problem Solving,* D. Weintraub, (ed.), pp. 83–102, North-Holland, Amsterdam.

Cote, Roger (1979) *Systematized Nomenclature of Medicine,* College of American Pathologists, Skokie, Illinois.

Darden, Lindley (1983) Reasoning by Analogy in Scientific Theory Construction, *Proc International Machine Learning Workshop,* pp. 32–40.

Finkel, A., Gordon, B., Baker, M. & Fanta, C. (1981) *Current Medical Information and Technology,* American Medical Association, Chicago.

Gordon, Michael (1983) Adaptive Subject Description in Document Retrieval, PhD Thesis, Dept of Computer and Communication Sciences, University of Michigan, Ann Arbor, MI.

Haas, Norman & Hendrix, Gary (1980) An Approach to Acquiring and Applying Knowledge, *Proc First Ann Nat'l Conf Artificial Intelligence,* pp. 235–239, American Assoc Artificial Intelligence.

Hindle, Don (1984) *FIDDITCH User's Manual,* Bell Labs.

Lenat, Douglas (1983) The Role of Heuristics in Learning by Discovery, in *Machine Learning,* T. Mitchell, (ed.) pp. 243–306. Tioga Publishing, Palo Alto, CA.

MEDLARS Management Section, (1982) *Online Services Reference Manual,* National Library of Medicine, Bethesda, MD.

Milli, Hafedh & Rada, Roy (1985) A Statistically Build Knowledge Base, *Proc Expert Systems in Government,* pp. 457–463, IEEE Computer Society Press.

Pollitt, S. E. (1983) End User Touch Searching for the Cancer Therapy Literature—Rule Based Approach, *Proc ACM/SIGIR Conf,* Assoc Comp Mach.

Rada, Roy (1984) Implicit Computation in Message Space of Parallel Machine, *Proc Conf Intelligent Systems and Machines,* pp. 424–428.

Rada, Roy (1985) Gradualness Facilitates Knowledge Refinement, *IEEE Transactions on Pattern Analysis and Machine Intelligence,* **7**, 5, pp. 523–530, September.

Rada, Roy, Humphrey, Susanne & Coccia, Craig (1985) A Knowledge-base for Retrieval Evaluation, *Proc ACM '85,* pp. 360–367.

Reeker, L. H. (1984) Adaptive Individualized Language Interfaces for Expert Systems, *Internal Proposal,* US Navy Center for Artificial Intelligence.

Rumelhart, David & Norman, Donald (1983) *Representation in Memory,* Center for Human Information Processing, La Jolla, CA.

Schank, Roger (1975) *Conceptual Information Processing,* North-Holland, Amsterdam.

Schank, Roger (1982) *Dynamic Memory: a theory of reminding and learning in computers and people,* Cambridge University Press, Cambridge, England.

Sparck Jones, Karen (1983) Intelligent Retrieval, *Proc Intelligent Inform Retr,* pp. 136–142, Aslib, London.

Walker, D. E. (1982) Natural Language Access Systems and the Organization and Use of Information, *Proc 9th Intern'l Computational Linguistics,* pp. 407–412, North-Holland, Amsterdam.

Appendix A

BUPA Medical Data

The data below was used as the training set for the experiment described in Chapter 4 (section 4.3). It was kindly provided by BUPA Medical Research Limited. Each line consists of measures on seven variables

MCV	Mean Corpuscular Volume
ALKPHOS	Alkaline Phosphotase
SGPT	Alamine Aminotransferase
SGOT	Aspartate Aminotransferase
GAMMAGT	Gamma-Glutamyl Transpeptidase
DRINKS	No. of half-pint equivalents per day
SELECTOR	Used to select training and test data

and makes up the record for a single male individual.

```
85,92,45,27,31,0,1          86,77,25,19,18,0.5,1
87,75,25,21,14,0,1          95,77,30,14,21,0.5,1
88,56,23,18,12,0,1          96,67,29,20,11,0.5,1
87,70,12,28,10,0,2          91,78,20,31,18,0.5,1
94,91,27,20,15,0.5,1        89,67,23,16,10,0.5,1
97,62,17,13,5,0.5,1         89,79,17,17,16,0.5,1
88,62,20,17,9,0.5,1         88,94,26,18,8,0.5,1
92,85,25,20,12,0.5,1        91,107,20,20,56,0.5,1
88,67,21,11,11,0.5,1        94,116,11,33,11,0.5,1
92,54,22,20,7,0.5,1         92,59,35,13,19,0.5,1
90,60,25,19,5,0.5,1         93,23,35,20,20,0.5,1
89,52,13,24,15,0.5,1        90,60,23,27,5,0.5,1
82,48,27,15,12,0.5,1        96,68,18,19,19,0.5,1
82,62,17,17,15,0.5,1        91,70,19,19,22,0.5,1
90,64,61,32,13,0.5,1        84,80,47,33,97,0.5,1
88,74,31,25,15,0.5,1        83,54,27,15,12,0.5,1
```

```
92,70,24,13,26,0.5,1          86,66,28,24,21,2,1
91,105,40,26,56,0.5,1         88,58,31,17,17,2,1
90,47,28,15,18,0.5,1          86,54,20,21,16,2,1
86,79,37,28,14,0.5,1          90,61,28,29,31,2,1
88,66,20,21,10,0.5,1          88,69,70,24,64,2,1
91,96,35,22,135,0.5,1         90,80,19,14,42,2,1
91,102,17,13,19,0.5,1         93,87,18,17,26,2,1
89,82,23,14,35,0.5,1          98,58,33,21,28,2,1
87,41,31,19,16,0.5,1          92,79,22,20,11,3,1
86,79,28,16,17,0.5,1          84,83,20,25,7,3,1
90,73,24,23,11,0.5,1          88,68,27,21,26,3,1
91,57,31,23,42,0.5,1          86,48,20,20,6,3,1
90,87,19,25,19,0.5,1          99,69,45,32,30,3,1
89,82,33,32,18,0.5,1          88,66,23,12,15,3,1
85,79,17,8,9,0.5,1            94,65,38,27,17,3,1
93,77,32,18,29,0.5,1          91,71,12,22,11,3,1
88,96,28,21,40,0.5,1          89,62,42,30,20,3,1
85,119,30,26,17,0.5,1         90,51,23,17,27,3,1
78,69,24,18,31,0.5,1          90,55,20,20,16,3,1
88,107,34,21,27,0.5,1         97,71,29,22,52,8,1
89,115,17,27,7,0.5,1          84,99,33,19,26,8,1
94,65,22,18,11,0.5,1          91,57,33,23,12,8,1
92,67,23,15,12,0.5,1          91,52,76,32,24,8,1
89,101,27,34,14,0.5,1         93,70,46,30,33,8,1
91,84,11,12,10,0.5,1          87,55,36,19,25,8,1
81,41,33,27,34,1,1            96,44,42,23,73,8,1
91,67,32,26,13,1,1            90,62,22,21,21,8,1
91,80,21,19,14,1,1            98,123,28,24,31,8,1
92,60,23,15,19,1,1            92,94,18,17,6,8,1
87,71,32,19,27,1,1            90,67,77,39,114,8,1
91,60,32,14,8,1,1             97,71,29,22,52,8,1
89,77,26,20,19,1,1            92,93,22,28,123,9,1
93,65,28,22,10,1,1            91,138,45,21,48,10,1
90,63,29,23,57,2,1            92,41,37,22,37,10,1
84,82,43,32,38,2,1            92,77,86,41,31,10,1
90,67,35,19,35,2,1            99,75,26,24,41,12,1
87,71,33,20,22,2,1            98,77,55,35,89,15,1
87,66,27,22,9,2,1             91,68,27,26,14,16,1
86,44,24,15,18,2,1            93,77,39,37,108,16,1
90,73,34,21,22,2,1            98,99,57,45,65,20,1
                              94,83,81,34,201,20,1
```

Appendix B

Sample BEAGLE Output

Below is some output produced by BEAGLE in the weather forecasting example. The overall successful prediction rate was 68% but for the examples in which it indicated confidence (i.e. those without question marks appended) the success rate was 65/92 or 70.65% which is rather good for an amateur. (See also Chapter 4.)

Simple Statistics

```
Simple statistics on data-set -- weather.dat

Variable                  min.        mean        max.
    1        DATE     1720.7000   9357.0371  13124.7002   C
    2     MINTEMP        0.6000      6.2709     13.1000   N
    3     MAXTEMP        4.6000     12.6901     23.3000   N
    4    MORNDAMP       57.0000     82.0604     96.0000   N
    5      EVEDAMP      28.0000     61.0330     96.0000   N
    6    RAINFALL        0.0000      1.7841     22.7000   N
    7     WINDMEAN       3.5000     10.2934     23.2000   N
    8     WINDGUST      13.0000     27.2747     62.0000   N
    9     SUNSHINE       0.0000      4.5055     13.5000   N
   10     PRESSURE     985.0000   1012.5824   1040.0000   N
   11      LASTSUN       0.0000      4.4522     13.5000   N
   12      NEXTSUN       0.0000      4.5434     13.5000   X
   13     LASTRAIN       0.0000      1.7841     22.7000   N
   14     NEXTRAIN       0.0000      1.8033     22.7000   N
   15     LASTWIND       3.5000     10.2912     23.2000   N
   16     NEXTWIND       3.5000     10.2879     23.2000   X

Run on 22-OCT-1985 at 10:46:35
```

Derived Rule-set

```
       ( NEXTRAIN >    0.100000)
$

( RAINFALL >      0.00)
$      75       45      14      48
(( SUNSHINE < WINDMEAN) > (( LASTRAIN <=   0.300000) + ( WINDGUST >=    45.00)))
$      50      18      39      75
(( PRESSURE -     997.00) <= MAXTEMP)
$      60      23      29      70
() $
              0.4890      182
000           6.0000       44
001           4.0000       10
010           2.0000        4
011           2.0000        4
100          13.0000       37
101          16.0000       23
110           8.0000       14
111          38.0000       46
```

Trial on Test Data (unseen)

```
          LEAF report, sorted on estimated values of:
       ( NEXTRAIN >    0.100000)
       Run on 19-OCT-1985 at 16:35:45
```

Rank	Pos.	Actual	Estimate		DATE	NEXTRAIN	(size)	
1	3	1.00	0.8189	+	04-FEB84	0.8	46	
2	30	0.00	0.8189		03-MARCH	0.0	46	
3	49	1.00	0.8189	+	22-MARCH	1.1	46	
4	50	1.00	0.8189	+	23-MARCH	2.9	46	
5	51	1.00	0.8189	+	24-MARCH	2.0	46	
6	52	1.00	0.8189	+	25-MARCH	11.5	46	
7	53	1.00	0.8189	+	26-MARCH	0.4	46	
8	64	1.00	0.8189	+	06-APRIL	3.4	46	
9	67	0.00	0.8189		09-APRIL	0.1	46	
10	70	1.00	0.8189	+	12-APRIL	0.4	46	
11	71	0.00	0.8189		13-APRIL	0.1	46	
12	102	1.00	0.8189	+	14-MAY	2.9	46	
13	108	1.00	0.8189	+	20-MAY	10.8	46	
14	115	0.00	0.8189		27-MAY	0.0	46	
15	5	1.00	0.6870	+	06-FEB84	1.5	23	
16	6	1.00	0.6870	+	07-FEB84	1.1	23	
17	20	1.00	0.6870	+	21-FEB84	5.9	23	
18	42	1.00	0.6870	+	15-MARCH	0.3	23	
19	48	1.00	0.6870	+	21-MARCH	3.0	23	
20	56	1.00	0.6870	+	29-MARCH	0.3	23	
21	57	1.00	0.6870	+	30-MARCH	1.6	23	
22	58	1.00	0.6870	+	31-MARCH	0.3	23	
23	59	0.00	0.6870		01-APRIL	0.1	23	
24	61	0.00	0.6870		03-APRIL	0.1	23	
25	62	1.00	0.6870	+	04-APRIL	1.3	23	
26	63	0.00	0.6870		05-APRIL	0.1	23	
27	65	1.00	0.6870	+	07-APRIL	1.7	23	
28	66	0.00	0.6870		08-APRIL	0.1	23	
29	68	1.00	0.6870	+	10-APRIL	5.1	23	
30	93	0.00	0.6870		05-MAY	0.0	23	
31	96	0.00	0.6870		08-MAY	0.0	23	
32	106	1.00	0.6870	+	18-MAY	1.0	23	
33	109	0.00	0.6870		21-MAY	0.0	23	
34	111	0.00	0.6870		23-MAY	0.1	23	
35	112	0.00	0.6870		24-MAY	0.1	23	
36	113	1.00	0.6870	+	25-MAY	8.9	23	
37	114	1.00	0.6870	+	26-MAY	6.8	23	
38	1	1.00	0.5659	+	02-FEB84	0.8	14	?
39	4	1.00	0.5659	+	05-FEB84	1.3	14	?
40	21	0.00	0.5659		22-FEB84	0.1	14	?
41	22	0.00	0.5659		23-FEB84	0.0	14	?
42	26	1.00	0.5659	+	27-FEB84	0.3	14	?

43	29	1.00	0.5659	+	02–MARCH	4.4	14	?
44	41	1.00	0.5659	+	14–MARCH	1.5	14	?
45	43	1.00	0.5659	+	16–MARCH	0.7	14	?
46	54	0.00	0.5659		27–MARCH	0.1	14	?
47	55	0.00	0.5659		28–MARCH	0.1	14	?
48	72	0.00	0.5659		14–APRIL	0.1	14	?
49	79	0.00	0.5659		21–APRIL	0.0	14	?
50	86	1.00	0.5659	+	28–APRIL	2.8	14	?
51	87	0.00	0.5659		29–APRIL	0.1	14	?
52	88	0.00	0.5659		30–APRIL	0.0	14	?
53	101	1.00	0.5659	+	13–MAY	22.3	14	?
54	103	0.00	0.5659		15–MAY	0.0	14	?
55	8	0.00	0.4978	+	09–FEB84	0.1	4	??
56	31	0.00	0.4978	+	04–MARCH	0.0	4	??
57	110	0.00	0.4978	+	22–MAY	0.1	4	??
58	47	1.00	0.4081		20–MARCH	0.8	10	?
59	77	1.00	0.4081		19–APRIL	2.7	10	?
60	90	0.00	0.4081	+	02–MAY	0.1	10	?
61	94	0.00	0.4081	+	06–MAY	0.0	10	?
62	95	0.00	0.4081	+	07–MAY	0.1	10	?
63	97	0.00	0.4081	+	09–MAY	0.1	10	?
64	2	1.00	0.3550		03–FEB84	4.6	37	
65	7	0.00	0.3550	+	08–FEB84	0.0	37	
66	9	0.00	0.3550	+	10–FEB84	0.1	37	
67	10	0.00	0.3550	+	11–FEB84	0.0	37	
68	14	0.00	0.3550	+	15–FEB84	0.0	37	
69	19	1.00	0.3550		20–FEB84	1.4	37	
70	24	1.00	0.3550		25–FEB84	0.6	37	
71	25	1.00	0.3550		26–FEB84	0.2	37	
72	27	0.00	0.3550	+	28–FEB84	0.1	37	
73	28	1.00	0.3550		29–FEB84	1.6	37	
74	33	1.00	0.3550		06–MARCH	0.3	37	
75	34	0.00	0.3550	+	07–MARCH	0.0	37	
76	37	0.00	0.3550	+	10–MARCH	0.0	37	
77	40	0.00	0.3550	+	13–MARCH	0.1	37	
78	44	0.00	0.3550	+	17–MARCH	0.0	37	
79	46	0.00	0.3550	+	19–MARCH	0.0	37	
80	60	0.00	0.3550	+	02–APRIL	0.1	37	
81	69	1.00	0.3550		11–APRIL	0.5	37	
82	73	0.00	0.3550	+	15–APRIL	0.0	37	
83	78	0.00	0.3550	+	20–APRIL	0.1	37	
84	81	0.00	0.3550	+	23–APRIL	0.0	37	
85	84	1.00	0.3550		26–APRIL	1.8	37	
86	85	1.00	0.3550		27–APRIL	4.4	37	
87	91	0.00	0.3550	+	03–MAY	0.1	37	
88	92	0.00	0.3550	+	04–MAY	0.1	37	
89	98	0.00	0.3550	+	10–MAY	0.1	37	
90	99	1.00	0.3550		11–MAY	0.8	37	
91	100	1.00	0.3550		12–MAY	2.3	37	
92	107	0.00	0.3550	+	19–MAY	0.1	37	
93	11	0.00	0.1442	+	12–FEB84	0.0	44	
94	12	0.00	0.1442	+	13–FEB84	0.0	44	
95	13	0.00	0.1442	+	14–FEB84	0.1	44	
96	15	0.00	0.1442	+	16–FEB84	0.0	44	
97	16	0.00	0.1442	+	17–FEB84	0.0	44	
98	17	0.00	0.1442	+	18–FEB84	0.0	44	
99	18	1.00	0.1442		19–FEB84	1.9	44	
100	23	0.00	0.1442	+	24–FEB84	0.1	44	
101	32	0.00	0.1442	+	05–MARCH	0.1	44	
102	35	0.00	0.1442	+	08–MARCH	0.0	44	
103	36	0.00	0.1442	+	09–MARCH	0.1	44	
104	38	0.00	0.1442	+	11–MARCH	0.0	44	
105	39	1.00	0.1442		12–MARCH	0.6	44	
106	45	1.00	0.1442		18–MARCH	0.2	44	
107	74	0.00	0.1442	+	16–APRIL	0.0	44	
108	75	0.00	0.1442	+	17–APRIL	0.0	44	
109	76	0.00	0.1442	+	18–APRIL	0.0	44	
110	80	0.00	0.1442	+	22–APRIL	0.1	44	
111	82	0.00	0.1442	+	24–APRIL	0.0	44	
112	83	0.00	0.1442	+	25–APRIL	0.1	44	
113	89	0.00	0.1442	+	01–MAY	0.0	44	
114	104	0.00	0.1442	+	16–MAY	0.0	44	

```
115  105      0.00      0.1442  +        17-MAY              0.1    44
116  116      0.00      0.1442  +        28-MAY              0.0    44
117  117      0.00      0.1442  +        29-MAY              0.0    44
118  118      0.00      0.1442  +        30-MAY              0.0    44
```

Crude success rate: 67.7966%
Mean target value =   0.4068

Success rate in non-queried groups =   70.6522% [92 cases].
Av. target value for all-YES group =   0.7143 [14 cases].
Av. target value for all-NO group =   0.1154 [26 cases].

Data-file was : weather.tst
Rule-file was : rain.rrr

Rule set being used (with Logical Target Expression):

Rule no.   1 :
(RAINFALL >   0.00)

Rule no.   2 :
((SUNSHINE < WINDMEAN) > ((LASTRAIN <=   0.300000) + (WINDGUST >=   45.00)))
Rule no.   3 :
((PRESSURE -   997.00)
 <= MAXTEMP)

Rules Encoded as Fortran Routines

```
          C*
Coded from rain.rrr during BEAGLE Run on 19-OCT-1985 at 16:37:38
          C*
          REAL FUNCTION MATH(V)
Converts Boolean to Real values:
          LOGICAL V
          IF (V)  MATH=1.0
          IF (.NOT. V)  MATH=0.0
          RETURN
          END
          C*
          LOGICAL FUNCTION BOOL(V)
Converts Real to Boolean values:
          BOOL = .FALSE.
          IF (V .GT. 0.0) BOOL=.TRUE.
          RETURN
          END
          C*
          INTEGER FUNCTION STAB(R,N)
Computes rule-signatures:
          LOGICAL R(10)
          IP = 0
          ID = 1
          J = N
          DO 100 I = 1,N
            IF (R(J)) IP = IP + ID
            ID = ID * 2
            J = J - 1
     100  CONTINUE
          STAB = IP
          RETURN
          END
          C*
          SUBROUTINE BEAGLE(ET,SIZE,IP,OK)
Calculates estimated Target Value from Signature table:
          COMMON /TAGS/ DATE, MINTEMP, MAXTEMP, MORNDAMP,
        #  EVEDAMP, RAINFALL, WINDMEAN, WINDGUST,
        #  SUNSHINE, PRESSURE, LASTSUN, NEXTSUN,
        #  LASTRAIN, NEXTRAIN, LASTWIND, NEXTWIND
          REAL MINTEMP
```

```
        REAL MAXTEMP
        REAL MORNDAMP
        REAL LASTSUN
        REAL NEXTSUN
        REAL LASTRAIN
        REAL NEXTRAIN
        REAL LASTWIND
        REAL NEXTWIND
        LOGICAL OK
        LOGICAL RULE (10)
        LOGICAL BOOL
        REAL MATH
        INTEGER STAB
        LOGICAL TV
C*
        Z = 0.0
        RULE( 1) = ( RAINFALL .GT.  Z)
        RULE( 2) = (MATH( SUNSHINE .LT.  WINDMEAN)
     #    .GT. (MATH( LASTRAIN .LE.  0.300000)
     #    + MATH( WINDGUST .GE.   45.00)))
        RULE( 3) = (( PRESSURE -    997.00)
     #    .LE.  MAXTEMP)
        IP = STAB(RULE, 3)
        OK = .TRUE.
        GOTO ( 1000,
     #   999,  999,  999, 1004, 1005,  999, 1007), IP+1
 999    ET =       16.4890 /       33.0000
        OK = .FALSE.
        SIZE =      33.0000
        RETURN
 1000   ET =        0.1442
        SIZE =      44
        RETURN
 1004   ET =        0.3550
        SIZE =      37
        RETURN
 1005   ET =        0.6870
        SIZE =      23
        RETURN
 1007   ET =        0.8189
        SIZE =      46
        RETURN
Cannot be reached, but Target follows for information only:
        TV = ( NEXTRAIN .GT.   0.100000)
        END
Created by VAX/BEAGLE
Conceived by Richard Forsyth
Copyright 1985, WARM BOOT Ltd.
Clever, eh?
C*
Coming up -- a minimal main program example:
Common block with variable names comes 1st.:
        COMMON /TAGS/ DATE, MINTEMP, MAXTEMP, MORNDAMP,
     #   EVEDAMP, RAINFALL, WINDMEAN, WINDGUST,
     #   SUNSHINE, PRESSURE, LASTSUN, NEXTSUN,
     #   LASTRAIN, NEXTRAIN, LASTWIND, NEXTWIND
        REAL MINTEMP
        REAL MAXTEMP
        REAL MORNDAMP
        REAL LASTSUN
        REAL NEXTSUN
        REAL LASTRAIN
        REAL NEXTRAIN
        REAL LASTWIND
        REAL NEXTWIND
        LOGICAL OK
Commence by getting/setting variable values.
Call Beagle decision routine somewhat like this:
        CALL BEAGLE(TE,S,IPOS,OK)
Continue by using TE, S, IPOS, OK as you wish.
Conclude in the normal Fortran fashion:
        STOP
        END
```

Glossary of Terms

adaptive control system
A system that uses feedback to adjust certain control parameters and thereby maintain desired performance in the face of disturbances in the environment.

AI
See *artificial intelligence*.

algorithm
A method for attaining a solution in a finite number of steps, usually forming the basis for a computer program. Unlike a heuristic method, an algorithm is guaranteed to work (but it may take a very long time).

architecture
The overall organization of a piece of computer hardware or software.

artificial intelligence (AI)
The study of ways of making machines, especially computers, solve problems intelligently.

attribute
See *feature*.

backtracking
Retracing the latest step in the search for a solution when it has led to a dead end. See also *depth-first search*.

backwards chaining
Reasoning backwards from hypotheses to the evidence needed to support or refute those hypotheses — e.g. working through a list of diseases to see if the symptoms are present or absent.

Bayes's rule
Reverend Bayes was a 18th century methodist clergyman who discovered a theorem concerning conditional probabilities. The formula is $P(H|E) = P(E|H)*P(H)/P(E)$ where H is a hypothesis and E is some evidence bearing on that hypothesis. Thus, for example, we can compute the probability of chicken pox given spots once we know the probability of spots given chicken pox (which is easier to estimate). Bayes's rule is widely used in expert systems.

beam search

A method of search in which all the descendant nodes of existing partial solutions are generated but only a fixed number of the most promising ones are preserved at each stage. So called because the technique explores the *search space* (q.v.) like a beam of light.

black-box methods

These are methods that ignore the internal structure of the phenomenon or its model and concentrate only on input–output behaviour.

bottom-up methods

Methods that work from raw data upwards towards a symbolic description of that data — e.g. in machine vision, working from the image to a description of what that image contains. See also *forward chaining* and *top-down methods*.

breadth-first search

A search technique in which all of the potential solutions at one level are examined before going on to the next level down.

bucket-bridge algorithm

This is a method of Credit Assignment (q.v.) suitable for problems where a number of rules have to cooperate in finding the solution to a multi-step problem. Rules that contribute to successful solutions are rewarded and share their reward with predecessor rules which assisted them. Likewise rules that contribute to unsuccessful solutions are penalized, and share their penalty with cooperating rules.

certainty factors

Numerical weightings, used in MYCIN for instance, to estimate the degree of truth of a given fact or conclusion.

classification

In libraries the classification system is a system for allocating a text to an appropriate subject category. In *pattern recognition* (q.v.) classification is the process of assigning to an input its appropriate class label. Many diagnostic problems are basically problems of classification, e.g. has this patient a stomach ulcer or gastric cancer?

cognitive graph

(See *semantic net*.

cognitive map

This term is used to describe the presumed neural structure formed by an experimental animal, such as a mouse, which learns to find its way through a maze.

concept formation

Inducing a general descriptions from examples (and normally also counter-examples). *Concept formation* is one form of *induction* (q.v.).

CPU

Central Processing Unit of a computer.

credit assignment

Identification of the rules or decisions responsible for success in reaching a goal. (Blame assignment is the process of identifying the steps responsible for failing to reach a goal.)

critic

The component of a learning system that evaluates proposed rules or concepts and carries out *credit assignment* (q.v.).

crossover

This is the crossing procedure in a *genetic algorithm* (q.v.) whereby portions of existing rules are cut up and spliced together to form a new rule. It is modelled on the exchange of DNA that takes place in sexual reproduction.

database

A collection of data, typically encoded as records where each record has a similar structure and describes the state of a particular object.

decision support system

A computer system that assists the human decision-maker.

decision tree

Decision trees contain tests that lead on to other tests, arranged in a treelike fashion. By applying the tests and following down the appropriate branches you eventually arrive at the correct category for an object or situation.

default value

Default values are values that apply in the absence of indications to the contrary. For instance, it might be a default property of birds that they can fly. Unless the system is specifically told that a bird is very young or flightless or dead, it will assume that it can fly.

demon

A Demon is a self-contained 'black box' performing a specific computation, very often triggered by events, i.e. not under the direct control of the main program sequence.

depth-first search

This strategy explores states in a Search Space by pursuing a single branch of the Search Tree until it hits a solution or a dead end. See also *backtracking*.

description language

The notation for *knowledge representation* (q.v.) that defines the kind of concepts or rules that can be induced by a learning algorithm.

descriptor

A variable or function used to describe an object or situation. Frequently the term Descriptor is applied to a binary attribute (having only the values true or false) which in logical terms is a Predicate. See also *feature*.

document

A textual item (e.g. a journal article or a book) which constitutes a unit of information in an Information Retrieval system.

domain

A domain is simply the subject area in which a given system works — for instance, geology or internal medicine. A Domain Specialist is a person who is an expert in that particular field of knowledge.

dynamic memory

This is a memory organization that does not just passively store information but continually readjusts itself to conform with new facts, especially when its expectations are disconfirmed.

evolutionary algorithm

An evolutionary algorithm is one that works by modelling the process of natural selection, first clearly described by Charles Darwin in 1859, in which better adapted organisms are more likely to survive and pass on their characteristics to their descendants.

expert system

Expert Systems are capable of offering advice or making intelligent decisions in a relatively narrow subject area. Typically expert systems solve problems that require years of training for human practitioners. Most expert systems contain an Inference Engine, which is a set of reasoning methods, and a Knowledge Base, which stores the system's expertise. The term is now applied so loosely, however, that it is gradually losing its meaning.

feature

A variable or single-argument predicate used in asserting one property of an object or situation.

feature space

In a *pattern recognition* (q.v.) problem where attributes are measured on numeric scales, any given pattern input can be regarded as a point in F-dimensional Feature Space (where F is the number of features).

field

An entry describing one aspect of a record in a database.

fifth-generation project

This Japanese project was announced in 1981. Briefly, the intention is to build a new generation of computer systems which match the human thinking process much more closely than traditional designs.

formal logic

This is the study of correct reasoning begun by Aristotle and other ancient Greeks and developed considerably in the 19th century by Boole, De Morgan, Frege and Russell. Recently logical reasoning has been mechanized in various ways, as for example in the language *Prolog* (q.v.)

forward chaining

This is a method of reasoning from evidence to conclusions adopted by some Expert Systems. It is simpler to program than *Backward Chaining* (q.v.) but leads to a less natural dialogue and does not make it easy for the system to answer How and Why questions.

frame

A frame is a data structure that recurs in many forms in AI. A frame describes some object or event. It has a number of Slots or Facets which are filled with data values that are *attributes* (q.v.) of the entity being described. Generally a Frame is more flexible than a *record* (q.v.) in that the number of slots is variable and the values in slots can be of any type.

fuzzy logic

Fuzzy Set Theory was founded by Zadeh in 1965. It is a generalization of Boolean Algebra which allows fractional truth values as well as 1 (true) and 0 (false), in an attempt to capture the fluidity of human reasoning. In Fuzzy Logic each proposition has a degree of truth, for example the statement 'she is beautiful' may have the truth value 0.75. (This is not meant to mean than 75% of a random sample would call her beautiful: it merely indicates that her grade of membership of the class of beautiful people is 75% of the maximum possible grade of membership.)

generalization

Generalization extends the scope of a concept or description to cover more examples. Generalization is an important operation in many rule–induction systems. This term is the opposite of *specialization* (q.v.).

genetic algorithm

See *evolutionary algorithm*.

glossary

List of mystifying definitions not containing the word you seek.

hacker

In Britain this refers to someone who breaks into private computer systems using the public telephone network; but in the USA it generally refers to compulsive programmer. Hence 'hacking'.

hardware

The physical equipment composing a computer system is called its Hardware. The programs it runs are termed Software.

heuristic rule

A Heuristic Rule is a rule of thumb that normally works but cannot always be relied on, such as 'only cross the road when the pedestrian light is green'. Humans use such rules all the time, and smart computers will have to use similar rules (even ones that sometimes fail) if they are to match human thinking. Many learning systems are designed to produce heuristic rules. The word 'heuristic' derives from the same Greek root as 'Eureka' and means 'serving to discover'.

hill-climbing

In an optimization problem one method of finding an optimum is always to take the next step of the search which leads to the biggest increase in the value being measured. This simple technique is known as Hill Climbing (or alternatively the method of 'steepest descent') by analogy with trying to find the summit of a mountain in dense fog by always moving towards. Its chief weakness is the likelihood of getting stuck on a local peak.

hypersphere classifier

A Hypersphere Classifier is one which assigns a pattern to its class by seeing which of a number of regions in the *feature space* (q.v.) contains the point defined by the input data. Geometrically each pattern region can be viewed as a hypersphere.

induction

This is the process of deriving general truths from particular instances. Inductive laws of rules can never be proved, though they can be disproved. Most of what we know through everyday experience and through scientific experimentation is inductive. Learning systems are designed to perform inductive inference by machine.

inference engine

This is the part of an Expert System that draws new conclusions from given facts.

information retrieval (IR)
This is the process of matching a user's Query against a large collection of Documents and picking out those documents which are relevant in some way to the query.

inheritance hierarchy
A *knowledge representation* (q.v.) in which items are held in a tree structure. Items at lower levels of the tree are said to 'inherit' properties belonging to their ancestors higher up the tree. For instance in an Inheritance Hierarchy of knowledge about animals it would not be necessary to store the fact that Pigeons lay eggs because this would be held as a *default value* (q.v.) of the description for birds in general, and that information would be inherited by the description of Pigeons.

inversion
This is an operator employed in *genetic algorithms* (q.v.) to reorder rule structures so that elements previously far apart are brought closer together and elements close together are separated. It affects subsequent *crossovers* (q.v.).

jargon
Jargon consists of words, phrases and syntactic usages which make communication easier between insiders in any field of study while making it harder for outsiders, thereby linguistically enforcing the elitism of expertise. Unless you use jargon liberally your career is likely to stagnate, especially in the computer industry.

keyword
This is a word or term selected for indexing a Document because it characterizes the contents of that document in some way.

knowledge acquisition
This refers to the eliciting, codifying and verification of knowledge from a human expert which is to be used in a computerized Expert System. Machine Learning is often seen as a way to by-pass this arduous process.

knowledge base
This is the part of an Expert System that contains the facts and Heurisitic Rules that give the system its expertise.

knowledge engineer
A Knowledge Engineer is someone who knows how to obtain knowledge from a human specialist and put it into a suitable form for use by machine.

knowledge representation
This refers to the choice of data structures to represent information in the computer.

learning programs
These programs are designed to improve their performance as they go along. To do so they require 'feedback' (i.e. they must be told when they make a mistake and when they get the right answer).

LISP
LISP is a programming language invented in 1960 which is much used today in AI work. It is good for processing lists and other complex symbolic data structures.

logic programming
Logic Programming describes the attempt of some AI researchers to transform computers from calculating engines to Inference Engines. The language *Prolog* (q.v.) is sometimes said to be a logic programming language.

machine learning
Machine learning systems improve their performance at a task automatically, generally by amending a Knowledge Base using inductive methods.

MEDLARS
Medical Literature Analysis and Retrieval System.

meta-rule
A Meta-rule is a rule about other rules, such as 'if a rule is very rarely true, try to generalize it'. The most sophisticated learning systems hold rules and meta-rules in the same format.

Monte Carlo method
A Monte Carlo method is one based on controlled randomness. Solutions are generated at random and evaluated, the best one being retained. An *evolutionary algorithm* (q.v.) is in effect a modified Monte Carlo procedure.

MOP
A Memory Organization Packet used as a component in some kinds of *dynamic memory* (q.v.).

mutation
One of the operators applied in Genetic Algorithms (q.v.). In AI (as in genetics) Mutation refers to a wide range of random changes that may modiry an information structures. Mutation is a 'background operator' with only a subsidiary role in the generation of new structures. See also *crossover* and *inversion*.

naturalistic selection
Generic term used to cover a variety of learning schemes drawing on Darwinistic principles.

noise
In information theory Noise refers to any source of distortion that can affect a message as it passes over a communications channel. In *pattern recognition* (q.v.) noise is used to cover various kinds of random or uncontrolled process that weaken the association between a stimulus pattern and the correct response, e.g. mistakes by the teacher, faulty instrument readings and so on.

object-oriented programming
A programming paradigm in which the main elements are objects (arranged in an *inheritance hierarchy* (q.v.) which communicate by passing messages.

parallel processing
A computer that uses parallel processing has many processors performing computations simultaneously. In certain applications parallel processing leads to significant gains of speed; but quite often multi-processor machines just replace one bottleneck (the CPU) with another (the shared memory or the communication channel between processors).

parameter adjustment
Altering the relative weighting of coefficients in a mathematical expression as a result of feedback about successes or failures. It is a primitive form of incremental learning.

parsing
This is a process whereby a sentence in a natural or formal language is analyzed into its constituents.

pattern recognition
Pattern Recognition systems take input data such as a picture or a voice-print and assign the input to one of two or more classes. Pattern recognition is a data-reduction task. Many expert systems are pattern recognizers at heart, and many learning systems learn to recognize patterns.

perception
This is the process of transforming the information given by the senses (like eyesight and touch) into a model of what is going on in the world. Animals, including humans, are good at perception; machines are not, yet. Intelligent machines will have to learn how to perceive their environments.

Perceptron
This term refers to a range of pattern recognizers using a single layer of threshold devices to classify input patterns. The Perceptron is a very simple model of what goes on in an animal's perceptual system.

predicate calculus
This is a form of symbolic logic where propositions are composed of predicates and relations between objects linked by operators such as AND or OR. Expressions may also be quantified. See *formal logic*.

production system
An Inference Engine made up of a large set of production rules, a working memory and a control regime that decides which productions to apply. Typically a production rule has a left half which matches patterns in the environment or in working memory and a right half that initiates actions or deposits messages in working memory.

programming language
A programming language is a set of rules for computing instructions for a computer. Programming languages have very strict formal rules, but natural languages (such as English and Chinese) have rules of grammar that are freer and less rigidly defined.

Prolog
This is a programming language based on logic. It is becoming popular for AI research.

query
A request for information.

query language
A Query Language is a set of rules governing the formulation of questions for a computer system. Typically query languages are used in Database systems and in Information Retrieval.

real time

A program that runs in 'real time' has to respond to events as they occur, before it is too late. For instance, the program controlling a nuclear power plant must close it down fast enough to prevent melt-down when things go amiss.

reconstructive memory

A kind of memory that does not store straightforward representations of events but retains enough information to enable it to reconstruct what happened afterwards. Human memory appears to be primarily reconstructive.

robotics

Robotics is the study of human-like machines that can perceive objects in the real world and manipulate them. It is still very much in its infancy. Today's robots lack the ability to make sense of their sensors. They are also deficient in learning ability.

rote learning

Learning by storage of facts, without generalization. Rote Learning systems are in effect very large tables or *databases* (q.v.).

rule-based system

Most Expert Systems are rule-based programs. Their 'knowledge' takes the form of *heuristic rules* (q.v.).

script

A high-level organized collection of facts and procedures used to organize a person's expectations.

search space

This refers to an abstract space of potential solutions. Many problems can be cast in a search framework (including the problem of Machine Learning) where the search space consists of nodes which are the potential or partial solutions and the links between nodes define ways of getting from one potential solution (e.g. a discrimination rule) to another (e.g. a modified rule). Searching does not only apply to overtly spatial problems such as finding the shortest route.

search tree

Programs that try to search intelligently for solutions grow tree-like structures which fan out as they consider the various options available at each stage and the consequences of picking each of those options. A special form of search tree is the 'game tree', where each branch leads to a move and further branches fan out from there to each counter-move, and so on.

selective forgetting

In a *rote memory* system (q.v.) there must be some way of periodically purging redundant or little-used knowledge, i.e. of Selective Forgetting.

semantic net

This is a *knowledge representation* (q.v.) in which nodes stand for objects and arcs linking nodes stand for the relations between those objects. Semantic Nets can be transformed into *frames* (q.v.) and vice versa, but the two styles of representation are convenient for a different range of tasks.

semantics

Semantics refers to the study of meaning in a language.

sensors

These are detectors that give a computer or a robot information about the outside world. For instance, a device for detecting infra-red rays would be a heat sensor. Robot sensors only provide raw information: the job of interpreting that information is complex. Human senses work rather differently. We do not see a speckled patch of reddish-grey; we see the wall of a building. (See also *perception*.)

signature table

A table in which combinations of *features* (q.v.) are used to index or address information concerning the state represented by that combination of features.

slot

A Slot is a field in a *frame*. It characterizes one aspect of the entitity represented by that frame.

software

See *hardware*.

specialization

Specialization is the opposite of *generalization* (q.v.). It narrows the scope of a concept or rule so that it covers fewer instances.

symbolic logic

Many learning systems produce symbolic logic expressions as rules. See also *formal logic*.

syntax

Syntax is the set of grammatical rules which distinguish well-formed from ill-formed sentences in natural or formal languages.

thesaurus

A Thesaurus is a lexicon organized by meaning, not in alphabetical order. In *information retrieval* (q.v.) a thesaurus may be used to match terms in a user's Query to related terms that are *keywords* (q.v.) in the Documents being sought.

training set

This is a Database of examples (togehter with the correct classification or expert decisions) which is given to a learning system to enable it to induce new knowledge. By contrast, a test data set contains data in a similar form which were not used during the training phase.

UIM

UIM stands for Ultra-Intelligent Machine. This phrase was coined by Jack Good to describe systems that are more intelligent than people. Many experts believe that UIMs will be created in the 21st century.

unit

A Unit is a kind of *frame* (q.v.).

VLSI

VLSI stands for Very Large Scale Integration. It describes the advanced processes now used to fabricate very large memory devices and very powerful processors on single chips of silicon.

working memory

In a *production system* (q.v.) the Working Memory is a storage area used for short-term information such as intermediate calculations and messages passed between rules. It corresponds roughly with the psychgological concept of STM (Short-Term Memory).

Bibliography

Aho, A., J. Hopcroft and J. Ullman, *Data Structures and Algorithms,* Addison-Wesley, Reading, MA, 1983.

Aleksander, Igor and Piers Burnett, *Reinventing Man,* Penguin Books, Middlesex, England, 1984.

Amarel, Saul, 'Problems of Representation in Heuristic Problem Solving', *Proc. Conf. Role of Language in Problem Solving*, pp. 11–32, North-Holland, Amsterdam, 1985.

Austin, Derek, 'The PRECIS System for Computer-Generated Indexes and its Use in the British National Bibliography', in *Subject Retrieval in the Seventies*, ed. T. Wilson, pp. 99–115, Greenwood Publishing Co., Westport, CT, 1972.

Austin, Derek, *PRECIS: A Manual of Concept Analysis and Subject Indexing*, British Library, London, 1984.

Banerji, R. B., 'Theory of Problem Solving: A Branch of Artificial Intelligence', *Proc. IEEE,* **70**, 12, pp. 1428–1448, 1982.

Bar-Hillel, Yehoshua, in *Language and Information: Selected Essays on their theory and application*, Addison-Wesley, Reading, MA, 1964.

Barr, A. and E. Feigenbaum, *Handbook of Artificial Intelligence, Vol. 1,* William Kaufman, Inc., Los Altos, CA, 1982.

Barr, A. and E. Feigenbaum, *Handbook of Artificial Intelligence, Vol. 2,* William Kaufman, Inc., Los Altos, CA, 1982.

Baskin, A. B. and A. H. Levy, 'MEDIKAS—An Interactive Knowledge Acquisition System, *Proc. Second Annual Symp. Computer Applic. Medical Care,* pp. 344–350, IEEE Computer Soc. Press, 1978.

Batchelor, Bruce G., *Practical Approaches to Pattern Classification,* Plenum Books, London, 1974.

Berliner, Hans, 'On the Construction of Evaluation Functions for Large Domains', *Proc. Intern'l Joint Conf. Art. Intell.,* pp. 53–55, 1979.

Bernstein, Lionel and Robert Williamson, 'Testing of a Natural Language Retrieval System for a Full Text Knowledge Base, *Jr. American Soc. Inform. Sc.*, **35**, 4, pp. 235–247, 1984.

Bethke, Albert 'Genetic Algorithms as Function Optimizers', Ph.D Thesis, Dept of Computer and Communication Sciences, University of Michigan, Ann Arbor, MI, 1980.

Blair, David and M. E. Maron, 'An Evaluation of Retrieval Effectiveness for a Full-Text Document-Retrieval System', *Communications of the ACM,* **28**, 3, pp. 289–299, March 1985.

Bledsoe, W. W. and I. Browning, 'Pattern Recognition & Reading by Machine', *Proc . Eastern Joint Computer Conf.*, 1959. Reprinted in Uhr (1966).

Bobrow, D. & T. Winograd, 'Overview of KRL, a Knowledge Representation Language', *Cognitive Science,* **1**, pp. 3–46, 1977.

Bonham, G. M., G. J. Nozicka, and F. N. Stokman, 'Cognitive Graphing and the Representation of Biomedical Knowledge, *Proc. Expert Systems in Government Conference*, IEEE Computer Society Press, 1985.

Brachman, Ronald, 'What IS-A Is and Isn't: An Analysis of Taxonomic Links in Semantic Networks, *Computer* **16**, 10, pp. 30–36, 1983.

Brooks, R. and J. Heiser, 'Transferability of a Rule-Based Control Structure to a New Knowledge Domain, *Proc. Third Annual Computer Applic. Medical Care,* pp. 56–63, IEEE Computer Soc. Press, 1979.

Buchanan, B. G. and Edward Feigenbaum, 'Dendral and Meta-Dendral: their Applications Dimension', *Artificial Intelligence,* **11**, 1978.

Buchanan, B. G. and Tom Mitchell, 'Model-Directed Learning of Production Rules', in *Pattern-Directed Inference Systems*, ed. Hays-Roth, Academic Press, New York, 1978.

Buchanan, Bruce, 'Scientific Theory Formation by Computer', in *Computer Oriented Learning Processes,* ed. J. C. Simon, Noordhoff, Leyden, 1976.

Carbonell, J., D. Scott, and D. Evans, *Toward the Automation of Content-Access Methods for Large-Scale Textual Databases,* Dept Computer Science, Carnegie-Mellon University, Pittsburg, PA, July 1984. Research proposal funded by National Library of Medicine.

Carbonell, Jaime, 'Learning by Analogy', in *Machine Learning,* ed. T. Mitchell, pp. 137–161, Tioga Publishing, Palo Alto, CA, 1983.

Carbonell, Jaime, 'AI Languages for Problem Solving', in *The Role of Language in Problem Solving,* ed. D. Weintraub, pp. 83–102, North-Holland, Amsterdam, 1985.

Collins, A. M. and E. F. Loftus, 'A Spreading Activation Theory of Semantic Processing', *Psychological Review,* **82**, pp. 407–428, 1975.

Conrad, Michael, 'Mutation-Absorption Model of the Enzyme', *Bull. Math. Bio.,* **41**, pp. 387–405, 1979.

Conrad, Michael, 'Bootstrapping on the Adaptive Landscape', *BioSystems,* **11**, pp. 167–182, 1979.

Conrad, Michael, *Adaptability: The Significance of Variability from Molecule to Ecosystem,* Plenum, New York, 1983.

Croft, Bruce and Roger Thompson, 'An Expert Assistant for Document Retrieval', *COINS Tech. Report 85–15,* University of Massachusetts, Amherst, MA, 1985.

Dahlberg, Ingetraut, 'Conceptual Definitions for INTERCONCEPT', *Intern. Classif.,* **8**, 1, pp. 16–22, 1981.

Dahlberg, Ingetraut, 'Conceptual Compatibility of Ordering Systems', *Intern. Classif.,* **10**, 1, pp. 5–8, 1983.

Darden, Lindley and Nancy Maull, 'Interfield Theories', *Philosophy of Science,* **44**, pp. 43–64, 1977.

Darden, Lindley, 'Reasoning by Analogy in Theory Construction', *Proc. Philosophy Science Assoc.,* pp. 147–165, 1982.

Darden, Lindley, 'Reasoning by Analogy in Scientific Theory Construction', *Proc. International Machine Learning Workshop,* pp. 32–40, June 1984.

Davis, Randall, 'TEIRESIAS: Applications of Meta-Level Knowledge', in *Knowledge-Based Systems in Artificial Intelligence,* ed. D. Lenat, pp. 229–491, McGraw-Hill, New York, 1982.

Devadason, F. J. and V. Balasubramanian, 'Computer Generation of Thesaurus from Structured Subject-Propositions', *Information Processing and Management,* **17**, pp. 1–11, 1981.

Dextre, S. G. and T. M. Clarke, 'A System for Machine-Aided Thesaurus Construction', *Aslib Proc.,* **33**, 3, pp. 102–112, 1981.

Dietterich, Thomas and Ryszard Michalski, 'Inductive Learning of Structural Descriptions', *Artificial Intelligence,* **16**, 1981.

Dietterich, Thomas, Bob London, Kenneth Clarkson, and Geoff Dromey, 'Learning and Inductive Inference', in *Handbook of Artificial Intelligence, Vol. 3,* ed. E. Feigenbaum, pp. 323–511, William Kaufmann, Inc., Los Altos, CA, 1982.

Enslow, P. H., 'Multiprocessor Organzation—a Survey', *ACM Computing Surveys* **9**, 1, pp. 103–129, 1977.

Erickson, K. A. and H. A. Simon, *Protocol Analysis, Verbal Reports as Data,* MIT Press, Cambridge, MA, 1984.

Ernst, G. and A. Newell, *GPS: A Case Study in Generality and Problem Solving,* Academic Press, New York, 1969.

Evens, Martha, Yih-Chen Wang, and James Vandendorpe, 'Relational Thesauri in Information Retrieval', *Jr. American Society Information Sci.,* **36**, pp. 15–27, 1985.

Fahlman, S., G. Hinton, and T. Sejnowski, 'Massively Parallel Architectures for AI: NETL, THISTLE, and Boltzmann Machines', *Proc. Amer. Assoc. Artif. Intelligence,* pp. 109–113, 1983.

Feldman, J. and D. Ballard, 'Connectionist Models and their Properties', *Cognitive Science* **6**, pp. 205–254, 1982.

Filman, Robert and Daniel Friedman, *Coordinated Computing: Tools and Techniques for Distributed Software,* McGraw-Hill, New York, 1984.

Fogel, L. J., A. J. Owens, and M. J. Walsh, *Artificial Intelligence through Simulated Evolution,* Wiley, New York, 1966.

Forsyth, Richard, *Expert Systems: Principles and Case Studies,* Chapman & Hall, London, 1984.

Fox, Edward, 'Extending the Boolean and Vector Space Models of Information Retrieval with P-Norm Queries and Multiple Concept Types', Ph.D Thesis, Dept. Computer Science, Cornell University, Ithaca, NY, 1983.

Garey, M. and D. Johnson, *Computers and Intractability,* Freeman, San Francisco, 1979.

Gomez, Fernando, 'Towards a Theory of Comprehension of Declarative Contexts', *Proc. 20th Meeting Assoc. Computational Linguistics*, Toronto, Canada, 1982.

Gordon, Michael, 'Adaptive Subject Description in Document Retrieval', Ph.D Thesis, Dept Computer and Communication Sciences, University of Michigan, Ann Arbor, MI, 1983.

Gottlieb, A. and J. Schwartz, 'Networks and Algorithms for Very-Large Scale Parallel Computation', *Computer* **15**, 1, pp. 27–36, 1982.

Grishman, R. and L. Hirschman, 'Question Answering from Natural Language Medical Data Bases', *Artificial Intelligence,* **11**, pp. 25–43, 1978.

Haas, Norman and Gary Hendrix, 'An Approach to Acquiring and Applying Knowledge', *Proc. First Ann. Nat'l Conf. Artificial Intelligence,* pp. 235–239, American Assoc. Artificial Intelligence, 1980.

Hart, Anna E., 'Experience in the Use of an Inductive System in Knowledge Engineering', in *Research & Development in Expert Systems*, ed. Max Bramer, Cambridge University Press.

Hendrix, Gary, 'Encoding Knowledge in Partitioned Networks', in *Associative Networks: the Representation and Use of Knowledge in Computers*, ed. N. V. Findler, Academic Press, New York, 1979.

Hendrix, G. G., E. D. Sacerdoti, D. Sagalowics, and J. Slocum, 'Developing a Natural Language Interface to Complex Data', *ACM Transactions on Database Systems,* **3**, 2, 1978.

Hinton, G. and J. Anderson, *Parallel Models of Associative Memory,* Erlbaum, Hillsdale, New Jersey, 1981.

Hinton, Geoff E., 'Learning in Parallel Networks', *Byte Magazine,* **10**, 4, 1985.

Holland, John, *Adaptation in Natural and Artificial Systems,* University of Michigan Press, Ann Arbor, Michigan, 1975.

Holland, John, 'Escaping Brittleness', *Proc. Intern'l Machine Learning Workshop,* pp. 92–96, 1983.

Howell, R. and R. Loy, 'Disease Coding by Computer: The Fruit Machine Method', *Brit. J. Prev. Soc. Med.,* **22**, pp. 178–181, 1968.

Hunt, Earl, *Experiments in Induction*, Academic Press, New York, 1966.

Hunter, Larry, 'Steps Toward Building a Dynamic Memory', *Proc. Third Intern'l Machine Learning Workshop,* 1985.

Jones, A. and J. Swartz, 'Experience Using Multiprocessor Systems—a Status Report', *ACM Computing Surveys* **23**, 2, pp. 121–166, 1980.

Kintsch, Walter, 'Memory for Text', in *Discourse Processing*, ed. W. Kintsch, pp. 186–204, North-Holland, Amsterdam, 1982.

Kirkpatrick, S., C. D. Gellatt, and M. D. Vecchi, 'Optimization by Simulated Annealing', *Science,* **220**, 1983.

Kolodner, Janet, *Retrieval and Organizational Strategies in Conceptual Memory*, Lawrence Erlbaum, Hillsdale, NJ, 1984.

Kuck, David, *The Structure of Computers and Computations, Vol. 1*, Wiley, New York, 1978.

Langley, Patrick, 'Data-driven Discovery of Physical Laws', *Cognitive Science,* **5**, 1977.

Larson, J. and Ryszard Michalski, 'Inductive Inference of VL Decision Rules', in *Pattern-Directed Inference Systems,* ed. Hays-Roth, Academic Press, New York, 1978.

Lebowitz, Michael, 'Concept Learning in a Rich Input Domain', *Proc. Internat'l Machine Learning Workshop,* pp. 177–182, 1983.

Lenat, Douglas, 'The Nature of Heuristics', *Artificial Intelligence,* **19**, 1982.

Lenat, Douglas, 'An Artificial Intelligence Approach to Discovery in Mathematics as Heuristic Search', in *Knowledge-Based Systems in Artificial Intelligence*, ed. L. Lenat, pp. 229–491, McGraw-Hill, New York, 1982.

Lenat, Douglas, 'The Nature of Heuristics', *Artificial Intelligence,* **19**, pp. 189–249, 1982.

Lenat, Douglas, 'The Role of Heuristics in Learning by Discovery', in *Machine Learning*, ed. T. Mitchell, pp. 243–306, Tioga Publishing, Palo Alto, CA, 1983.

Litoukhin, J., 'Toward an Integrated Thesaurus of the Social Sciences', *Intern. Classif.,* **7**, 2, pp. 56–59, 1980.

Luhn, H. P., 'The Automatic Creation of Literature Abstracts', *IBM Jr. Res. Devel.,* **2**, 2, pp. 159–165, April 1958.

Machinery, Association of Computing, 'The Full Category System', *Computing Reviews,* January 1984.

Maron, M. E. and J. K. Kuhns, 'On Relevance, Probabilistic Indexing, and Information Retrieval', *Jr. Assoc. Computing Mach.,* **3**, 1960.

McCarn, D. B., 'MEDLINE: an Introduction to On-Line Searching', *Jr. American Soc. Inform. Sci.,* **31**, 3, pp. 181–192, May 1980.

Medicine, National Library of, 'MEDLARS, the Computerized Literature Retrieval Service', DHEW NIH 79–1286, US Government Printing Office, Bethesda, MD, January 1979.

Medicine, National Library of, 'Medical Subject Headings, Tree Structures, 1985', *NLM-MED-84-04*, Bethesda, MD, July 1984.

Medicine, National Library of, *Programs and Services, Fiscal Year 1983*, US Government Printing Office, Bethesda, MD, March 1984.

Michalski, Ryszard and J. B. Larson, *Selection of Most Representative Training Examples & Incremental Generation of VL1 Hypotheses*, University of Illinois, Urbana, 1978. Report 867.

Michalski, Ryszard, J. Carbonell and T. Mitchell eds. *Machine Learning*, Tioga Press, Palo Alto, 1983.

Michalski, Ryszard and R. L. Chilausky, 'Learning by Being Told and Learning from Examples', *J. Policy Analysis & Information Systems*, **4**, 1980.

Michalski, Ryszard, 'A Theory and Methodology of Inductive Learning', in *Machine Learning*, ed. T. Mitchell, pp. 83–134, Tioga Publishing, Palo Alto, CA, 1983.

Michie, Donald and Roger Chambers, 'Boxes: an Experiment in Adaptive Control', in *Machine Intelligence,* **2**, ed. Michie, Edinburgh University Press, Edinburgh, 1968.

Michie, Donald and Rory Johnston, *The Creative Computer,* Pelican Books, Harmondsworth, 1985.

Mili, Hafedh and Roy Rada, 'A Statistically Build Knowledge Base', *Proc. Expert Systems in Government*, IEEE Computer Society Press, pp. 457–463, October 1985.

Minsky, Marvin and Seymour Papert, *Perceptrons,* MIT Press, Massachusetts, 1969.

Mitchell, Thomas, 'Generalization as Search', *Artificial Intelligence,* **18**, 2, pp. 203–226, 1982.

Mitchell, Tom, Paul Utgoff, and Ranan Banerji, 'Learning by Experimentation: Acquiring and Refining Problem-Solving Heuristics', in *Machine Learning*, ed. T. Mitchell, pp. 163–190, Tioga Press, Palo Alto, CA, 1983.

Neville, R. and P. Mars, 'Hardware Design for a Hierarchical Structure Stochastic Learning Automaton', *Jr. Cybernetics and Inform. Sc.,* **2**, pp. 30–35, 1979.

Newell, A. and H. A. Simon, 'Computer Science as Empirical Inquiry: Symbols and Search', *Communications of the ACM,* **19**, 3, pp. 113–126, 1976.

Niehoff, Robert and Greg Mack, 'The Vocabulary Switching System', *Intern. Classif.,* **12**, 1, pp. 2–6, 1985.

Nilsson, Nils, *Principles of Artificial Intelligence,* Tioga Press, Palo Alto, 1980.

Osherson, D., M. Stob, and S. Weinstein, 'Ideal Learning Machines', *Cognitive Science,* **6**, 3, pp. 277–290, 1982.

Ozkaharan, E. A., 'Desirable Functionalities of Database Architectures', *Proc. of IFIP World Congress*, 1983.

Pearl, Judea, 'On the Discovery and Generation of Certain Heuristics', *AI Magazine* **4**, pp. 23–34, 1983.

Pietilainen, Pirkko, 'Possibility for Intelligent Feedback in On-line Searching', *Online Review,* **7**, 5, pp. 391–396, 1983.

Politikas, Peter and Sholom Weiss, 'Using Empirical Analysis to Refine Expert System Knowledge Bases', *Artificial Intelligence,* **22**, pp. 23–48, 1984.

Pollock, J. J. and A. Zamora, 'Automatic Spelling Correction in Scientific and Scholarly Text', *Communications of ACM,* **27**, pp. 358–368, 1984.

Popper, Karl, *The Logic of Scientific Discovery*, Basic Books, New York, 1959.

Quillian, M. R., 'Semantic Memory', in *Semantic Information Processing*, ed. M. Minsky, MIT Press, Cambridge, MA, 1968.

Quinlan, John Ross, *Induction over Large Databases*, Stanford University, 1979. Report HPP–79–14.

Quinlan, John Ross, 'Semi-autonomous Acquisition of Pattern-based knowledge', in *Introductory Readings in Expert Systems*, ed. Donald Michie, Gordon & Breach, 1982.

Quinqueton, Joel and Jean Sallentin, *Algorithms for Learning Logical Formulas*, William Kaufmann, CA, 1983.

Rada, Roy and Lynn Evans, 'Automated Problem Encoding System for Ambulatory Care', *Computers and Biomedical Research,* **12**, pp. 131–139, 1979.

Rada, Roy, 'Evolutionary Structure and Search', Ph.D Thesis, Dept of Computer Science, University of Illinois, Urbana, IL, 1981.

Rada, Roy, 'Evolution and Gradualness', *BioSystems,* **14**, pp. 211–218, 1981.

Rada, Roy, 'Characterizing Search Spaces', *Proc. Intern'l Joint Conf. Art. Intell.*, pp. 780–782, 1983.

Rada, Roy, Yvonne Rhine, and Janice Smallwood, 'Rule Refinement', *Proc. Soc. Computer Applic. Medical Care*, pp. 62–65, IEEE Press, 1984.

Rada, Roy, 'Probabilities and Predicates in Knowledge Refinement', *Proc. IEEE Workshop on Principles of Knowledge-Based Systems*, pp. 123–128, 1984.

Rada, Roy, 'Implicit Computation in Message Space of Parallel Machine', *Proc. Conf. Intelligent Systems and Machines*, pp. 424–428, 1984.

Rada, Roy, Susanne Humphrey, and Craig Coccia, 'A Knowledge-base for Retrieval Evaluation', *Proc. ACM '85*, pp. 360–367, 1985.

Rada, Roy, Ellen Brown, Susanne Humphrey, Alexandra Suh, and Craig Coccia, 'Relevance on a Biomedical Classification Structure', *Proc. Expert Systems in Government*, pp. 532–537, October 1985.

Rada, Roy, 'Gradualness Facilitates Knowledge Refinement', *IEEE Transactions on Pattern Analysis and Machine Intelligence*, pp. 523–530, September 1985.

Radecki, T., 'Similarity Measures for Boolean Search Request Formulation', *Jr. American Society Information Sc.*, pp. 8–17, 1982.

Reeker, L. H., 'A Problem Solving Theory of Syntax Acquisition', *Journal of Structural Learning,* **2**, 4, pp. 1–10, 1971.

Reeker, L. H., 'The Computational Study of Language Acquisition', in *Advances in Computers,* **15**, ed. Rubinoff, pp. 181–237, Academic Press, New York, 1976.

Rich, Elaine, *Artificial Intelligence,* McGraw-Hill, New York, 1983.

Ritchie, G. D. and F. K. Hanna, 'AM: A Case Study in AI Methodology', *Artificial Intelligence,* **23**, pp. 249–268, 1984.

Rosenblatt, Frank, 'The Perceptron: a Probabilistic Model for Information-Storage and Organization in the Brain', *Psychological Review,* **65**, 1958.

Rosenblatt, Frank, *Principles of Neurodynamics*, Spartan Books, New York, 1962.

Rosenbloom, P., J. Laird, J. McDermott, A. Newell, and E. Orciuch, 'R1-Soar: An Experiment in Knowledge-Intensive Programming in a Problem-Solving Architecture', *Proc. IEEE Workshop on Principles of Knowledge-Based Systems*, pp. 65–72, IEEE Computer Soc. Press, Silver Spring, MD, 1984.

Rumelhart, David and Donald Norman, *Representation in Memory*, Centre for Human Information Processing, La Jolla, CA, June 1983.

Sager, J. C., H. L. Somers, and J. McNaught, 'Thesaurus Integration in the Social Sciences, Part 1: Comparison of Thesauri', *Intern. Classif.,* **8**, 3, pp. 133–137, 1981.

Salton, Gerard, 'Automatic Text Analysis', *Science,* **168**, pp. 335–343, April 1970.

Salton, Gerard, 'Some Hierarchical Models for Automatic Document Retrieval', *American Documentation,* **14**, 3, pp. 213–222.

Salton, Gerard and Michael McGill, *Introduction to Modern Information Retrieval*, McGraw-Hill, New York, 1983.

Samuel, Arthur, 'Some Studies in Machine Learning Using the Game of Checkers', *IBM Journal of Research & Development,* **3**, 1959.

Samuel, Arthur, 'Some Studies in Machine Learning Using the Game of Checkers, Part II', *IBM Journal of Research & Development,* **11**, 1967.

Schank, Roger, *Conceptual Information Processing,* North-Holland, Amsterdam, 1975.

Schank, Roger, Janet Kolodner, and Gerald DeJong, 'Conceptual Information Retrieval', in *Information Retrieval Research*, ed. P. W. Williams, pp. 94–116, Butterworths, London, 1981.

Schank, Roger, *Dynamic Memory: a theory of reminding and learning in computers and people*, Cambridge University Press, Cambridge, England, 1982.

Section, Medical Subject Headings, *Medical Subject Headings, Annotated Alphabetical List, 1985*, National Library of Medicine, Bethesda, MD, 1984. Publication PB84–223156.

Selfridge, Oliver, 'Pandemonium: a Paradigm for Learning', *NPL Symposium on Mechanization of Thought Processes*, HMSO, London, 1959. Reprinted in Uhr, 1966.

Selfridge, Oliver and Ulric Neisser, 'Patten Recognition by Machine', *Scientific American,* **203**, 1960.

Shapiro, M. J. and G. M. Bonham, 'A Cognitive Process Approach to Collective Decision-Making', in *Cognitive Dynamics and International Politics*, ed. C. Jonsson, Frances Pinter, London, 1982.

Shortliffe, Edward, *Computer-Based Medical Consultations: MYCIN*, Elsevier, New York, 1976.

Simon, H. and A. Newell. *Human Problem Solving*, Prentice-Hall, Englewood Cliffs, NJ, 1972.

Simon, Herbert, 'Why Should Machines Learn', in *Machine Learning*, ed. T. Mitchell, pp. 25–38, Tioga Press, Palo Alto, CA, 1983.

Sklansky, Jack and Gustav Wassel, *Pattern Classifiers and Trainable Machines,* Springer-Verlag, New York, 1981.

Smith, Stephen F., *Flexible Learning of Problem-Solving Heuristics through Adaptive Search*, William Kaufmann, CA, 1983.

Sparck-Jones, Karen, *Automatic Keyword Classification for Information Retrieval*, Butterworth, London, 1971.

Sparck-Jones, Karen, 'Intelligent Retrieval', *Proc. Intelligent Inform. Retr.*, pp. 136–142, Aslib, London, March 1983.

Soergel, Dagobert, 'A General Model for Indexing Languages: the Basis for Compatibility and Integration', in *Subject Retrieval in the Seventies*, ed. T. Wilson, pp. 36–61, Greenwood Publishing Co., Westport, CT, 1972.

Soergel, Dagobert, *Indexing Languages and Thesauri: Construction and Maintenance*, Wiley, New York, 1974.

Soergel, Dagobert, 'Automatic and Semi-Automatic Methods as an Aid in the Construction of Indexing Languages and Thesauri', *Intern. Classif.*, **1**, 1, pp. 34–39, 1974.

Sudarshan, B., 'Development of Reference Retrieval System with Simultaneous Building of Thesaurus', *Lib. Sc.*, **16**, 3, pp. 77–83, September 1979.

Svenonius, Elaine, 'Compatibility of Retrieval Languages: Introduction to a Forum', *Intern. Classif.*, **10**, 1, pp. 2–4, 1983.

Swanson, D. G., 'Searching Natural Language Text by Computer', *Science*, **132**, pp. 1099–1104, October 1960.

Swartout, William, 'XPLAIN: A System for Creating and Explaining Expert Consulting Systems', *Artificial Intelligence*, **21**, 3, pp. 285–325, 1983.

Tong, R., V. Askman, and J. Cunningham, 'RUBRIC: an Aritficial Intelligence Approach to Information Retrieval', *Proc. 1st Intern'l Workshop on Expert Database Systems*, October 1984.

Tong, Richard, D. Shapiro, J. Dean, and B. McCune, 'A Comparison of Uncertainty Calculi in an Expert System for Information Retrieval', *Proc. Intern'l Joint Conf. Art. Intell.*, pp. 194–197, 1983.

Uhr, Leonard and C. Vossler, 'A Pattern Recognition Program that Generates, Evaluates and Adjusts its own Operators', *Proc. Western Joint Computer Conf.*, 1961.

Uhr, Leonard, 'Pattern Recognition Computers as Models for Form Perceptors', *Psychological Bulletin*, **60**, 1963.

Uhr, Leonard, *Pattern Recognition*, Wiley, New York, 1966.

Waltz, David, 'An English Language Question Answering System for a Large Relational Database', *Communications of ACM*, **21**, pp. 526–539, 1978.

Waltz, David, 'Event Shape Diagrams', *Proc. National Conf. Artificial Intelligence,* pp. 84–87, 1982.

Wilkes, M. V., 'Beyond Today's Computers', *Information Processing '77,* pp. 1–5, North-Holland, Amsterdam, 1977.

Winston, Patrick, *Artifical Intelligence*, 2nd ed., Addison-Wesley, Massachusetts, 1984.

Winston, Patrick, *The Psychology of Computer Vision*, McGraw-Hill, New York, 1975.

Yovits, M., G. Jacobi, and G. Goldstein, *Self-organizing Systems 1962*, Spartan Books, Washington, DC, 1962.

Zeigler, Bernard P., *Multifacetted Modeling and Discrete Event Simulation,* Academic Press, London, England, 1984.

Zipf, G. K., *Human Behaviour and the Principle of Least Effort*, Addison-Wesley, Reading, MA, 1949.

Index